Except for plainchant, each track w/same name is combined

ANTHOLOGY OF SCORES TO

A HISTORY of USIC IN WESTERN CULTURE

Volume I: Antiquity through the Baroque Era

Second Edition

MARK EVAN BONDS

Department of Music
University of North Carolina at Chapel Hill

PEARSON

Prentice Hall

Upper Saddle River, New Jersey 07458

Library of Congress Cataloging-in-Publication Data

Bonds, Mark Evan.
    A history of music in Western culture / Mark Evan Bonds.—2nd ed.
      p. cm.
    Includes bibliographical references and index.
    ISBN 0-13-193104-0 (main textbooks)
    1. Music—History and criticism. I. Title.

ML160.B75 2006
780′.9—dc22

            2004043171

President, Humanities/Social Sciences:
  Yolanda de Rooy
AVP/Director of Production and
  Manufacturing: Barbara Kittle
Editor-in-Chief: Sarah Touborg
Acquisitions Editor: Christopher T. Johnson
Editorial Assistant: Evette Dickerson
Marketing Manager: Sheryl Adams
Marketing Assistant: Cherron Gardner

Managing Editor: Lisa Iarkowski
Production Editor: Joseph Scordato
Production Assistant: Marlene Gassler
Permissions Supervisor: Ron Fox
Manufacturing Manager: Nick Sklitsis
Manufacturing Buyer: Ben Smith
Creative Design Director: Leslie Osher
Interior and Cover Design: Laura Gardner

This book was set in 9/11 Times Roman by A-R Editions, Inc. and was printed and bound by
The Courier Companies. The cover was printed by Phoenix Color Corp.

Credits and acknowledgments borrowed from other sources and reproduced, with permission,
in this textbook appear on pages 310–313.

Pearson Education Ltd
Pearson Education Singapore, Pte. Ltd
Pearson Education, Canada, Ltd
Pearson Education—Japan

Pearson Education Australia PTY, Limited
Pearson Education North Asia Ltd
Pearson Educacion de Mexico, S.A. de C.V.
Pearson Education Malaysia, Pte. Ltd

PEARSON
Prentice
Hall

10 9 8 7 6 5 4 3 2 1
ISBN 0-13-193113-X

CONTENTS

1 Epitaph of Seikilos (1st century C.E.)

CD1   Track 1

p. 8

No form

As long as you live, be happy;
do not grieve at all.
Life's span is short;
time exacts the final reckoning.

This brief piece, dating from the first century C.E., is in the Ionian *tonos,* occupying an octave on E that includes C♯ and F♯, with special prominence given to the pitch A. This last pitch, the middle note of the octave on E, constitutes the *mese* ("mean") of the range. "In all good music," comments the author of the *Problems* (possibly Aristotle) "*mese* occurs frequently, and all good composers have frequent recourse to *mese,* and, if they leave it, they soon return to it, as they do to no other note." Songs like this one are known to have been accompanied on the lyre or some similar instrument, but the accompaniment itself was never notated and remains a matter of considerable speculation.

Performance notes: Only the vocal line is notated, but this does not preclude the addition of instruments. Here, the lyra (lyre) plays the melody through once in its entirety before and then again after the vocalist has sung her part with the lyra doubling the vocal line an octave below. The instrumentalist is playing the lyra with a plectrum, similar to a modern-day guitar pick.

2 Plainchant **Mass for Easter Sunday**

CD1   Track 2

p. 38

No form

a) **Introit (Propers)**

Resurrexi, et adhuc tecum sum, alleluia:
posuisti super me manum tuam, alleluia:
mirabilis facta est scientia tua,
alleluia, alleluia.

Domine, probasti me, et cognovisti me:
tu cognovisti sessionem meam,
et resurreccionem meam.

I arose and am still with thee, alleluia:
thou hast laid thy hand upon me, alleluia;
thy knowledge is become wonderful,
alleluia, alleluia.

Lord, thou hast proved me, and known me:
thou hast known my sitting down
and my rising up.

b) Kyrie (Ordinary)

Kyrie eleison. Lord have mercy.
Christe eleison. Christ have mercy.
Kyrie eleison. Lord have mercy.

c) Gloria (Ordinary)

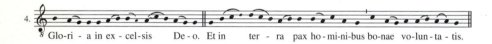

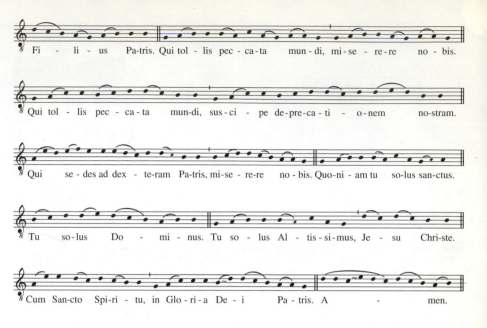

Gloria in excelsis Deo.
Et in terra pax hominibus bonae voluntatis.
Laudamus te. Benedicimus te.
Adoramus te. Glorificamus te.
Gratias agimus tibi propter magnam gloriam tuam.
Domine Deus, Rex caelestis.
Deus Pater omnipotens.
Domine Fili unigenite Jesu Christe.
Domine Deus, Agnus Dei, Filius Patris.
Qui tollis peccata mundi,
miserere nobis.
Qui tollis peccata mundi,
suscipe deprecationem nostram.
Qui sedes ad dexteram Patris,
miserere nobis.
Quoniam tu solus sanctus.
Tu solus Dominus.
Tu solus Altissimus, Jesu Christe.
Cum Sancto Spiritu,
in Gloria Dei Patris. Amen.

Glory to God in the highest.
And on earth peace to men of good will.
We praise thee, we bless thee,
we adore thee, we glorify thee.
We give thee thanks for thy great glory.
O Lord God, King of heaven,
God the Father almighty.
O Lord, the only begotten Son, Jesus Christ.
O Lord God, Lamb of God, Son of the Father.
Thou who takest away the sins of the world,
have mercy on us.
Thou who takest away the sins of the world,
receive our prayer.
Thou who sittest at the right hand of the Father,
have mercy on us.
For thou only art holy,
thou only art Lord,
thou only art most high, O Jesus Christ,
with the Holy Ghost,
in the glory of God the Father. Amen.

d) Collect (Propers)

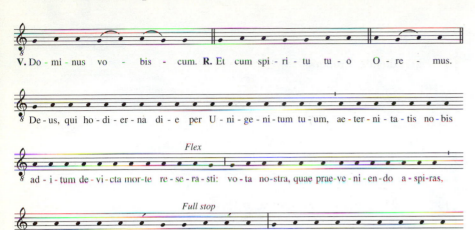

V. Do - mi - nus vo - bis - cum. R. Et cum spi - ri - tu tu - o   O - re - mus.

De - us, qui ho - di - er - na di - e per U - ni - ge - ni - tum tu - um, ae - ter - ni - ta - tis no - bis

Flex

ad - i - tum de - vi - cta mor - te re - se - ra - sti: vo - ta no - stra, quae prae - ve - ni - en - do a - spi - ras,

Full stop

et - i - am ad - ju - van - do pro - se - que - re. Per e - um - dem Do - mi - num no - strum

Je - sum Chri - stum Fi - li - um tu - um: qui te - cum vi - vit et re - gnat in u - ni - ta - te

Spi - ri - tus San - cti De - us, per o - mni - a sae - cu - la sae - cu - lo - rum. A - men.

Dominus vobiscum.
Et cum spiritu tuo. Oremus.

Deus, qui hodierna die per Unigenitum tuum,
aeternitatis nobis aditum devicta morte reserasti:
vota nostra, quae praeveniendo aspiras,
etiam adjuvando prosequere.

Per eumdem Dominum nostrum
Jesum Christum Filium tuum:
qui tecum vivit et regnat
in unitate Spiritus Sancti Deus,
per omnia saecula saeculorum. Amen.

The Lord be with you.
And with thy spirit. Let us pray.

O God, who this day by thine only-begotten Son
didst conquer death, opening unto us the gates
of everlasting life; to the desires of our hearts
which thou inspirest, do thou, by thy gracious help,
enable us to attain.

Through the same Jesus Christ,
our Lord, thy Son,
who with thee
in the unity of the Holy Ghost lives and reigns God,
world without end. Amen.

e) Epistle (Propers)

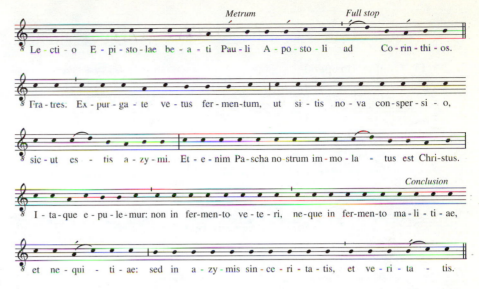

Metrum *Full stop*

Le - cti - o E - pi - sto - lae be - a - ti Pau - li A - po - sto - li ad   Co - rin - thi - os.

Fra - tres. Ex - pur - ga - te ve - tus fer - men - tum, ut si - tis no - va con - sper - si - o,

sic - ut es - tis a - zy - mi. Et - e - nim Pa - scha no - strum im - mo - la - tus est Chri - stus.

Conclusion

I - ta - que e - pu - le - mur: non in fer - men - to ve - te - ri, ne - que in fer - men - to ma - li - ti - ae,

et ne - qui - ti - ae: sed in a - zy - mis sin - ce - ri - ta - tis, et ve - ri - ta - tis.

Lectio Epistolae beati Pauli Apostoli
ad Corinthios.
Fratres: Expurgate vetus fermentum,
ut sitis nova conspersio,
sicut estis azymi.
Etenim Pascha nostrum immolatus est Christus.
Itaque epulemur:
non in fermento veteri,
neque in fermento malitiae,
et nequitiae:
sed in azymis sinceritatis,
et veritatis.

Reading of the Epistle of St. Paul the Apostle
to the Corinthians.
Brethren, purge out the old leaven,
that you may be a new paste,
as you are unleavened;
for Christ our passover is sacrificed.
Therefore let us feast,
not with the old leaven,
nor with the leaven of malice
and wickedness,
but with the unleavened bread of sincerity
and truth.

f) Gradual (Propers)

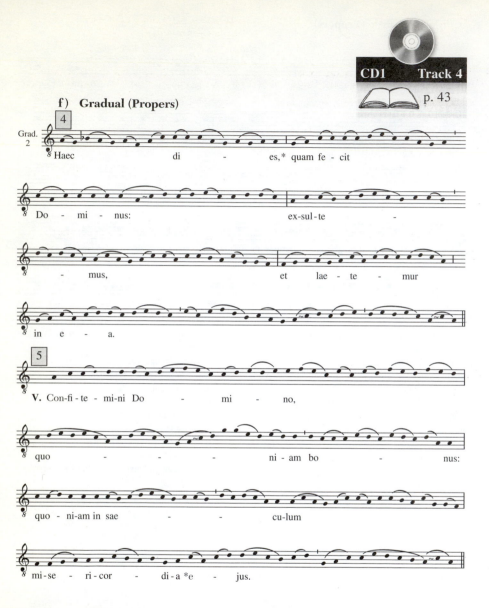

Grad. 2 — Haec di - es,* quam fe - cit

Do - mi - nus: ex-sul -te - mus, et lae - te - mur in e - a.

5

V. Con-fi - te - mi-ni Do - mi - no, quo - ni - am bo - nus:

quo - ni-am in sae - cu-lum mi-se - ri-cor - di-a *e - jus.

g) Alleluia (Propers)

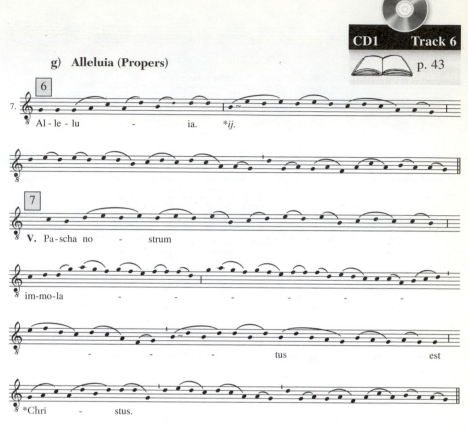

7. — Al - le - lu - ia. *ij.

V. Pa-scha no - strum im-mo-la - tus est

*Chri - stus.

Alleluia.
Pascha nostrum immolatus est Christus.

Alleluia.
Christ our passover is sacrificed.

Haec dies, quam feci Dominus:
exsultemus, et laetemur in ea.

This is the day which the Lord hath made:
let us be glad and rejoice therein.

Confitemini Domino, quoniam bonus:
quoniam in saeculum misericordia ejus.

Give praise to the Lord, for he is good;
for his mercy endureth forever.

h) **Sequence (Propers)**

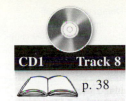
CD1   Track 8
p. 38

780   Officium et Missa in die Paschae

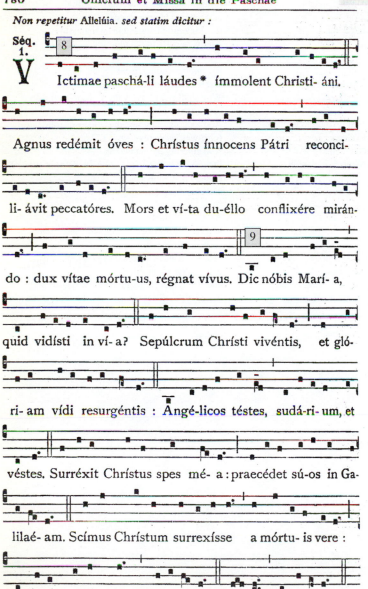

Non repetitur Allelúia. *sed statim dicitur :*

Séq. 1. [8] Ictimae paschá-li láudes * ímmolent Christi-áni.

Agnus redémit óves : Chrístus ínnocens Pátri reconci-

li-ávit peccatóres. Mors et ví-ta du-éllo conflixére mirán-

do : dux vítae mórtu-us, régnat vívus. [9] Dic nóbis Marí-a,

quid vidísti in ví-a? Sepúlcrum Chrísti vivéntis, et gló-

ri-am vídi resurgéntis : Angé-licos téstes, sudá-ri-um, et

véstes. Surréxit Chrístus spes mé-a : praecédet sú-os in Ga-

lilaé-am. Scímus Chrístum surrexísse a mórtu-is vere :

tu nóbis, víctor Rex, mi-se-ré-re.   Amen. (Alle-lú-ia.)

1. Victimae paschali
   laudes immolent Christiani.

2. Agnus redemit oves:
   Christus innocens Patri reconciliavit peccatores.

3. Mors et vita duelo conflixere mirando:
   dux vitae mortuus, regnat vivus.

4. Dic nobis Maria, quid vidisti in via?
   Sepulcrum Christi viventis,
   et gloriam vidi resurgentis:

5. Angelicos testes, sudarium, et vestes.
   Surrexit Christus spes mea:
   praecedet suos in Galilaeam.

6. Scimus Christum surrexisse a mortuis vere:
   tu nobis, victor Rex, miserere.

1. To the Paschal Victim let Christians
   offer songs of praise.

2. The Lamb has redeemed the sheep.
   Sinless Christ has reconciled sinners to the Father.

3. Death and life have engaged in miraculous combat.
   The leader of life is slain, (yet) living he reigns.

4. Tell us, Mary, what you saw on the way?
   I saw the sepulchre of the living Christ
   and the glory of His rising;

5. The angelic witnesses, the shroud and vesture.
   Christ my hope is risen.
   He will go before his own into Galilee.

6. We know that Christ has truly risen from the dead.
   Thou conqueror and king, have mercy on us.

i) Gospel (Propers)

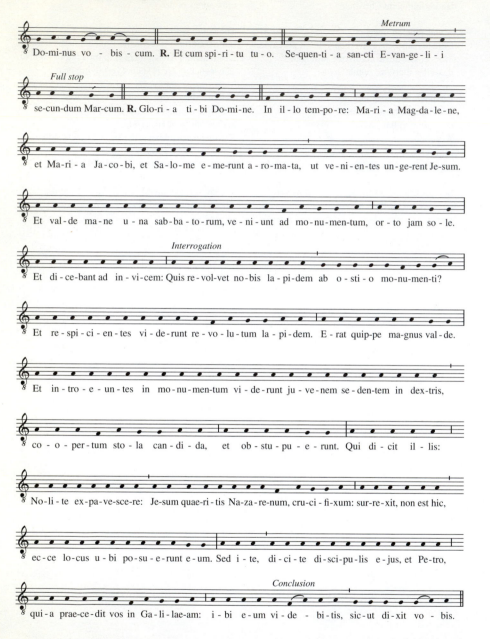

Dominus vobiscum.
Et cum spiritu tuo.
Sequentia sancti Evangelii
secundum Marcum.
Gloria tibi Domine.

In illo tempore:
Maria Magdalene, et Maria Jacobi,
et Salome emerunt aromata,
ut venientes ungerent Jesum.
Et valde mane una sabbatorum,
veniunt ad monumentum,
orto jam sole.
Et dicebant ad invicem:
Quis revolvet nobis lapidem
ab ostio monumenti?
Et respicientes viderunt revolutum lapidem.
Erat quippe magnus valde.
Et introeuntes in monumentum
viderunt juvenem sedentem in dextris,
coopertum stola candida,
et obstupuerunt.
Qui dicit illis:
Nolite expavescere:
Jesum quaeritis Nazarenum, crucifixum:
surrexit, non est hic,
ecce locus ubi posuerunt eum.
Sed ite, dicite discipulis ejus,
et Petro, quia praecedit vos in Galilaeam:
ibi eum videbitis, sicut dixit vobis.

The Lord be with you.
And with thy spirit.
Continuation with the holy Gospel
according to Mark.
Glory to thee, O Lord.

At that time,
Mary Magdalene, and Mary the mother of James,
and Salome bought spices,
that they might come and anoint Jesus.
And very early in the morning,
the first day of the week they came to the sepulchre,
the sun being then risen:
and they said one to another,
Who shall roll us away the stone from the door
of the sepulchre?
And looking, they saw the stone was rolled away:
for it was very great.
And entering the sepulchre,
they saw a young man sitting on the right side,
clothed in a white robe,
and they were astonished.
He said to them:
Be not affrighted;
you seek Jesus of Nazareth, who was crucified;
he is risen, he is not here;
behold the place where they laid him.
But go, tell his disciples,
and Peter, that he goeth before you into Galilee:
there you shall see him, as he told you.

j) Credo (Ordinary)

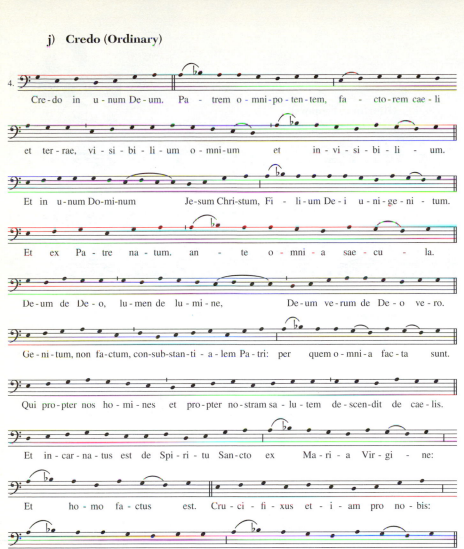

4.
Cre - do in u - num De - um. Pa - trem o - mni - po - ten - tem, fa - cto - rem cae - li

et ter - rae, vi - si - bi - li - um o - mni - um et in - vi - si - bi - li - um.

Et in u - num Do - mi - num Je - sum Chri - stum, Fi - li - um De - i u - ni - ge - ni - tum.

Et ex Pa - tre na - tum. an - te o - mni - a sae - cu - la.

De - um de De - o, lu - men de lu - mi - ne, De - um ve - rum de De - o ve - ro.

Ge - ni - tum, non fa - ctum, con - sub - stan - ti - a - lem Pa - tri: per quem o - mni - a fac - ta sunt.

Qui pro - pter nos ho - mi - nes et pro - pter no - stram sa - lu - tem de - scen - dit de cae - lis.

Et in - car - na - tus est de Spi - ri - tu San - cto ex Ma - ri - a Vir - gi - ne:

Et ho - mo fa - ctus est. Cru - ci - fi - xus et - i - am pro no - bis:

sub Pon - ti - o Pi - la - to pas - sus et se - pul - tus est.

Et re - sur - re - xit ter - ti - a di - e, se - cun - dum Scri - ptu - ras.

Et a - scen - dit in cae - lum: se - det ad dex - te - ram Pa - tris.

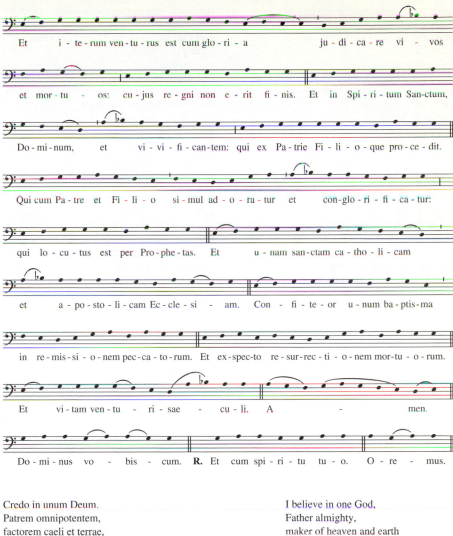

Et i - te - rum ven - tu - rus est cum glo - ri - a ju - di - ca - re vi - vos

et mor - tu - os: cu - jus re - gni non e - rit fi - nis. Et in Spi - ri - tum San - ctum,

Do - mi - num, et vi - vi - fi - can - tem: qui ex Pa - trie Fi - li - o - que pro - ce - dit.

Qui cum Pa - tre et Fi - li - o si - mul ad - o - ra - tur et con - glo - ri - fi - ca - tur:

qui lo - cu - tus est per Pro - phe - tas. Et u - nam san - ctam ca - tho - li - cam

et a - po - sto - li - cam Ec - cle - si - am. Con - fi - te - or u - num ba - ptis - ma

in re - mis - si - o - nem pec - ca - to - rum. Et ex - spec - to re - sur - rec - ti - o - nem mor - tu - o - rum.

Et vi - tam ven - tu - ri sae - cu - li. A - men.

Do - mi - nus vo - bis - cum. **R.** Et cum spi - ri - tu tu - o. O - re - mus.

Credo in unum Deum.	I believe in one God,
Patrem omnipotentem,	Father almighty,
factorem caeli et terrae,	maker of heaven and earth
visibilium omnium et invisibilium.	and of all things visible and invisible.
Et in unum Dominum Jesum Christum,	And in one Lord Jesus Christ,
Filium Dei unigenitum.	the only-begotten Son of God,
Et ex Patre natum.	born of the Father
ante omnia saecula.	before all ages.
Deum de Deo, lumen de lumine,	God of God, light of light,
Deum verum de Deo vero.	true God of true God.
Genitum, non factum,	Begotten, not made,
consubstantialem Patri:	being of one substance with the Father,
per quem omnia facta sunt.	by whom all things were made.

Qui propter nos homines et propter nostram salutem descendit de caelis.	Who for us men and for our salvation came down from heaven.
Et incarnatus est de Spiritu Sancto ex Maria Virgine:	And was made incarnate by the Holy Ghost of the Virgin Mary,
Et homo factus est.	and was made man.
Crucifixus etiam pro nobis:	And was crucified for us
sub Pontio Pilato passus et sepultus est.	under Pontius Pilate. He suffered and was buried.
Et resurrexit tertia die,	And the third day he rose again
secundum Scripturas.	according to the Scriptures.
Et ascendit in caelum:	And ascended into heaven,
sedet ad dexteram Patris.	and sitteth on the right hand of the Father.
Et iterum venturus est cum gloria	And he shall come again with glory to judge
judicare vivos et mortuos:	the quick and the dead;
cujus regni non erit finis.	of whose kingdom there shall be no end.
Et in Spiritum Sanctum, Dominum,	And in the Holy Ghost,
et vivificantem:	Lord and giver of life,
qui ex Patrie Filioque procedit.	who proceedeth from the Father and the Son.
Qui cum Patre et Filio simul adoratur	Who, together with the Father and the Son,
et conglorificatur:	is worshiped and glorified;
qui locutus est per Prophetas.	who spake by the prophets.
Et unam sanctam catholicam	And one holy, Catholic,
et apostolicam Ecclesiam.	and Apostolic Church.
Confiteor unum baptisma	I acknowledge one baptism
in remissionem peccatorum.	for the remission of sins.
Et exspecto resurrectionem mortuorum.	And I look for the resurrection of the dead,
Et vitam venturi saeculi. Amen.	and the life of the world to come. Amen.
Dominus vobiscum.	The Lord be with you.
Et cum spiritu tuo.	And with thy spirit.
Oremus.	Let us pray.

k) Offertory (Propers)

p. 39

Terra tremuit, et quievit,
dum resurgeret in judicio Deus,
alleluia.

The earth trembled and was still
when God arose in judgment,
alleluia.

l) Preface (Ordinary)

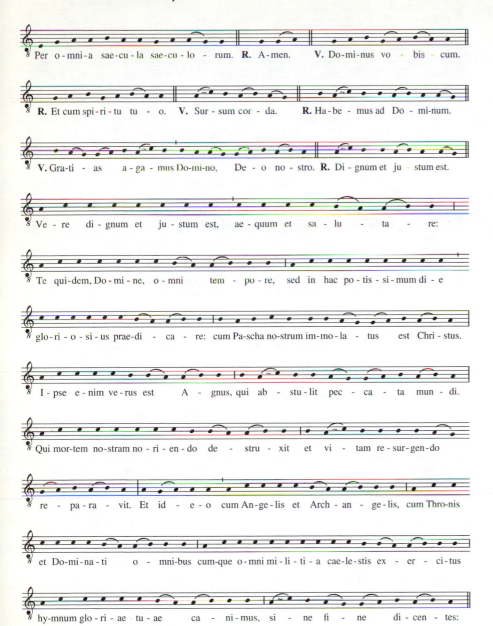

Per o-mni-a sae-cu-la sae-cu-lo-rum. **R.** A-men. **V.** Do-mi-nus vo-bis-cum.

R. Et cum spi-ri-tu tu-o. **V.** Sur-sum cor-da. **R.** Ha-be-mus ad Do-mi-num.

V. Gra-ti-as a-ga-mus Do-mi-no, De-o no-stro. **R.** Di-gnum et ju-stum est.

Ve-re di-gnum et ju-stum est, ae-quum et sa-lu-ta-re:

Te qui-dem, Do-mi-ne, o-mni tem-po-re, sed in hac po-tis-si-mum di-e

glo-ri-o-si-us prae-di-ca-re: cum Pa-scha no-strum im-mo-la-tus est Chri-stus.

I-pse e-nim ve-rus est A-gnus, qui ab-stu-lit pec-ca-ta mun-di.

Qui mor-tem no-stram no-ri-en-do de-stru-xit et vi-tam re-sur-gen-do

re-pa-ra-vit. Et id-e-o cum An-ge-lis et Arch-an-ge-lis, cum Thro-nis

et Do-mi-na-ti o-mni-bus cum-que o-mni mi-li-ti-a cae-le-stis ex-er-ci-tus

hy-mnum glo-ri-ae tu-ae ca-ni-mus, si-ne fi-ne di-cen-tes:

Per omnia saecula saeculorum.   Amen.
Dominus vobiscum.
Et cum spiritu tuo.
Sursum corda.
Habemus ad Dominum.
Gratias agamus Domino, Deo nostro.
Dignum et justum est.
Vere dignum et justum est,
aequum et salutare:
Te quidem, Domine, omni tempore,
sed in hac potissimum
die gloriosius praedicare:
cum Pascha nostrum immolatus est Christus.
Ipse enim verus est Agnus,
qui abstulit peccata mundi.
Qui mortem nostram noriendo
destruxit et vitam
resurgendo reparavit.
Et ideo cum Angelis et Archangelis,
cum Thronis et Dominati omnibus
cumque omni militia caelestis
exercitus hymnum gloriae tuae canimus,
sine fine dicentes:

World without end,   Amen.
The Lord be with you.
And with thy spirit.
Lift up your hearts.
We have lifted them up unto the Lord.
Let us give thanks to the Lord our God.
It is meet and just.
It is truly meet and just,
right and profitable to extol thee indeed
at all times, O Lord,
but chiefly with highest praise
to magnify thee on this day
when for us was sacrificed Christ our passover.
For he is the true Lamb
who has taken away the sins of the world;
who by dying himself
has destroyed our death;
and by rising again has bestowed a new life on us.
And therefore with the angels and archangels,
with the thrones and dominations,
and with all the array of the heavenly Host,
we sing a hymn to thy glory
and unceasingly repeat:

m) Sanctus (Ordinary)

Sanctus, *Sanctus, Sanctus Dominus, Deus Sabaoth.
Pleni sunt caeli et terra gloria tua.
Hosanna in excelsis. Benidictus qui venit
in nomine Domine. Hosanna in excelsis.

[Canon]

Per omnia saecula saeculorum. R. Amen.

Sanctus, Sanctus, Sanctus	Holy, holy, holy,
Dominus, Deus Sabaoth.	Lord God of Hosts.
Pleni sunt caeli et terra gloria tua.	The heavens and earth are full of thy glory.
Hosanna in excelsis.	Hosanna in the highest.
Benidictus qui venit in nomine Domine.	Blessed is he who comes in the name of the Lord.
Hosanna in excelsis.	Hosanna in the highest.
Per omni a saecula saeculorum. Amen.	World without end. Amen.

n) Pater noster (Ordinary)

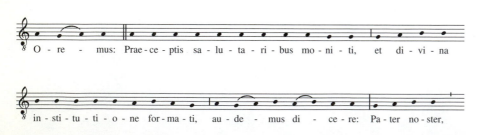

O-re - mus: Prae-ce-ptis sa-lu-ta-ri-bus mo-ni-ti, et di-vi-na

in-sti-tu-ti-o-ne for-ma-ti, au-de-mus di-ce-re: Pa-ter no-ster,

qui es in cae-lis: San-cti-fi-ce-tur no-men tu-um: Ad-ve-ni-at

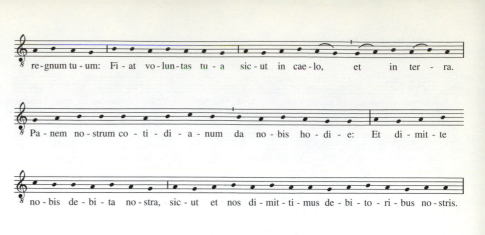

re-gnum tu-um: Fi-at vo-lun-tas tu-a sic-ut in cae-lo, et in ter-ra.

Pa-nem no-strum co-ti-di-a-num da no-bis ho-di-e: Et di-mit-te

no-bis de-bi-ta no-stra, sic-ut et nos di-mit-ti-mus de-bi-to-ri-bus no-stris.

Et ne nos in-du-cas in ten-ta-ti-o-nem. R. Sed li-be-ra nos a ma-lo.

Per o-mni-a sae-cu-la sae-cu-lo-rum. R. A-men.

Pax Do - mi-ni sit sem-per vo-bis - cum. R. Et cum spi-ri-tu tu-o.

Oremus:	Let us pray:
Praeceptis salutaribus moniti,	Thereto admonished by wholesome precepts,
et divina institutione formati,	and in words taught us by God himself,
audemus dicere:	we presume to say:
Pater noster, qui es in caelis:	Our Father, who art in heaven;
Sanctificetur nomen tuum:	hallowed by thy name:
Adveniat regnum tuum:	thy kingdom come:
Fiat voluntas tua sicut in caelo, et in terra.	thy will be done on earth as it is in heaven.
Panem nostrum cotidianum da nobis hodie:	Give us this day our daily bread;
Et dimitte nobis debita nostra,	and forgive us our trespasses
sicut et nos dimittimus debitoribus nostris.	as we forgive those who trespass against us.
Et ne nos inducas in tentationem.	And lead us not into temptation.
Sed libera nos a malo.	But deliver us from evil.
Per omnia saecula saeculorum. Amen.	World without end, Amen.
Pax Domini sit semper vobiscum.	The peace of the Lord be with you always.
Et cum spiritu tuo.	And with thy spirit.

o) Agnus Dei (Ordinary)

Agnus Dei,
qui tollis peccata mundi:
miserere nobis.
Agnus Dei,
qui tollis peccata mundi:
miserere nobis.
Agnus Dei,
qui tollis peccata mundi:
dona nobis pacem.

Lamb of God,
who takest away the sins of the world,
have mercy on us.
Lamb of God,
who takest away the sins of the world,
have mercy on us.
Lamb of God,
who takest away the sins of the world,
give us peace.

CD1 Track 11
p. 39

p) Communion (Propers)

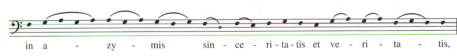

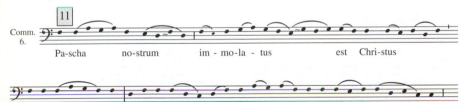

Pascha nostrum immolatus est Christus alleluia:
itaque epulemur in azymis
sinceritatis et veritatis,
alleluia, alleluia, alleluia.

Christ our passover is sacrificed, alleluia:
therefore let us feast with the unleavened bread
of sincerity and truth,
alleluia, alleluia, alleluia.

q) Post-Communion (Ordinary)

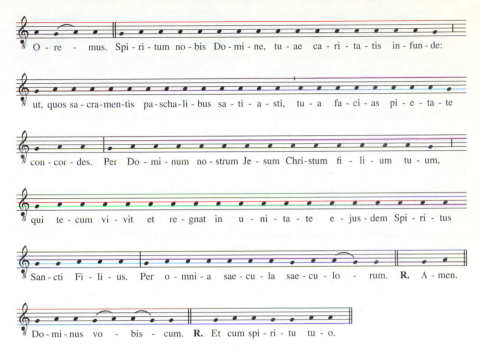

Oremus.
Spiritum nobis Domine,
tuae caritatis infunde:
ut, quos sacramentis paschalibus satiasti,
tua facias pietate concordes.
Per Dominum nostrum
Jesum Christum filium tuum,
qui tecum vivit et regnat
in unitate ejusdem Spiritus Sancti Filius.
Per omnia saecula saeculorum. Amen.
Dominus vobiscum. Et cum spiritu tuo.

Let us pray.
Impart to our souls, O Lord,
the Spirit of thy love,
that those whom thou hast fed with this Paschal mystery
may be united in harmony by thy merciful goodness.
Through Jesus Christ,
our Lord, thy Son,
who with thee lives and reigns
in the same unity of the Holy Ghost.
World without end. Amen.
The Lord be with you. And with thy spirit.

r) Ite, missa est (Ordinary)

Ite, missa est, alleluia, alleluia.
Deo gratias, alleluia, alleluia.

Go, the Mass has been said, alleluia, alleluia.
Thanks be to God, alleluia, alleluia.

The sung portions of the Mass consist of elements whose texts are fixed and unchanging—the Ordinary—and elements whose texts vary according to the particular Sunday or feast day within the liturgical year—the Propers. The Kyrie, Gloria, Credo, Sanctus, and Agnus Dei are the main elements of the Ordinary. (The *Pater noster*—the Lord's Prayer—and the concluding *Ite, missa est* are also unchanging but are recited in a formulaic fashion.) The remaining elements belong to the Ordinary. Several of them—the Collect, Epistle, Gospel, Preface, and Post-Communion, are of relatively little musical interest, as they are sung according to a formulaic pattern centering on a single recitation tone. These items are not included on the present recording. But the Introit, Gradual, Alleluia, Sequence, Offertory, and Communion are musically rich and varied, and they constitute the bulk of the chant repertory for the Mass.

The Introit, Offertory, and Communion are sometimes called "action chants" because they accompany actions of the priest and his attendants who are celebrating Mass. The Introit is sung during the procession into the church, the Offertory during the presentation of the bread and wine, the Communion during the distribution of the bread and wine. These chants are typically built around a psalm verse. *Resurrexi,* the Introit for the Mass on Easter Sunday, for example, incorporates a psalm verse (*Domine, probasti me…*) that is essentially recitational, centering on a single "recited" note (here, the pitch A). But the much longer introduction to the Psalm verse (*Resurrexi…alleluia*) is freely composed in terms of both its text and its music. The setting is neumatic, with melismas of four and five notes distributed liberally throughout. The Offertory and Communion for Easter are even more elaborate, with long melismas on the repeated word *alleluia* in both. The remaining items of the Ordinary—the Kyrie, Sanctus, Agnus Dei, and *Ite missa est,* all of which feature relatively brief texts—are also predominantly neumatic with a mixture of syllabic and mildly melismatic passages.

The most elaborate chants in the Mass are the Gradual and Alleluia, along with the Tract, which replaces the Alleluia during the penitential seasons of Advent and Lent. These chants feature relatively brief texts. The Alleluia for Easter Sunday (Anthology No. 2g), for example, consists of only six words. To recite such a short text in the same manner as the Epistle or Gospel would create an exceptionally brief unit of music. This kind of text demands a more elaborate presentation, and the Alleluia repertory in particular is known for its florid, exuberant melodies, especially on the final syllable of the word *alleluia,* a passage known as the *jubilus* (derived from the same root word as the word "jubilation").

The Gradual, Alleluia, and Tract are called responsorial chants because the chorus alternates with ("responds to") the soloist or a small group of soloists. In the Gradual for Easter Sunday, *Haec dies,* the soloist intones the opening two words (up to the asterisk marked in the score), at which point the chorus enters (*quam fecit Dominus…*). (Modern performances, including the one here, no longer observe this distinction between soloist and chorus in the intonation.) This entire unit is known as the respond. The subsequent psalm verse, taken from the Psalm 118:1 (*Confitemini Domino…*) is then sung by the soloist. In earlier times, the chorus's part of the respond would be repeated, but this practice had disappeared by the 13th century.

Alleluias are performed in a slightly different manner. The soloist intones the opening word (up to the asterisk in the score), then the chorus repeats this same passage exactly. The chorus proceeds to sing the *jubilus,* an elaborate melisma, and the soloist then sings the verse (*Pascha nostrum…*), with the chorus joining in on the final phrase (here, *Christus*). Finally, the soloist sings the opening *alleluia* and the chorus enters directly with the *jubilus.*

3 Plainchant **Vespers on Trinity Sunday**

Companion CD   Track 1

p. 41

a) Antiphon *Laus Deo Patri*

To God the Father, to the Son co-equal, and to the Spirit proceeding, let praise resound unceasingly from the lips of all creation, throughout all ages, world without end.

b) Psalm 112 *Laudate Pueri*

1. Laudá-te pú-*e-ri* Dóminum : * laudá-*te nómen* Dómi-ni.

2. Sit nómen Dómini *bene*dictum, * ex hoc nunc, et *usque* in saéculum. (E : saéculum.)

3. A sólis órtu usque *ad oc*cásum, * laudábile *nómen* Dómini. (E : Dómini.)

4. Excélsus super ómnes *géntes* Dóminus, * et super caélos *glória* éjus.

5. Quis sicut Dóminus Déus nóster, qui in *áltis* hábitat, * et humília réspicit in ca*élo et in* térra?

6. Súscitans a *térra* inopem, * et de stércore *érigens* páuperem : (E : páuperem.)

7. Ut cóllocet éum *cum prin*cipibus, * cum princípibus *pópuli* súi.

8. Qui habitáre fácit stéri*lem in* dómo, * mátrem fili*órum lae*tántem.

1. PRAISE the LORD, ye servants; * O praise the Name of the LORD.
2. Blessed be the Name of the LORD * from this time forth for evermore.
3. The LORD'S Name is praised * from the rising up of the sun unto the going down of the same.
4. The LORD is high above all nations, * and his glory above the heavens.
5. Who is like unto the LORD our God, that hath his dwelling so high, * and yet humbleth himself to behold the things that are in heaven and earth!
6. He taketh up the simple out of the dust, * and lifteth the poor out of the mire;
7. That he may set him with the princes, * even with the princes of his people.
8. He maketh the barren woman to keep house, * and to be a joyful mother of children.

The chants for the Divine Office (Matins, Lauds, etc.) center on the singing or recitation of Psalms. Each Psalm recitation in the Divine Office was preceded and followed by a more musically varied antiphon. At Vespers on Trinity Sunday, for example, Psalm 112, *Laudate pueri,* is recited to the fourth psalm tone and is both preceded and followed by the antiphon *Laus Deo Patri.*

Antiphons tend to be relatively brief. Though syllabic, they are more melodically varied than the psalm recitations they frame. *Laus Deo Patri,* in Mode 4, begins and ends on the E and covers a melodic span down to the C below and the B above. The melodic intervals are largely conjunct (that is, by step); there is no interval larger than a third in this particular antiphon. The melody as a whole traces a gentle upward progression, followed by a slow descent, and a brief rise just before the end, when it cadences on the original pitch of E.

Psalms, whose texts are much longer than those of antiphons, are recited syllabically to one of the eight melodic formulas known as psalm tones (see Textbook Example 1-2). Textually, psalm verses fall into two more or less equal halves, and the music of the psalm tones reflects this structure. Each half centers on a recitation tone that is repeated often enough to accommodate all the words of the verse at hand. The first half of each psalm tone ends in a mediant (mid-way) cadence, indicated in the notation here with a solid line through the staff: the unshaded square neume can be repeated as needed according to the number of syllables in the text at this point. The second half ends in a more distinctive cadence—in the case of the Fourth Psalm Tone shown here, this is a step-wise descent down to the pitch E. This formula is repeated until all the appointed verses of the psalm have been sung. The two halves of the psalm tone were often sung antiphonally; in the performance here, the soloist sings the first half of each verse, and the chorus sings the second. At the end of the psalm, the Doxology ("Glory be to the Father. . .") is sung to the same psalm tone. At this point, the original antiphon is repeated in its entirety. Thus the antiphon creates what might be thought of as a set of bookends for the psalm. (Note: Because of different numbering systems, Psalm 112 is numbered 113 in some editions of the Psalms.)

4 Plainchant Hymn **Pange lingua gloriosi corporis mysterium** (late 13th century)

CD1   Track 12

p. 41

1. Pan- ge lin- gua glo- ri- o- si Cor- po- ris mys- te- ri- um,

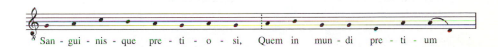

San- gui- nis- que pre- ti- o- si, Quem in mun- di pre- ti- um

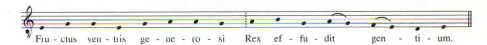

Fru- ctus ven- tris ge- ne- ro- si Rex ef- fu- dit gen- ti- um.

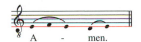

A- men.

1. Pange lingua gloriosi Corporis mysterium, Sanguinisque pretiosi, Quem in mundi pretium Fructus ventris generosi Rex effudit gentium.	1. Sing, my tongue, the Savior's glory of His flesh the mystery sing; of the Blood, all price exceeding, shed by our immortal King, destined, for the world's redemption, from a noble womb to spring.
2. Nobis datus, nobis natus Ex intacta Virgine, Et in mundo conversatus, Sparso verbi semine, Sui moras incolatus Miro clausit ordine.	2. Of a pure and spotless Virgin born for us on earth below, He, as Man, with man conversing, stayed, the seeds of truth to sow; then He closed in solemn order wondrously His life of woe.
3. In supremae nocte coenae, Recumbens cum fratribus, Observata lege plene Cibis in legalibus, Cibum turbae duodenae Se dat suis manibus.	3. On the night of that Last Supper, seated with His chosen band, He the Pascal victim eating, first fulfills the Law's command; then as Food to His Apostles gives Himself with His own hand.

4. Verbum caro, panem verum
   Verbo carnem efficit:
   Fitque sanguis Christi merum,
   Et si sensus deficit,
   Ad firmandum cor sincerum
   Sola fides sufficit.

5. Tantum ergo Sacramentum
   Veneremur cernui:
   Et antiquum documentum
   Novo cedat ritui:
   Praestet fides supplementum
   Sensuum defectui.

6. Genitori, Genitoque
   Laus et jubilatio,
   Salus, honor, virtus quoque
   Sit et benedictio:
   Procedenti ab utroque
   Compar sit laudatio.
   Amen.

   (St. Thomas Aquinas, 1225–1274)

4. Word-made-Flesh, the bread of nature
   by His word to Flesh He turns;
   wine into His Blood He changes;—
   what though sense no change discerns?
   Only be the heart in earnest,
   faith her lesson quickly learns.

5. Down in adoration falling,
   Lo! the sacred Host we hail;
   Lo! o'er ancient forms departing,
   newer rites of grace prevail;
   faith for all defects supplying,
   where the feeble senses fail.

6. To the everlasting Father,
   and the Son who reigns on high,
   with the Holy Ghost proceeding
   forth from Each eternally,
   be salvation, honor, blessing,
   might and endless majesty.
   Amen.

   [from *Liturgia Horarum,*
   trans. Fr. Edward Caswall (1814–1878)]

Hymns tend to be syllabic in style. They typically feature multiple strophes, as in the hymn for the Feast of Corpus Christi, *Pange lingua gloriosi corporis mysterium*. Hymns played an important role in the Divine Office. In contrast to liturgical or scriptural texts, hymn texts were newly written and provided an important outlet for the expression of religious ideals and belief. The text of *Pange lingua gloriosi corporis mysterium* was written by none other than Thomas Aquinas (1225–1274), one of the most important theologians of the medieval church. Its melody, by an unknown composer, bears the melodic hallmarks of a later chant style, with a strong sense of melodic symmetry and direction.

5   Ordo virtutum (excerpt) (ca. 1150)
Hildegard von Bingen (1098–1179)

CD1   Track 13
p. 51

IV

[The Devil attempts to break into the circle of the Virtues to retrieve the Soul, but he is repulsed by them. It would be appropriate for them to repel the Devil by throwing flowers at him.

Victory and Chastity will take up a chain and, with the help of one or more of the other Virtues, will bind the Devil, who will be left lying on the floor until the the end of the production.]

72. The Devil

Que es, aut unde venis?
Who are you, and from whence do you come?

Tu amplexata es me, et ego foras eduxi te.
You have embraced me, and I have led you forth.

Sed nunc in reversione tua confundis me;
But now in your turning back you confuse me;

Ego autem pugna mea deiciam te!
But I will hurl you down with my assault.

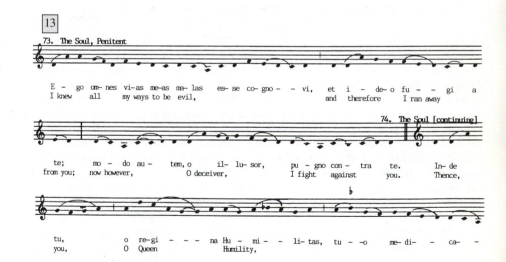

73. The Soul, Penitent

E - go om- nes vi- as me- as ma- las es- se co- gno - - vi, et i - de- o fu - - gi a
I knew all my ways to be evil, and therefore I ran away

74. The Soul [continuing]

te; mo - do au - tem, o il - lu- sor, pu - gno con - tra te. In- de
from you; now however, O deceiver, I fight against you. Thence,

tu, o re- gi - - - na Hu - mi - - li- tas, tu - -o me- di - - ca -
you, O Queen Humility,

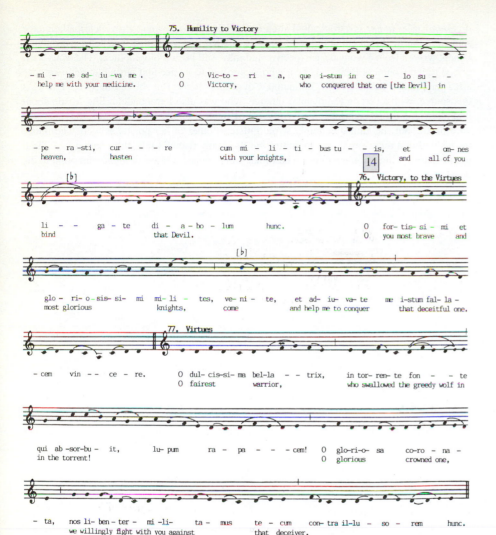

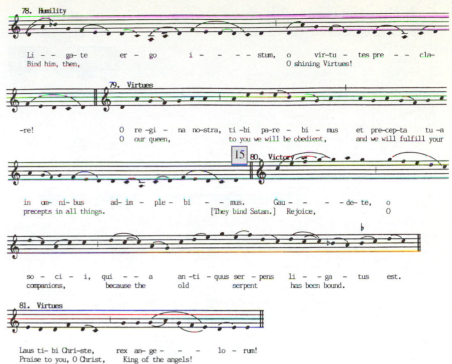

Hildegard von Bingen's *Ordo virtutum* ("Play of Virtues") is a freely composed drama not connected with any existing chant or ritual but composed instead to texts and melodies entirely of Hildegard's own creation. The plot of this morality play—a dramatized allegory of good versus evil—centers on a series of disputes between the devil and sixteen Virtues, each of which is represented by a different singer. Dramatized performances of such dialogues varied widely by time and location, as well as by their place in the liturgy. They were sometimes presented as tropes of the Introit at Mass, sometimes as additions to Matins.

Each character of Hildegard's drama has its own musical profile. "The Penitent Soul," heard at the beginning of this excerpt, sings in a relatively low range when addressing the devil but moves into a higher range when she turns to the Blessed Virgin Mary, the "Queen of Humility." Hildegard also highlights the climactic moment when Satan is bound and thereby symbolically defeated. At this moment, "Victory" sings a high melisma on the word *Gaudete* ("rejoice"). The music up until this point has been largely syllabic and in a lower range. Throughout the entire drama, Satan himself has no music at all: he shouts his lines. It would seem that hell, for Hildegard, was a world without music.

Performance notes: The entrance of the bells at the climactic moment of Satan's binding is not indicated in the preserved sources of this work but is very much in keeping with the spirit of the moment. The sources also do not indicate very much in the way of staging and the movement of the singers; these, too, must be interpolated into any live performance.

6 A chantar (early 13th century)
Beatriz de Dia (d. ca. 1212)

[handwritten: troubador song]

[handwritten: syllabic]

[handwritten annotations: Pure sound, minimal vibrato, High... / Sustained string note, woman comes in octave above / E / form follows poetry / troubador song—genera]

A chantar m'es al cor is a troubadour song in Occitan (also known as Provençal), a language spoken in the medieval era in the southern part of what is now France. The song is a moving lament written from a woman's perspective and may well be autobiographical. The song is ascribed to the Countess Beatriz de Dia, who, according to an account written about a century after her death, was married to Guillaume, Count of Poitiers. But she fell in love, or so says this source, with a certain Raimbaut d'Orange, who was also a troubadour. She "made about him many good and beautiful songs." Only one of Beatriz's poems—*A chantar*—has survived with music, but she almost certainly wrote music to other of her poems as well. The music moves within a relatively narrow ambitus, but its steady rise and fall, culminating in a climb to the melody's highest pitch in the penultimate line, imparts a sense of intense emotion to the words.

[handwritten: range]

A chantar m'es al cor que non deurie
tant mi rancun cele a qui sui amigs,

et si l'am mais que nule ren qui sie;
non mi val ren beltat ni curtesie
ne ma bontaz ne mon pres ne mon sen;
altresi sui enganade et tragide
qu'eusse fait vers lui desavinence.

To sing I must of what I'd rather not,
so much does he of whom I am the lover
    embitter me;
yet I love him more than anything in the world.
To no avail are my beauty or politeness,
my goodness, or my virtue and good sense.
For I have been cheated and betrayed,
as if I had been disagreeable to him.

CD1   Track 16

p. 56

Cantigas de Santa Maria, no. 140:
A Santa Maria dadas (ca. 1270–1290)

CD1　Track 17

p. 57

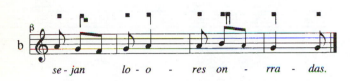

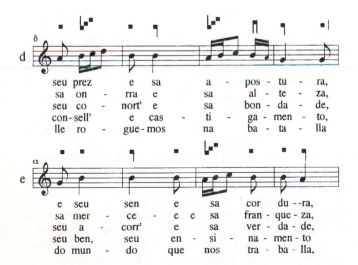

A Santa Maria dadas	*To Holy Mary be*
sejan loores onrradas.	*given respectful praises.*

1. Loemos a sa mesura,
   seu prez e sa apostura,
   e seu sen e sa cordura,
   mui máis ca cen mil vegadas.
   A Santa Maria...

   Let us praise her dignity,
   her worth and her gracefulness,
   and her judgment and her wisdom,   5
   much more than a hundred thousand times.
   To Holy Mary,,,

2. Loemos a sa nobreza,
   sa onrra e sa alteza,
   sa mercee e sa franqueza,
   e sas vertudes preçadas.
   A Santa Maria...

   Let us praise her nobility,
   her honour and her rank,
   her mercy and her openness,   10
   and her treasured virtues.
   To Holy Mary...

CANTIGA 140

3. Loemos sa lealdade,
   seu conort' e sa bondade,
   seu acorr' e sa verdade,
   con loores mui cantadas.
   A Santa Maria...

   Let us praise her loyalty,
   her consolation and her bounty,
   her help and her truth,   15
   with praises ever sung.
   To Holy Mary...

4. Loemos seu cousimento,
   consell' e castigamento,
   seu ben, seu ensinamento
   e sas graças mui grãadas.
   A Santa Maria...

   Let us praise her attentiveness,
   her counsel and admonition,
   her goodness, her learning   20
   and her graces so fine.
   To Holy Mary...

5. Loando-a, que nos valla
   lle roguemos na batalla
   do mundo que nos traballa,
   e do dem' a denodadas.
   A Santa Maria...

   In praising her, let us ask her
   that she be a strength to us in the battle
   against this world, which causes us travail,   25
   and against the devil, with valour.
   To Holy Mary...

The preserved repertory of *cantigas* ("songs") from the Iberian Peninsula—present-day Spain and Portugal—is quite small. Only two sources transmit the poetry with melodies. One of these is a large and sumptuously illustrated manuscript containing more than 400 *Cantigas de Santa Maria,* songs in Honor of the Virgin Mary (see illustration, Textbook, p. xx). This source was prepared for (and possibly composed in part by) Alfonso el Sabio ("The Wise"), king of Castille and Leon from 1252 until 1284. Although sacred in subject matter, these songs were not liturgical. Their poetic and musical style, moreover, is consistent with what we know of the secular songs that were written in this place and time. The texts of the *cantigas* are written in Gallo-Portuguese, and most are set syllabically in strophic form with a refrain.

Scholars have long debated the extent of Arabic influence on the music of this repertory. Large portions of the Iberian Peninsula had been under Muslim rule since the 8th century, and the impact of this culture on the regions of what are now Spain and Portugal extended to virtually every aspect of life. Exactly how much musical influence is to be found in the *Cantigas de Santa Maria* remains unclear, however.

Performance notes: The accompanying instrument heard on this recording is a dulcimer, a zither-like instrument struck with two small wooden sticks. The fact that only the vocal line is preserved in notated form in no way precludes the addition of one or more instruments that might serve to introduce the voice and double its line.

8 Palästinalied, (ca. 1200)
Walther von der Vogelweide (ca. 1170–1230)

CD1   Track 18

p. 60

1. Nu alrest leb' ich mir werde,
   sît mîn sundic ouge ersiht.
   Lant daz hêre und ouch die erde,
   dem man vil der êren giht.

   Mir'st geschehn, des ich ie bat,
   ich bin komen an die stat,
   da got mennischlîchen trat.

1. Now for the first time I am alive,
   For my sinful eyes have beheld
   the land here and the very earth
   to which mankind gives such honor.

   I have that for which I so long prayed,
   I have come to the place
   where God walked as man.

In German-speaking lands, the *Minnesinger* (literally, singers of *Minne,* or "courtly love") developed their own repertory of songs. Walther von der Vogelweide's *Palästinalied* provides a good example of this repertory. Chivalry, the praise of God, and the praise of noblewomen are recurrent themes in this repertory. Like many *Minnelieder* (*Lieder* means "songs"), Walther's *Palästinalied* is written in bar form, consisting of two musically identical statements (called *Stollen*) and a final closing statement (the *Abgesang*), creating the pattern of AAB. It is largely syllabic, and it tells of a crusader knight's thrill at standing on the same ground as Christ had during his lifetime. (The First Crusade had captured Jerusalem in 1099, permitting Christians to make pilgrimages to the holy city.) Like the songs of the troubadours and trouvères, the *Minnelieder* were almost certainly performed to the accompaniment of instruments, but no notated source of this accompaniment has been preserved.

Performance notes: The plucked instrument heard in the accompaniment is an *'ud,* a short-necked lute without frets common in northern Africa and the Middle East. It is a forerunner of the lute, whose name is a corruption of the French *l'ud* ("the *'ud*"). The bowed stringed instrument is a rebec, a small, three-stringed instrument also of Middle Eastern origin.

9 Melismatic organum, **Kyrie Cunctipotens genitor deus** (Codex Calixtinus, ca. 1120–1130)

CD1 Track 20
p. 63

Cunctipotens genitor Deus, omni creator, eleyson.
Fons et origo boni pie luxque perennis, eleison.

Salvificet pietas tua nos bone rector, eleison.

Criste Dei forma virtus Patrisque sophia, eleyson.
Plasmatis humani factor lapsi reparator, eleison.

Ne tua damnetur jhesu factura benigne, eleison.

Amborum sacrum spiramen nexus amorque, eleyson.
Procedens fomes vitae fons purificans vis, eleison.

Purgator culpe venie largitor opimae, offensas dele sancto nos munere reple spiritus alme.

Omnipotent Father, God, creator of all, have mercy.
Fountain and origin of all good, holy and eternal light, have mercy.

May your holiness bring us salvation, O good Leader, have mercy.

Christ, appearance of God, power and wisdom of the Father, have mercy.
Maker of human flesh, savior of the fallen, have mercy.

Let not your creation be damned, O goodly Jesus.

Sacred breath of both, and combined love, have mercy.
Active former of life, fountain purifying us, have mercy.

Redeemer of sin, greatest dispenser of pardon, remove our misdeeds, fill us with holy reward, O nurturing Spirit.

(text and melody from additional source: Paris, Bibl. Nat. lat. 887, f.56, shown here in italics)

Melismatic organum introduced multiple notes in the *vox organalis* against a single note in the chant. This allowed for a much wider use of dissonance between the organal voice and the chant. This type of organum is particularly prevalent in manuscripts from northern Spain and from southwestern France, particularly the abbey of St. Martial, in what is now southern France. This particular organum comes from the Codex Calixtinus, a text written around 1120–1130 as a guide and songbook for pilgrims on their way to Santiago de Compostela, the site of the shrine of Saint James the Apostle, in what is now northwestern Spain. This two-part organum is built on the plainchant Kyrie *Cunctipotens genitor deus* (see Textbook, p. 48). Each unit of this chant (Kyrie, Christe, Kyrie) is sung twice, first with an organal voice above, then in its original monophonic form (corresponding to m. 9, 18, 24 in the transcription here).

Performance notes: While the pitches of the original notation are fairly clear, the alignment of the two is often ambiguous. The edition here suggests one possible approach to making the two voices consonant; the performance suggests another. The opening and closing harmonies of each melodic unit (demarcated by a rest in the score) are always consonant at the unison, fifth, or ocatve; the way in which the two voices converge in the middle of each phrase remains open to interpretation.

10 Organum **Haec dies** (mid- to late 12th century) (ca. 1150)
Léonin (?) (fl. mid- to late 12th century)

CD1 Track 23

p. 65

R. Haec dies [quam fecit dominus: exsultemus
   et laetemur in ea.]
V. Confitemini Domino, quoniam bonus:
   quoniam in saeculum [misericordia eius].

R. This is the day [which the Lord hath made;
   let us rejoice and be glad in it.]
V. Give thanks unto the Lord; for he is good:
   for [his mercy endureth for ever].

(Ps. 118: 24, 29)
N.B. The text in brackets is performed in
plainchant, not organum, and therefore does
not appear in the original score.

This organum setting of the Easter plainchant Gradual *Haec dies* (Anthology 1/#4) is part of the *Magnus liber organi*. Based on the account of the author known as Anonymous IV, it is ascribed to Léonin, the 12th-century composer who worked in and around the Cathedral of Notre Dame in Paris.

To understand the structure of organum, we must first understand the structure of the original chant. In this case, *Haec dies* is a responsorial chant, portions of which were performed by a soloist (or small group of soloists singing in unison) in the Middle Ages, other portions of which are performed by a chorus responding to the soloist. Léonin left unchanged the choral portions of these chants, which continued to be performed monophonically by the chorus, but he wrote lengthy two-voice organa for those portions of the chants performed by the soloist (or soloists). His organum setting of the Easter plainchant Gradual *Haec dies* may be diagrammed as follows:

Respond		Verse	
Soloist	Chorus	Soloist	Chorus
Two-part organum	Plainchant	Two-part organum	Plainchant
Haec dies	*quam fecit Dominus…*	*Confitemini Domino…*	*misericordia ejus.*

Léonin's organal sections are either in free organum (also known as "unmeasured organum") or in measured organum (also known as "discant organum"). In free organum, the duplum voice moves rapidly against the slower-moving notes of the original chant. It was used in passages that in the original chant are neumatic (up to five or six notes per syllable), as on the opening words *Haec dies*. In measured organum, the two voices move at about the same speed in what is essentially a note-against-note style. This type of organum was used in passages that are melismatic in the original chant (many notes per syllable), such as on the word *Domino,* and, toward the end, on the words *in saeculum.*

Performance notes: As is so often the case in early polyphony, questions of rhythmic interpretation are far more troublesome than questions of pitch. The edition here interprets the entire organum in modern-day notation; but this does not reflect the kind of rhythmic fluidity that was probably used in actual performances of organum during the 12th century, particularly in the sections of free organum (as at the beginning, m. 1–51). The measured organum (m. 70–98, for example) is somewhat better served by this form of notation; the rhythmic coordination of the two voices here is less ambiguous. Some recent performances of organum have doubled the sustained lower voices with instruments, but there is some controversy over whether or not this would have been the practice in the medieval church. The recording here is entirely vocal.

No. 10 Léonin: *Haec dies* ■ 21

11 Clausula **In saeculum** (second half of 12th century)

in seculum   forever

The desire to gloss existing chants did not end with the composition of organum. Composers like Perotin also composed many *clausulae*—brief polyphonic sections of discant organum—that could be substituted at will into the appropriate section of a larger existing work of organum. The *clausula* (to use its singular form) is thus not an independent composition that can be performed on its own. The tenor voice of a typical *clausula,* in fact, often consists of only a single word or even just a syllable or two of a longer word.

    A single source typically provides *clausulae* for several different passages within the same organum, and even multiple *clausulae* for the same passage. The Florence manuscript of the *Magnus liber organi,* for example, contains no fewer than ten different *clausulae* for the passage on the words *in saeculum* (or *seculum*) within the Gradual *Haec dies.* In performing organum, singers were free to substitute whichever *clausula* or *clausulae* they desired in any combination. Alternatively, they could use no *clausulae* at all. From a liturgical point of view what is important here is that regardless of the combination of *clausulae* chosen, all the notes and words of the original chant would be present in one form or another.

    Stylistically, *clausulae* are no different from the music they were written to replace. Within the complete organum of the Gradual *Haec dies* in the manuscript known as W1, for example, the passage on the words *in saeculum* is set in measured organum. The many *clausulae* that might be substituted for this passage are also in measured organum (note-against-note); the *clausula* given here, from the manuscript known as W2, is somewhat longer than the passage it was written to replace, although others on the same text are sometimes shorter and sometimes about the same length. This particular *clausula* happens to state the original chant melody (in the lower voice) twice, beginning at m. 1 and at m. 15.

12 Motet **Lonc tens ai mon cuer/ In seculum** (early 13th century)

CD1   Track 28

p. 69

1. *Lonc tens ai mon cuer assis*	1. I have fixed my heart on
2. *en bien amer.*	2. loving well for a long time.
3. N'onques vers amours ne fis	3. Never did I do anything to love
4. riens a blaumer;	4. which would incur blame.
5. ainz me sui mout entremis	5. Rather, I have made every effort
6. de lui loer.	6. to praise him.
7. Or ne puis mes endurer,	7. Now I can hold out no longer:
8. si m'a conquis;	8. he has conquered me;
9. de sa joie m'a si pris,	9. his joy has captured me so securely
10. n'i puis durer.	10. that I cannot go on.
11. Par mi sunt si pleur et si ris,	11. I am given to tears, then to laughter.
12. tout truis amer;	12. I find everything bitter;
13. quant le quit meillor trover,	13. when I think I will find love better,
14. lors me fet pis.	14. then he does something worse.
15. *Dieus quant je me doi*	15. God, when I should be
16. *la nuit reposer,*	16. resting at night,
17. *resveillent moi*	17. love's sweet pains
18. *li doz mal d'amer.*	18. waken me.

Although *clausulae* may have been fragmentary from a liturgical point of view, consisting of only a few syllables or words, the longer ones constituted a musical whole that began and ended in the same mode; the very word *clausula* itself comes from a Latin root meaning to cadence or conclude. The only thing *clausulae* lacked to be performed separately was a text.

In the venerable medieval tradition of troping, some unknown individual or group of individuals working in the late 12th or early 13th century had the idea of underlaying a new text to the duplum of an existing *clausula* and performing the new work outside the liturgy of the church. Thus was born the genre of the motet (from the French word *mot,* meaning "word"). The term was fitting because the text for the duplum in many of the earliest motets was in the vernacular, not Latin. It is the presence of a contrasting text in the upper voice or voices that distinguishes the motet from its immediate ancestor, the *clausula.* The texted duplum was known as the *motetus* because it had words.

Musically, there are only minor differences between the *clausula* on *in seculum* (Anthology No. 11) and the motet *Lonc tens ai mon cuer / In seculum* found in a mid-13th-century manuscript. (By convention, the titles of 13th-century motets consist of the first word or words of each voice in order from top to bottom.) The text for the motetus—a love song—is decidedly secular. The introduction of secular words into what had previously been a sacred work is something found repeatedly in the repertory of medieval motets.

13   Motet **Huic main / Hec dies**
(early 13th century)

CD1   Track 29
p. 71

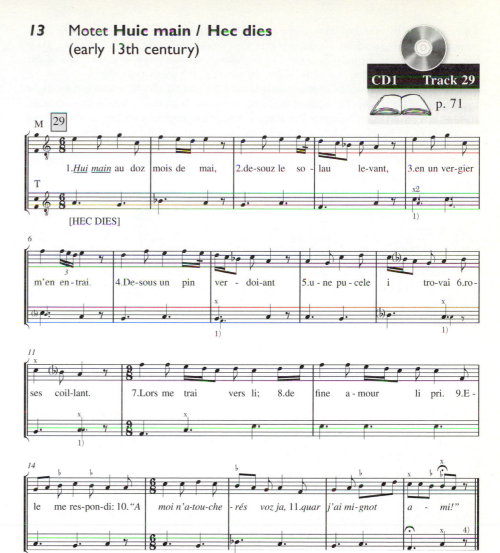

1. *Hui main* au doz mois de mai,	1. This morning, in the sweet month of May,
2. desouz le solau levant,	2. just as the sun was rising,
3. en un vergier m'en entrai.	3. I entered an orchard.
4. Desous un pin verdoiant	4. There under a lush green pine
5. une pucele i trovai	5. I found a maiden
6. roses coillant.	6. gathering roses.
7. Lors me trai vers li;	7. Forthwith I approached her
8. de fine amour li pri.	8. and courteously declared my love for her.
9. Ele me respondi:	9. She answered me:
10. *"A moi n'atoucherés voz ja,*	10. "You will never touch me,
11. *quar j'ai mignot ami!"*	11. for I have a handsome sweetheart!"

Separated from its liturgical context, the tenor of a motet was no longer a sacred object—a portion of a larger plainchant—and composers were quick to take advantage of this fact. They began to manipulate the musical content of the tenor in various ways. In one version of the opening of the motet *Huic main / Hec dies,* for example, the anonymous composer uses the first eight notes of the chant in a conventional fashion but then breaks off, repeating these eight notes not once but twice. (The score in the anthology shows both this version and an alternate version from a different source.) The notes of the chant resume with the words *De fine amour...,* but the opening eight notes come back one more time at the very end, to the words *moi n'a toucherés.* Although derived from a chant, this tenor has clearly lost not only its liturgical function but also its original musical shape, serving instead as the point of departure for an essentially new composition.

14 Motet **A Paris / On parole / Frese nouvele** (late 13th century)

CD1   Track 30

p. 71

a mes-tier, 10. pour so-la - cier 11. be-les da-mes a de-vis: 12. Et tout ce truev[e] on a Pa-ris.

en - tre-deus 8. de men - re feur pour ho - mes de - si-teus.

ve - le, mue-re fran - ce, mue-re, mue-re fran - ce!]

Triplum
1. On parole de batre et de vanner
2. et de foïr et de hanner;
3. mais ces deduis trop me desplaisent,
4. car il n'est si bone vie que d'estre a aise
5. de bon cler vin et de chapons
6. et d'estre aveuc bons compaignons,
7. liés et joiaus,
8. chantans, truffans et amorous,
9. et d'avoir, quant a mestier,
10. pour solacier
11. beles dames a devis:
12. Et tout ce truev[e] on a Paris.

Duplum
1. A Paris soir et matin
2. truev[e] on bon pain et bon cler vin,
3. bone char et bon poisson,
4. de toutes guises compaignons,
5. sens soutie, grant baudour,
6. biaus joiaus dames d'ounour;
7. et si truev[e] on bien entredeus
8. de menre feur pour homes desiteus.

Tenor
1. Frese nouvele, muere france,
   muere, muere france!
2. Frese nouvele, muere france,
   muere, muere france!
3. Frese nouvele, muere france,
   muere, muere france!
4. Frese nouvele, muere france,
   muere, muere france!

Triplum
The talk is of theshing and winnowing,
of digging and ploughing.
Such pastimes are not at all to my liking.
For there is nothing like having one's fill
of good clear wine and capons,
and being with good friends,
hale and hearty,
singing, joking and in love,
and having all one needs
to give pleasure to beautiful women
to one's heart's content.
All of this is to be had in Paris.

Duplum
Morning and night in Paris
there is good bread to be found, good clear wine,
good meat and fish,
all manner of friends
of lively minds and high spirits,
fine jewels and noble ladies
and, in the meantime,
prices to suit a poor man's purse.

Tenor
Fresh strawberries! Nice blackberries!
Blackberries, nice blackberries!
Fresh strawberries! Nice blackberries!
Blackberries, nice blackberries!
Fresh strawberries! Nice blackberries!
Blackberries, nice blackberries!
Fresh strawberries! Nice blackberries!
Blackberries, nice blackberries!

—Translated by Michael J. Freeman

The anonymous motet *A Paris / On parole / Frese nouvele* bears no relationship at all to any preexistent work. It is based on a newly composed tenor with its own self-contained (if very brief) text in French. The tenor states its eight-measure unit of text and music a total of four times. At least one of the two upper voices, in turn, overlaps the cadential points of the tenor, thus creating a sense of forward momentum even while articulating points of rest within the three-voice texture. The text of the tenor—*Frese nouvele, muere france* ("Fresh strawberries! Nice blackberries!")—is a street vendor's call, the 13th-century-equivalent of a peanut vendor's cry in a baseball stadium. As such, it justifies both the musical and textual repetition it receives here.

The motetus and triplum of this same motet present two texts different from each other and different yet again from that of the tenor. The resulting polytextual motet is typical of the genre in the second half of the 13th century. The three texts of *A Paris / On parole / Frese nouvele* are all related in content. Above the street-vendor's cry in the tenor, the triplum and duplum extol the virtues of Paris: good bread, good wine, good friends, even good prices "to suit a poor man's purse." The texts of many other 13th-century motets are more diverse; some are even polyglot, with a motetus in Latin and a triplum in French, or vice versa. Subject matter is often equally unrelated. It is not unusual, for example, to find a sacred Latin motetus juxtaposed with a French triplum whose text is a love poem. The distinction between sacred and secular was not nearly so sharp in the medieval era as it would be in later centuries. Still, one senses in at least some of these compositions a real delight in the contrasting images they evoke. It is also likely that they contain references that would have been familiar in the 13th century but are no longer readily grasped today.

Performance notes: This recording begins with a complete statement of the tenor line by itself, followed by the tenor and motetus together, followed at last by the addition of the triplum. This additive approach to performance, although not indicated in the score, allows for each voice to be heard with special clarity.

15　Conductus **Flos ut rosa floruit**
(second half of 13th century)

CD1　Track 31
p. 73

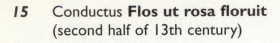

I.

Flos ut ro - sa flo - ru - it, quan-do Virgo ge - nu - it Ma - ri - a

6

Sal - va - to - rem om - ni - um, sum-mi Pa-tris Fi - li - um, *no-va ge - ni - tu - ra.*

12
II.

Qui di - vi - na gra - ci - a de - scen-dit ad in - fe-ra hu - ma - na,

17

Et sal - va - vit om - ni - a sum-ma cum po - ten - ci - a, *no-va ge - ni - tu - ra.*

23 III.

Can -te -mus hym - num glo-ri - e, can -ti -co le - ti - ci - e lau - dan - do,

28

Sol - lem-pni-zan - tes ho - di -e re - gi re-gum iu - sti - ci - e gra - ci - as a - gen-do.

34 IV.

Qui na -tus est de vir - gi -ne mi -sti -co spi - ra - mi-ne, *no-va ge - ni - tu - ra.*

40

Er - go no - stra con - ci - o psal - lat cum tri - pu - di - o

44

be - ne - di - cat Do - - - - - - - - - mi - no.

I. Flos ut rosa floruit, quando Virgo genuit Maria
Salvatorem omnium, summi Patris Filium, *nova genitura.*

II. Qui divina gracia descendit ad infera humana,
Et salvavit omnia summa cum potencia, *nova genitura.*

III. Cantemus hymnum glorie, cantico leticie laudando,
Sollempnizantes hodie regi regum iusticie gracias agendo.

IV. Qui natus est de virgine mistico spiramine, *nova genitura.*
Ergo nostra concio psallat cum tripudio benedicat Domino.

I. A flower bloomed like a rose, when the Virgin Mary gave birth
To the Savior of all people, the Son of the highest Father, *in a birth of utter newness.*

II. In divine grace he came down to humanity below
And saved us all with his immense power, *in a birth of utter newness.*

III. Let us sing a hymn of glory, praising him with a song of joy,
And celebrate today by giving thanks to the justice of the king of kings.

IV. He was born of a virgin by a mystical spirit, *in a birth of utter newness.*
Therefore let this group dance and sing praises and bless the Lord.

The conductus offered yet another outlet for composers wishing to write either monophonic or polyphonic music in the late 12th and early 13th centuries. These works, for one, two, three, or occasionally four voices, are not based on borrowed material of any kind. The texts consist of freely composed poetry written in metered verse that lend themselves to syllabic and strongly metrical musical settings. In the polyphonic conductus, all voices move in roughly the same rhythm. The note-against-note part-writing in this genre is so distinctive in fact that this manner of composition in medieval music has since come to be called "conductus style." Conducti (or conductus; both can be used as plurals) derive their name from the Latin word *conducere,* meaning "to escort," and these pieces were probably first used as processionals—that is, as music to be performed while a priest and his attendants entered and left the church.

Rhythmically, the notation of these pieces is ambiguous. They do not follow the system of modal rhythm evident in the measured sections of organum, clausula, and motet, but probably adhere to the modal rhythm of the texts themselves. Most sources align the voices with some care, using vertical lines to clarify the relationship of the different parts. The long melisma at the end of the last strophe of *Flos ut rosa floruit* is a characteristic feature of the genre known as a *cauda,* a term derived from the Latin word for "tail," the same root word from which "coda" would eventually evolve.

16 Garrit Gallus / In nova fert / Neuma

from the Roman de Fauvel (ca. 1315)

Philippe de Vitry (?) (1291–1361)

Companion CD   Track 3

p. 79

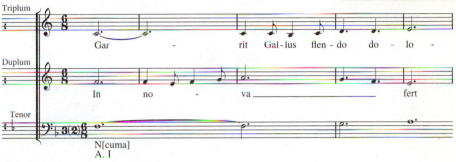

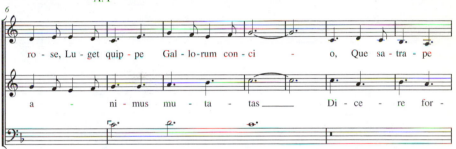

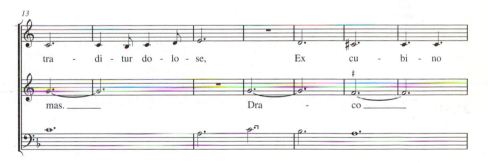

TRIPLUM

Garrit Gallus flendo dolorose	The cock babbles, lamenting sorrowfully,
Luget quippe Gallorum concio.	for the whole assembly of cocks*
Que satrape traditur dolose,	mourns because, while serving vigilantly,
Ex cubino sedens officio.	it is trickily betrayed by the satrap.
Atque vulpes, tamquam vispilio	And the fox,† like a grave robber,
in Belial vigens astucia	thriving with the astuteness of Belial,
De leonis consensu proprio	rules as a monarch with the consent
Monarchisat, atat angaria	of the lion himself.‡ Ah, what slavery!
Rursus, ecce. Jacob familia	Lo, once again Jacob's family
Pharaone altero fugatur;	is exiled by another Pharaoh.
Non ut olim lude vestigia	Not, as formerly, able to escape
Subintrare potens, lacrimatur.	to the homeland of Judah, they weep.
In deserto fame flagellatur.	Stricken by hunger in the desert,
Adiutoris carens armatura.	lacking the help of arms,
Quamquam clamat, tamen spoliatur,	although they cry out, they are robbed;
Continuo forsan moritura.	perhaps speedily they will die.

* Gallus: cock; or Gauls (the French)
† Enguerran de Marigny, chief councillor of the
  French king
‡ Philip IV the Fair

O miserum exulum vox dura!	O harsh voice of the wretched exiles;
O Gallorum garritus doloris,	O sorrowful babbling of the cocks,
Cum leonis cecitas obscura	since the dark blindness of the lion
Fraudi paret vulpis proditioris.	submits to the fraud of the traitorous fox.
Eius fastus sustinens erroris	you who suffer the arrogance of his misdeeds,
Insurgito: alias labitur	rise up,
Et labetur quod haves honoris,	or what you have of honor is being or
Quod mox in facinis tardis ultoribus itur.	will be lost, because if avengers are slow
	men soon turn to evil doing.

DUPLUM

In nova fert animus mutatas	My heart is set upon speaking of forms
Dicere formas.	changed into new (bodies).§
Draco nequam quam olim penitus	The evil dragon that renowned Michael once
Mirabilis crucis potencia	utterly defeated by the miraculous power
Debellavit Michael inclitus,	of the Cross,
Mox Absalon munitus gracia,	now endowed with the grace of Absalom,
Mox Ulixis gaudens facundia,	now with the cheerful eloquence of Ulysses,
Mox lupinis dentibus armatus,	now armed with wolfish teeth
Sub Tersitis miles milicia	a soldier in the service of Thersites,
Rursus vivit in vulpem mutatus,	lives again changed into a fox
Cauda cuius, lumine privatus	whose tail the lion deprived
Leo, vulpe imperante, paret.	of sight obeys, while the fox reigns.
Oves suggit pullis saciatus.	He sucks the blood of sheep and is satiated
	with chickens.
Heu! suggere non cessat et aret	Alas, he does not cease sucking and still thirsts;
Ad nupcias carnibus non caret.	he does not abstain from meats at the wedding feast.
Ve pullis mox, ve ceco leoni!	Woe now to the chickens, woe to the blind lion.
Coram Christotandem ve draconi.	In the presence of Christ, finally, woe to the dragon.

—RICHARD HOPPIN

§ Ovid *Metamorphoses,*1,1.

One of the twelve surviving manuscripts of the *Roman de Fauvel* includes a number of interpolated musical compositions, ranging from short, monophonic pieces to large-scale polyphonic motets. The polyglot (multilingual) motet *Garrit gallus / In nova fert / Neuma* may be by Philippe de Vitry himself, who refers to it in his treatise *Ars nova* to illustrate certain features of the *ars nova* or "new art."

The untexted tenor of *Garrit gallus / In nova fert / Neuma* is freely composed and bears the simple indication *Neuma,* a kind of generic designation for a melisma. The tenor is structured according to the principle of isorhythm, a term coined in the 20th century to describe a technique common to many motets and mass movements written between roughly 1300 and 1450. An isorhythmic tenor is one based on a fixed rhythmic and melodic pattern that is repeated at least once (and usually more often) over the course of an entire work. Isorhythm became the preferred structure of the motet in the 14th century.

The rhythmic pattern of an isorhythmic tenor is called its *talea* (meaning "cutting" or "segment"); the melodic pattern is called its *color* (a term borrowed from rhetoric and used to describe certain techniques of repetition). Although *talea* and *color* are sometimes of the same length within a given tenor, more often they arc not. The *talea* of the tenor of *Garrit gallus / In nova fert / Neuma* (see the example) is stated six times in succession, beginning at measures 1, 11, 21, 31, 41, and 51. The *color,* in contrast, is three times as long and is stated in its entirety only twice, beginning at measures 1 and 31.

The *talea* of the tenor in *Garrit gallus / In nova fert / Neuma.*

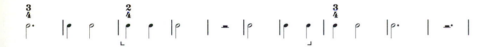

17 Messe de Nostre Dame: Kyrie
(ca. 1360)

Guillaume de Machaut (ca. 1300–1377)

CD1   Track 32

p. 81

three times

three times

Guillaume de Machaut's *Messe de Nostre Dame* ("Mass of Our Lady") is the only 14th century polyphonic setting of the complete Mass Ordinary known to have been written by a specific composer. Machaut differentiates between movements with large quantities of text and those with relatively little text. The former are set in a predominantly syllabic, conductus-like fashion (note-against-note), while the latter are set in the style of an isorhythmic motet. Whatever their differences in style, all the movements are based on a plainchant version of the appropriate element of the Ordinary. Thus the tenor of the isorhythmic Kyrie derives from the plainchant Kyrie *Cunctipotens Genitor Deus* (see Anthology 1/#9, above). The *talea* (the rhythmic pattern) of the tenor in the first Kyrie is extremely brief (only four measures in modern transcription), and the only rest comes at the very end of the *talea*, which helps articulate each successive return. The *color* (the melodic pattern), adhering to the pitches of the chant exactly, is stated only once. In a practice that became common around the middle of the 14th century, Machaut includes a voice known as the contratenor (meaning "against the tenor") that occupies the same range as the tenor. The contratenor, like the tenor, is isorhythmic, but its *talea* in the first Kyrie is longer. It is fully stated twice—in m. 1–12 and 13–25—then restated partially in the last two measures. By virtue of its length and internal rests, it keeps the motion of the lower voices moving forward. The *color* of the contratenor, unrelated to any preexisting melody, is stated only once. The motetus (duplum) and triplum move freely in more rapid rhythms. In the Christe and the final Kyrie, the *talea* of the tenor and contratenor voices coincide.

The melodic character of Machaut's Kyrie is typical of mid-14th century polyphony: somewhat angular, with large leaps (an upward seventh in the contratenor of Kyrie I in m. 17, an upward major sixth in m. 21–22), hockets (from the Latin word for "hiccough") in m. 10 and 22, and a good deal of syncopation throughout.

The principal cadences follow the standard formulas of the day, with the two structural voices—the highest-sounding voice and the tenor, which together provide the basic harmonic intervals—moving from a sixth to an octave or from a third to a fifth. Such cadences are found in Machaut's Kyrie at m. 80 (sixth to an octave in the tenor and the triplum, the highest-sounding voice at this point) and at m. 27 (third to fifth in the tenor and triplum).

18 Je puis trop bien ma dame comparer
(ca. 1350?)

Guillaume de Machaut

CD1 Track 35
p. 83

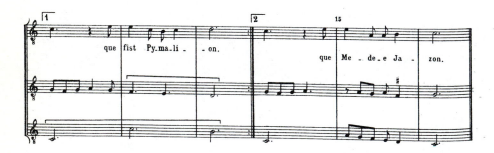

1. Je puis trop bien ma dame comparer	I can all too well compare my lady
2. A l'image que fist Pymalion.	To the image which Pygmalion made.
3. D'ivoire fu, tant belle et si sans per	It was of ivory, so beautiful, without peer,
4. Que plus l'ama que Medée Jazon.	That he loved it more than Jason did Medea.
5. Li folz toudis la prioit,	Out of his senses, he prayed to it unceasingly,
6. Mais l'image riens ne le respondoit.	But the image answered him not.
7. Einse me fait celle qui mon cuer font,	Thus does she, who makes my heart melt, treat me,
8. *Qu'ades la pri et riens ne me respont.*	*For I implore her ever, and she answers me not.*

By the middle of the 14th century, three *formes fixes*—literally "fixed forms," or structural patterns—had established themselves as the most important varieties of secular song in France: the ballade, virelai, and the rondeau. These were at once both poetic and musical forms, each with its own characteristic pattern of rhyme and musical repetition, with at least one line of refrain—that is, the same words sung to the same music in every strophe (or verse). Musically, each of these forms consists of two parts, conventionally labeled A and B. The first ending of a repeated part (A, B, or both) is known as its *ouvert* ("open") and the second ending as its *clos* ("close").

The text of the ballade usually consists of three strophes of seven or eight lines, the last of which is a refrain. The rhyme pattern varies. That of Machaut's ballade *Je puis trop bien ma dame comparer* ("I may well compare my lady") is ababccdD. (Lowercase letters indicate lines of text that are different in each strophe; uppercase letters indicate the refrain, which is identical throughout, both textually and musically.) Other typical rhyme patterns for the ballade include ababbcbC, ababcdE, and ababcdeF.

Musically, the ballade falls into two distinct sections, the first of which is always repeated and the second of which is sometimes repeated. The music thus unfolds in the pattern AAB (like Machaut's *Je puis trop bien ma dame comparer*, see the following table) or AABB.

RELATION OF TEXT AND MUSICAL STRUCTURE IN MACHAUT'S BALLADE *JE PUIS TROP BIEN MA DAME COMPARER*		
Strophe 1	**Rhyme scheme**	**Musical structure**
Je puis trop bien ma dame comparer	a	A, first ending (*ouvert*)
A l'ymage que fist Pymalion.	b	
D'yvoire fu, tant belle et si sans per	a	A, second ending (*clos*)
Que plus l'ama que Medea Jazon.	b	
Li folz toudis la prioit,	c	B
Mais l'ymage riens ne lie respondoit.	c	
Einsi me fait celle qui mon cuer font,	d	
Qu'ades la pri et riens ne me respont.	D (refrain)	

Ballades tend to be the most melismatic of all the *formes fixes* used in 14th-century France, with a rhythmically active uppermost voice. Machaut's *Je puis trop* is highly florid, yet the cadences are carefully aligned to the structure of the poetry. As in Machaut's four-part setting of the Mass, the tenor and contratenor lines weave in and out of one another.

Guillaume de Machaut

CD1   Track 37

p. 84

Douce dame jolie,	Fair sweet lady,

Douce dame jolie,
Pour Dieu ne pensés mie
Que nulle ait signourie
Seur moy, fors vous seulement.

i Qu'adès sans tricherie Chierie

Vous ay, et humblement
Tous les jours de ma vie Servie

Sans vilein pensement.

Helas! et je mendie
D'esperance et d'aïe;
Dont ma joie est fenie,
Se pité ne vous en prent.

Dous dame jolie . . .

ii Mais vo douce maistrie
    Maistrie
Mon cuer si durement
Qu'elle le contralie
    Et lie
En amours, tellement

Qu'il n'a de riens envie
Fors d'estre en vo baillie;
Et se ne li ottrie
Vos cuers nul aligement.

Douce dame jolie . . .

Fair sweet lady,
for God's sake do not think
that any woman has mastery
over me, save you alone.

For always without deceit
I have cherished you,
and humbly
served you
all the days of my life
without any base thought.

Alas! I am bereft
of hope and help;
and so my joy is ended,
unless you pity me.

But your sweet mastery
masters
my heart so harshly
as to torment it
and bind it
with love, so much so

that it desires nothing
but to be in your power;
and yet your heart grants it
no relief.

iii Et quant ma maladie
        Garie
     Ne sera nullement
     Sans vous, douce anemie,
        Qui lie
     Estes de mon tourment.

     A jointes mains deprie
     Vo cuer, puis qu'il m'oublie,
     Que temprement m'ocie,
     Car trop langui longuement.

     Douce dame jolie . . .

And since my sickness
will not be cured
in any way
save by you, sweet enemy,
who are glad
at my distress,

then with hands clasped I pray
that your heart, since it neglects me,
may kill me soon,
for I have languished too long.

Guillaume de Machaut's *Douce dame jolie* ("Sweet pretty lady") is a virelai, another of the *formes fixes*. Each strophe of the virelai follows the pattern AbbaA. The refrain, in other words, is sung at the beginning and end of each strophe. Virelais are typically set in a syllabic fashion. About three-fourths of Machaut's 33 virelais have come down to us as monophonic works, though this does not preclude the possibility that other voices were added, either as accompaniment or in the form of improvised counterpoint. Virelais, like all songs of this period, could also be performed instrumentally, without any text at all.

RELATION OF TEXT AND MUSICAL STRUCTURE IN MACAHUT'S VIRELAI *DOUCE DAME JOLIE*	
Rhyme scheme	Musical structure
A (refrain)	A
b	B, first ending (*ouvert*)
b	B, second ending (*clos*)
a	A
A (refrain)	A

Performance notes: The notated sources of this music transmit only the melodic line with its text. The performance here is purely vocal; other performance options might be on a solo instrument like the rebec without any voice at all; with voice and instrument, with the instrument doubling the vocal line; or with voice and an instrumental providing a contrasting accompanimental line.

20 Ma fin est mon commencement
(ca. 1350–1360?)
Guillaume de Machaut

CD1   Track 38

p. 84

Ma fin est mon commencement	My end is my beginning
Et mon commencement ma fin.	and my beginning my end.
Et teneure vraiement.	And holds indeed.
Ma fin est mon commencement.	My end is my beginning.
Mes tiers chans trois fois seulement	My third part three times only
Se retrogardę et einsi fin.	is retrograde and ends thus.
Ma fin est mon commencement	My end is my beginning
Et mon commencement ma fin.	and my beginning my end.

The rondeau (plural: rondeaux) consists of eight lines of text set to music following the scheme ABaAabAB. Guillaume de Machaut's rondeau *Ma fin est mon commencement* ("My End is My Beginning") is a particularly ingenious application of the form. The cantus (the highest voice) and the tenor—in a direct musical representation of the text—are exact retrogrades of each other. In other words, the cantus line, sung backwards from end to the beginning, is exactly the same as what the tenor sings forward from beginning to end. The contratenor line, in turn, reverses itself at midpoint: it moves forward from m. 1 to the cadence at m. 20, then retraces its steps backward from m. 21 to the end. The idea that beginnings and endings are one in the same is deeply rooted in Christian theology, which holds that every birth entails a death, which in turn marks the beginning of another birth, into eternal life.

21 **Tout par compas** (early 15th century)
Baude Cordier (fl. early 15th century)

CD1 Track 39
p. 85

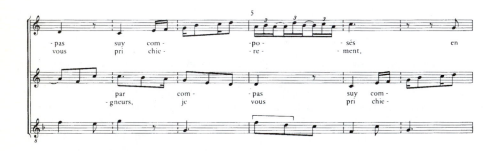

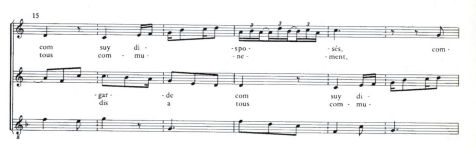

No. 21 Cordier: *Tout par compas*

Tout par compas suy composés	With a compass was I composed,
En ceste ronde proprement	Properly, as befits a roundelee,
Pour moy chanter plus seurement.	To sing me more correctly.
Regarde com suy disposés,	Just see how I am disposed,
Compaing, je te pri chierement:	Good friend, I pray you kindly:
Tout par compas suy composés	With a compass was I composed,
En ceste ronde proprement	Properly, as befits a roundelee,
Trois temps entiers par toy posés	Three times around my lines you posed,
Chacer me pues joyeusement,	You can chase me around with glee
S'en chantant as vray sentement.	If in singing you're true to me.
Tout par compas suy composés	With a compass was I composed,
En ronde proprement	Properly, as befits a roundelee,
Pour moy chanter plus seurement.	To sing me more correctly.
Seigneurs, je vous pri chierement,	Good lords, I pray you kindly,
Priés pour celi qui m'a fait.	Pray for her who made me.
Je dis a tous communement:	I say to all of you in common:
Seigneurs, je vous pri chierement,	Good lords, I pray you kindly,
Que Dieu a son definement	That God may, at her death,
Li doint pardon de son meffait.	Pardon her misdeeds.
Seigneurs, je vous pri chierement	Good lords, I pray you kindly,
Priés pour celi qui m'a fait.	Pray for her who made me.

Baude Cordier's rondeau *Tout par compas* ("In a circle I am composed") is notated in the form of a circle (see illustration, Textbook, p. 87). The two upper voices constitute a canon, in which one voice follows the other in strict imitation. The rhythms are often intricate, but the notational difficulties of this and other works of the *ars subtilior* should not obscure their emotional intensity. Listening to them without the benefit (or burden) of the score, one can perhaps better appreciate them as music and not mere technical artifice.

22 Ecco la primavera (second half of 14th century)
Francesco Landini (ca. 1325–1397)

CD2 Track 1
p. 88

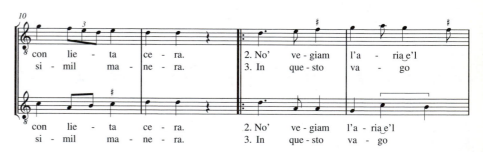

Ecco la primavera
che 'l cor fa rallegrare;
temp'è da 'nnamorare
e star con lieta cera.

No' vegiam l'aria e 'l tempo
che pur chiama allegreza;
in questo vago tempo
ogni cosa ha vagheza.

L'erbe con gran frescheza
e fiori copron prati
e gli alberi adornati
sono in simil maniera.

The time of Spring has come
which makes the heart rejoice;
it's time to fall in love
and to be of good cheer.

We see the air and weather
bringing about gladness;
in this lovely time
every thing has loveliness.

The meadows with fresh grass
and with flowers are covered;
and the trees are adorned
in a similar manner.

The Italian *ballata* (plural: *ballate*) of the 14th century is formally similar to the French virelai of the same period (not, as one might expect, to the ballade). The poetic form of the ballata is AbbaA, with a refrain framing the internal lines of each strophe. Most ballate have three strophes, but some have only one; most are polyphonic (usually for two or three voices), but there are a few monophonic ones as well.

Landini's *Ecco la primavera* ("Behold, Spring"), for two voices, exemplifies the ballata genre. It features smooth melodic lines that project the text syllabically, though not all ballate are quite this syllabic. The openings of the first and second section of the music are said to "rhyme," in that they share certain features of rhythm and melody, as do the corresponding cadential measures of the two sections. This kind of musical rhyme can be found in many ballate.

23 Non al suo amante (ca. 1340–1360)

Jacopo da Bologna (fl. 1340–1360)

CD2 Track 2

p. 88

Non al suo amante più Diana piacque
Quando per tal ventura tutta nuda
La vide in mezzo de le gelide acque.

Ch'a me la pastorella alpestra e cruda,
Posta a bagnar un leggiadretto velo
Ch'a l'aura il vago e biondo capel chiuda.

Tal che mi fece quando gli arde'l cielo,
Tutto tremar d'un amoroso gielo.
—Francesco Petrarca (1304–1374)

[The goddess] Diana never pleased her lover more
when by chance he saw her quite naked
among the chilly waters.

That I [was pleased] by a rustic, curel shepherdess
intent on washing the graceful wispy veil
that protects her pretty blond hair from the breeze.

So that although the sky burned hot
my whole body trembled with the cold chill of love.

The 14th century Italian madrigal began as a literary form, which by the 1340s had crystallized into a series of two or three strophes, each consisting of three lines, with a two-line ritornello (refrain) at the very end. Musical settings of this poetry clearly reflect its textual structure. The ritornello is almost invariably set in a contrasting meter, as in Jacopo da Bologna's *Non al suo amante* ("Never to her lover"), with a triple-meter ritornello at the end of each duple-meter strophe. Composers of madrigals often set the end (and sometimes the beginning) of individual lines to elaborate melismas. Almost all the trecento madrigal repertory is for two voices, with the upper voice the more florid of the two. Although the tenor is often texted, it lends itself equally well to instrumental performance.

Performance notes: In this performance, the lower voice is given over entirely to a citole, a plucked instrument similar to a lute but with a box-like body and wire strings.

A poste messe veltri et gran mastini "Te, te Villan te, te Baril!" Chiamando, "Ciof, ciof, quì quì, ciof	All in their places, greyhounds, mastiffs ready, "Hey, hey, Villán," "Hey, Hey, Baríl" . . . And shout "Ciof, ciof . . . here . . . here . . . ciof,"
Bracchi e segui per boschi aizzando,	Urging brachs and bloodhounds on the outing.
"Ecco, ecco là, ecco là!" "Guarda, guarda quà." "Lassa, lassa, lassa." "O tu, o tu, o tu." "Passa passa passa."	This way, that way . . . where? Look, look, over there . . . Slow! . . . slow! . . . slow! Hey you . . . you . . . you . . . Go! . . . go! . . . go! . . .
La cerbia uscì al grido e al l'abbaio. Bianca lattata col collar di vaio.	Midst shouts and barks, the doe emerged at bay, Milky white, with neck of spotted gray.
A ricolta bu, bu, bu, bu, bu bu, bu, bu, bu, bu, sanza corno, Tatim tatim tatim tatim tatim titon titon titon tatim tatim tatim tatim sonava per iscorno No no no no no.	To rally! Bu, bu, bu, bu, bu Bu, bu, bu, bu, bu, without the horn, Tatim, tatim, tatim, tatim, tatim, Titon, titon, titon, tatim, tatim, Tatim, tatim, it sounded as in scorn . . . No, no, no, no, no!

25 Doctorum principem / Melodia suavissima / Vir mitis (ca. 1410)
Johannes Ciconia (ca. 1370–1412)

CD2   Track 7
p. 89

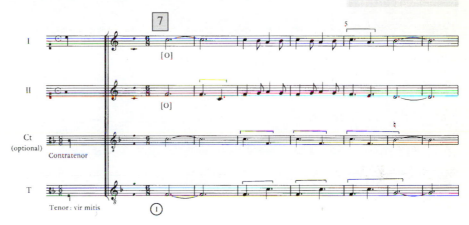

The *caccia* (plural: *cacce*) takes its name from the same root word as the English word "chase." Caccia texts often deal, aptly, with hunting, though they can also depict such lively scenes as fires, street vendors' cries, and the bustle of the marketplace. The music, usually for three voices, features two canonic upper parts and an independent tenor. Many (but not all) cacce conclude with a ritornello that can be monophonic, polyphonic, or canonic. Although written monophonically, the ritornello in Lorenzo da Firenze's *A poste messe* ("In their positions") can also be realized canonically.

Performance notes: Two of the three voices are here performed on instruments: the upper line on a recorder, the middle line on a cornetto, a type of wooden horn. In the canonic ritornello (notated with only a single line), the voice begins, followed by the cornetto; the recorder enters at the appropriate point as the third voice, but begins with the music notated at m. 85.

No. 25 Ciconia: *Doctorum principem / Melodia suavissima / Vir mitis*

A: *Voice I:*

1. [O] Doctorum principem super ethera revocant virtutum digna merita.

   Ergo vive voci detur opera,

   promat mentis fervor, intus concita.

1. The fitting merits of his deed extol the prince of teachers to beyond the skies.

   Therefore let sincerely summoned care be given to living voice,

   let fervour of mind show forth.

2. O Francisce Zabarelle, gloria,
   doctor, *h*onos et lumen Patavorum,
   vive felix de tanta victoria;
   pro te virescit fama, P*at*avorum.

2. O Francesco Zabarella, glory,
   teacher, honour, light of Padua,
   live contented at such a triumph.
   Padua's fame will increase because of thee.

3. O Francisce Zabarelle, pabula
   parasti pastoribus armentorum,
   quibus pascant oves; grata secula

   te pro munete revocant laborum.

3. O Francesco Zabarella, thou hast provided
   nourishment for the shepherds of the flocks,
   on which they may graze their sheep. A grateful world

   proclaims thee as reward for thy labours.

B: *Voice II:*

1. [O] Melodia suavissima cantemus,
   tangant voces melliflue sidera,
   concordi*e* carmen liram sonemus,
   resonet per choros pulsa cithara.

1. Let us sing with sweetest melody,
   let our mellifluous voices reach the stars,
   let us sound the harmonious lyre,
   let the plucked cithara resound throughout the choirs.

2. O Francisce Zabarelle, protector,
   imo verus pater rei publice,
   illos ad se vocat terum conditor,
   qui fortu*ne* miserentur lubrice.

2. O Francesco Zabarella, protector,
   yea, true father of the commonweal,
   the Maker calls unto himself
   those that have pity for fleeting misfortune.

3. O Francisce Zabarelle, causas
   specularis omnium creatorum;

   tuas posteri resonebunt musas
   per omnia secula seculorum.

3. O Francesco Zabarella,
   thou dost watch over the affairs of all creatures:

   posterity will resound thy praises
   for ever and ever.

Johannes Ciconia's *Doctorum principem / Melodia suavissima / Vir mitis* is an example of a new kind of work, the civic motet, written in praise of a particular person or place—in this case, Francesco Zabarella, an official at the court of Padua in northern Italy and Ciconia's protector and patron. The *color* of the isorhythmic tenor is stated three times (marked with "I," "II," and "III" in the score), each time in a different mensuration; thus, although the pitches of the tenor line repeat, the rhythmic pattern changes with each statement. The optional contratenor is constructed in the same way. The voice-leading—with many hockets, a relatively free treatment of dissonance (especially in the contratenor), and cadential parallel fifths—is stylistically typical of the late 14th and early 15th centuries.

26 Sumer is icumen in (ca. 1250)

Anonymous

CD2 Track 10 p. 89

MIDDLE ENGLISH:

Sumer is icumen in,	Summer has come in,
Lhude sing cuccu.	Loudly sing, cuckoo!
Groweth sed and bloweth med,	Grows the seed and blooms the meadow,
And springth the wde nu.	And the woods springs anew.
Sing cuccu.	Sing, cuckoo!
Awe bleteth after lomb,	The ewe bleats after her lamb,
Lhouth after calve cu;	The cow lows after her calf;
Bulluc sterteth,	The bull jumps, the stag leaps,
bucke verteth.	Merrily sing, cuckoo!
Murie sing cuccu.	Cuckoo, cuckoo,
Cuccu, cuccu.	Well sing you, cuckoo.
Wel singes thu cuccu.	Nor stop now!
Ne swik thu naver nu.	Sing cuckoo now, sing cuckoo!
	Sing cuckoo now, sing cuckoo!

LATIN:

Perspice christicola: quae dignacio!	Behold, Christian, what dignity!
Caelicus agricola, pro vitis vicio,	The celestial farmer [God], because of the weakness of life [the vine]
Filio non parcens exposuit mortis exicio;	Did not spare his son, but exposed him to the fate of death;
Qui captivos semivivos a supplicio	He who gives life to those half-alive captives,
Vitae donat et secum coronat in coeli solio.	delivers them from punishment,
Resurrexit Dominus.	and crowns them in the heavenly throne.
	The Lord is risen.

PES:

Sing cuccu nu, Sing cuccu.	Sing cuckoo now, Sing cuckoo.
Sing cuccu, Sing cuccu nu.	Sing cuckoo, Sing cuckoo now.

The oldest known canon in Western music, this setting of the anonymous poem *Sumer is icumen in* testifies to the predilection of late medieval English composers for thirds. Believed to have been written around 1250, it consists of a *rota*—or round for two voices—that unfolds over a two-part *rondellus,* in which the two voices exchange phrases (A and B) continuously, following this scheme:

```
A    B    A    B
B    A    B    A
```

The work is preserved in a manuscript that includes both Latin and English texts; there is some debate about which is the older version of the text, but they seem in any event to be separate—this is not, in other words, a polylingual motet. The original manuscript's instructions for performing the work direct that it be "sung by four companions, but it should not be sung by fewer than three, or two at the least, in addition to those who sing the *pes* [that is, the *rondellus* in the two lower voices]."

Performance notes: The canonic writing in this work is such that it can be realized in performance in many different ways. The present recording begins with the two voices of the *pes,* followed by a single voice in the upper range throughout an entire strophe; eventually as many as four voices sing in canon above the *pes.*

27   Edi be thu, heven-queene

(late 13th century)

Anonymous

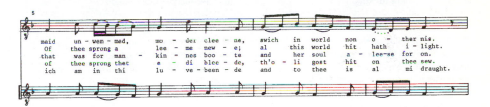

[1] This part may also be sung.

[2] Small notes to be used only in vocal performance.

1. Edi be thu, heven-queene,
folkes froovre and engles blis,
maid unwemmed, moder cleene,
swich in world non other nis.
On thee hit is wel ethseen
of alle wimmen thu hast the pris.
Mi sweete levdi, heer mi been
and rew of me yif thi will is.

2. Thu astiye so dairewe
deleth from the derke night.
Of thee sprong a leeme newe;
al this world hit hath ilight.
Nis no maid of thine hewe,
so fair, so scheene, so rudi, so bright;
mi sweet levdi, of me thu rew
and have merci of thi knight.

3. Sprunge blostm of one roote,
th'oli gost thee rest upon;
that was for mankinnes boote
and her soul aleese for on.
Levdi milde, soft and swoot,
ich crie merci, ich am thi mon,
to honde bothen and to foot
on alle wise that ich kon.

1. Blessed be thou, queen of heaven,
people's comfort and angel's bliss,
maid unblemished, mother pure,
such as no other is in the world.
In thee it is very evident
that of all women thou hast the highest place.
My sweet lady, hear my prayer
and show pity on me if it is thy will.

2. Thou didst rise up as dawn
divides from the dark night.
From thee sprang a new sunbeam;
it has lit all this world.
There is no maid of thy complexion—
so fair, so beautiful, so ruddy, so bright;
my lady sweet, on me show pity,
and have mercy on thy knight.

3. Blossom sprung from a single root,
the Holy Ghost rested upon thee;
that was for mankind's salvation,
and to free their souls in exchange for one.
Gentle lady, soft and sweet,
I beg forgiveness, I am thy man,
both hand and foot,
in every way that I can be.

This anonymous song makes liberal use of thirds and sixths as consonant intervals. The rhythmic interpretation of this and similar songs of the 14th century is open to debate. Although the original source for this song carefully aligns the two parts, it leaves ambiguous the duration of the notes. The edition here follows the regular meters of the text, though this is only one of several possibilities. Either or both parts could be performed vocally or instrumentally.

28   La quinte estampie real (second half of 13th century)
Anonymous

CD2   Track 12

p. 49

The *estampie* (from the same root word as "stamp," as in stamping one's foot) was a type of medieval dance. Like other notated dance music of the Medieval era, it is characterized by short repeated sections called *puncta* ("points"). These modular units could be repeated, varied, and embellished at will according to the needs of the dance. In the *Quinte estampie real* ("Fifth Royal *Estampie*"), each *punctum* ("point") is repeated immediately, with a first and then a second ending comparable to the *ouvert* and *clos* of contemporary vocal forms. Here, the same pair of endings serves for all four *puncta*. Dances of this era were highly stylized, with elaborate steps executed at times by individual couples, at times by large groups dancing as a unit. The round dance is an example of the latter category: it called for a group of dancers to hold hands and move in a circle with lively stepping. Dancing was a social activity practiced at all levels of society, from the nobles of the royal courts to the lowliest peasants.

Performance notes: Medieval dances could be (and by all accounts were) performed on almost any combination of instruments. In this recording, we hear two recorders and a *bendir,* a medieval counterpart of today's snare drum, with strings stretched beneath the drumhead to create a slight rattling sound on impact.

29 Quam pulchra es (ca. 1410–1430)

John Dunstable (ca. 1390–1453)

CD2   Track 13

p. 113

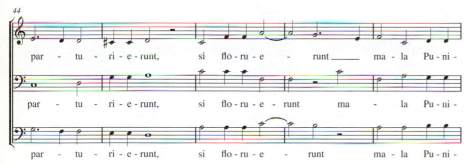

Quam pulchra es et quam decora,
　carissima in deliciis.
Statura tua assimilata est palme,
　et ubera tua botris.
Caput tuum ut Carmelus,
　collum tuum sicut turris eburnea.
Veni, dilecte mi,
egrediamur in agrum,
et videamus si flores fructus parturierunt,
　si floruerunt mala Punica.
Ibi dabo tibi ubera mea.
Alleluia.

How fair and pleasant you are,
　O loved one in delights.
You are stately as a plam tree,
　and your breasts are like its clusters.
Your head crowns you like Carmel:
　your neck is like an ivory tower.
Come, my beloved,
let us go forth into the fields,
and see whether the grape blossoms have opened
　and the pomegranates are in bloom
There I will give you my love.
Alleluia.

—The Song of Solomon 7:6–12

—Adapted from the Revised Standard Version
of the Bible

Dunstable's *Quam pulchra es* ("How fair you are"), a motet written sometime before 1430 on a text from the Song of Solomon, illustrates the panconsonant style associated in the early 15th century with the *contenance anglosie* (the "English guise"). Its three voices are of more or less equal weight; none of them derives from preexistent material. They all have the same rhythmic profile and they combine repeatedly to form triads that move in blocks, almost like a chorale or hymn. The intervals resulting from the interrelationship of the three voices are overwhelmingly consonant: dissonances, such as the E in the uppermost voice in m. 2, are few in number and rhythmically brief. The texture here is similar to that of the polyphonic conductus, yet the rhythms and vertical alignment of sonorities clearly distinguish Dunstable's motet from that earlier form.

30 Flos florum (ca. 1425–1430)
Guillaume Du Fay (1397–1474)

CD2 Track 15 p. 113

Flos florum,
Fons hortorum,
Regina polorum,

Spes veniae,
Lux laetitiae,
Medicina dolorum,

Virga recens,
Et virgo decens,
Forma bonorum:

Parce reis
Et opem fer eis
In pace piorum,

Pasce tuos,
Succure tuis,
Miserere tuorum!

Flower of flowers,
Fount of gardens.
Queen of heaven,

Hope of pardon,
Light of joy,
Cure of pain,

Staff that guides,
Decorous maiden,
Model of goodness:

Spare the guilty
And bring them reward
Through the peace of the righteous,

Feed thine own,
Help thine own,
Have mercy upon thine own.

This brief work is an example of a *cantilena* motet, which features a florid, lyrical top voice over a pair of slower-moving lower voices. The influence of the *contenance angloise* is clearly evident here. In spite of the rhythmic contrast among the voices, the intervals resulting from their interaction are strongly oriented toward thirds and triads, with triadic cadences at m. 7, 11, 40, and 59. The fifth nevertheless retains its traditional pride of place as the final cadential interval, as in Dunstable's *Quam pulchra es* (Anthology 1/#29).

31 Conditor alme siderum (ca. 1430?)

Guillaume Du Fay

Companion CD Track 4

p. 113

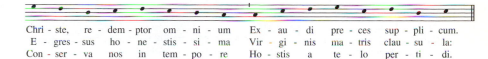

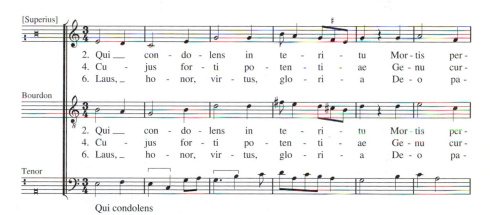

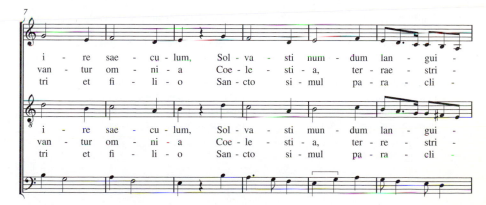

dum, Do - nans re - is___ re - me - di - um.
a, Nu - tu fa - ten - tur sub - di - ta.
to In sae - cu - lo - rum sae - cu - la.

dum, Do - nans re - is___ re - me - di - um.
a, Nu - tu fa - ten - tur sub - di - ta.
to In sae - cu - lo - rum sae - cu - la.

A - men.

Du Fay was an important figure in the development of fauxbourdon, a compositional technique that emerged around 1430. A fauxbourdon is an unnotated line that runs parallel to the uppermost of two notated lines, usually at the interval of a fourth below. The resulting harmonic texture is rich in thirds and sixths. The Advent hymn *Conditor alme siderum* ("Bountiful creator of the stars") alternates between plainchant (in the odd-numbered strophes) and three-voiced polyphony. In the polyphonic sections, the two higher voices sing a rhythmically patterned and slightly embellished version of the original plainchant. Interestingly, the earliest preserved version of this work transmits the plainchant melody in mensural notation, bringing it into alignment with the rhythm of the alternating polyphony. This source also transcribes only one of the two upper voices in the polyphonic sections, the "bourdon." The third voice is indicated simply by the word *fauxbourdon* ("false bourdon") written in the margin.

Conditor alme siderum,	Creator of the stars of night,
Aeterna lux credentium,	Thy people's everlasting light,
Christe, redemptor omnium	Jesu, Redeemer, save us all,
Exaudi preces supplicum.	and hear Thy servants when they call.
Qui condolens in teritu	Thou, grieving that the ancient curse
Mortis perire saeculum,	should doom to death a universe,
Solvasti mundum languidum,	hast found the medicine, full of grace,
Donans reis remedium.	to save and heal a ruined race.
Vergente mundi vespere	Thou camest, the Bridegroom of the Bride,
Uti sponsus de thalamo	as drew the world to evening tide,
Egressus honestissima	proceeding from a virgin shrine,
Virginis matris clausula:	the spotless Victim all divine.
Cujus forti potentiae	At whose dread Name, majestic now,
Genu curvantur omnia	all knees must bend, all hearts must bow;
Coelestia, terraestria,	and things celestial Thee shall own,
Nutu fatentur subdita.	and things terrestrial Lord alone.
Te deprecamur agie	O Thou whose coming is with dread,
Venture iudex saeculi	to judge and doom the quick and dead,
Conserva nos in tempore	preserve us, while we dwell below,
Hostis a telo pertidi.	from every insult of the foe.
Laus, honor, virtus, gloria	To God the Father, God the Son,
Deo patri et filio	and God the Spirit, Three in One,
Sancto simul paraclito	laud, honor, might, and glory be,
In saeculorum saecula. Amen.	from age to age eternally. Amen.

32 Nuper rosarum flores (1436)

Guillaume Du Fay

CD2 Track 18

p. 114

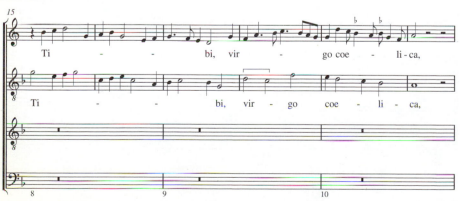

Nuper rosarum flores
Ex dono pontificis
Hieme licet horrida,
Tibi, virgo coelica,
Pie et sancte deditum
Grandis templum machinae
Condecorarunt perpetim.

Recently roses [came]
as a gift of the Pope,
although in cruel winter,
to you, heavenly Virgin.
Dutifully and blessedly is dedicated
[to you] a temple of magnificent design.
May they together be perpetual ornaments.

Hodie vicarius	Today the Vicar
Jesu Christi et Petri	of Jesus Christ and Peter's
Successor EUGENIUS	successor, Eugenius,
Hoc idem amplissimum	this same most spacious
Sacris templum manibus	sacred temple with his hands
Sanctisque liquoribus	and with holy waters
Consecrare dignatus est.	he is worthy to consecrate.
Igitur, alma parens,	Therefore, gracious mother
Nati tui et filia,	and daughter of your offspring,
Virgo decus virginum,	Virgin, ornament of virgins,
Tuus te FLORENTIAE	your, Florence's, people
Devotus orat populus,	devoutly pray
Ut qui mente et corpore	so that together with all mankind,
Mundo quicquam exoravit,	with mind and body, their
	entreaties may move you.
Oratione tua	Through your prayer,
Cruciatus et meritis	your anguish and merits,
Tui secundum carnem	may [the people] deserve to
Nati domini sui	receive of the Lord,
Grata beneficia	born of you according to the flesh,
Veniamque reatum	the benefits of grace
Accipere mereatur.	and the remission of sins.
Amen.	Amen.

—Translation by William Bowen

Even the sections for only two voices exhibit a sonority quite different from that of earlier music. In the two-voiced Italian caccia of the 14th century, for example, parallel seconds, fourths, fifths, sevenths, and octaves predominate. The most common intervals in the duo sections in Du Fay's work, in comparison, are thirds, sixths, and tenths, and each voice maintains its own distinct melodic profile.

The sections featuring four or (when the motetus divides) five voices—that is, those sections containing the double cantus firmus in the Tenor and Tenor II lines—follow the outline of a consistent harmonic progression, moving from the principal tonal center (on G, sounded nine times within each return of the double cantus firmus) to a fifth higher (on D, sounded six times) and then to a major third above the tonal center (on B♭). Although it would be anachronistic to speak in terms of a harmonic progression here—like their medieval counterparts, Renaissance composers thought of harmony as a by-product of polyphonic voice-leading—this kind of patterned sonority would certainly have struck contemporary listeners as being quite different from the motets of the previous generation.

The new sonority characteristic of Renaissance style coexisted for a time with traditional approaches to musical structure. Indeed, some of Du Fay's most significant early works are organized according to the medieval technique of isorhythm even as they explore new sonorities. The motet *Nuper rosarum flores* ("The Rose Blossoms"), written for the consecration of the newly completed dome of the Cathedral in Florence on 25 March 1436, provides a revealing example of this mixing of old and new.

The *cantus firmus*—the term composers of the time were now using for the "fixed melody" that served as the basis of a composition—derives from the opening of the Introit *Terribilis est locus iste* ("Awesome is this place"), a chant employed (appropriately enough) in ceremonies for the dedication of a new church. Du Fay applies the *cantus firmus* in an unusual way here, stating it canonically in two voices, beginning in m. 29. The melody in the Tenor II line is stated a fifth above the melody in the Tenor, and each voice is based on a different isorhythm, so that the two voices move at different speeds.

In spite of its archaic isometric structure, the sonorities of *Nuper rosarum flores* are decidedly progressive. The music is full of what would now be called root position triads. The lowest line of Du Fay's motet is not always the basis—or root—of the harmony, but the lowest-sounding voice usually is, whether it occurs in the Tenor, Tenor II, or motetus part. Thus the lowest-sounding voice consistently provides the root of the triad sounding above it.

33 Ave Maria . . . virgo serena

(ca. 1475–1485?)

Josquin des Prez (ca. 1450–1521)

CD2 Track 26

p. 117

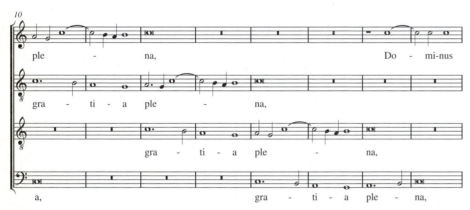

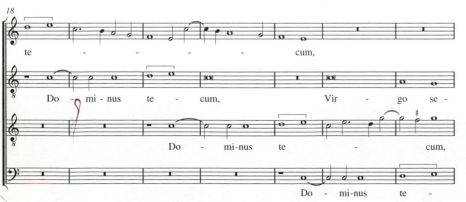

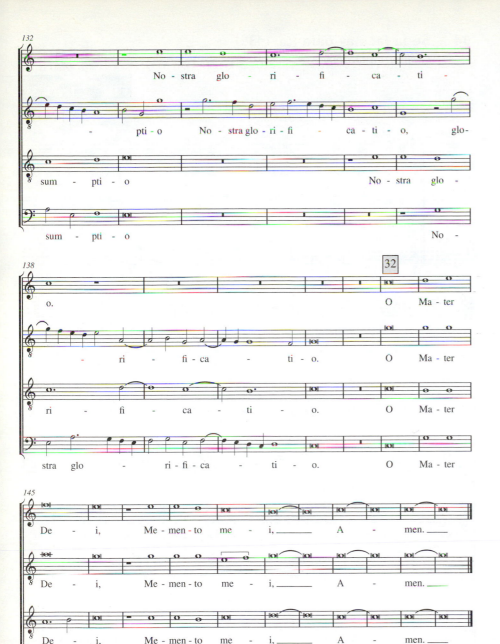

Ave Maria, gratia plena:
Dominus tecum, Virgo serena

Ave cuius conceptio,
solemni plena gaudio,
Caelestia, terrestria,
nova replet laetitia.

Ave cuius nativitas,
nostra fuit solemnitas,
Ut lucifer lux oriens,
verum solem praeveniens.

Ave pia humilitas,
Sine viro fecunditas,
Cuius annuciatio
nostra fuit salvatio.

Ave vera virginitas,
immaculata castitas,
Cuius purificatio
nostra fuit purgatio.

Ave praeclara omnibus,
angelicis virtutibus,
Cuius fuit assumptio,
nostra glorificatio.

O Mater Dei,
memento mei.
Amen.

Hail Mary, full of grace;
The Lord is with you, serene virgin.

Hail, whose conception,
full of solemn joy,
fills the heavens and the earth
with new rejoicing.

Hail, whose birth
was our festival,
As the light-bearing dawn
heralds the true sunrise.

Hail, blessed humility,
fruitful without a man
whose annunciation
was our salvation.

Hail, true virginity,
immaculate chastity,
whose purification
was our cleansing.

Hail, foremost
among all angelic virtues,
Whose assumption was
our glorification.

O Mother of God,
remember me.
Amen.

This motet illustrates the growing importance of pervading imitation in the last quarter of the 15th century. By its very nature, pervading imitation requires all voices to sing essentially the same musical ideas, making all voices more or less equal in their melodic and rhythmic profiles. The resulting homogeneity of texture is a characteristic feature of much Renaissance music written from the late 15th century onward.

Josquin's motet opens with a series of imitative entries that move systematically from the highest to the lowest voice. A new theme (m. 8) enters before the Bassus has finished its statement of the first idea. This new theme, in turn, is taken up by each of the other voices in succession. Yet another theme enters in the Superius (m. 16), overlapping once again with the Bassus. The process repeats yet again beginning in m. 23, this time beginning in the Altus and overlapping with both Tenor and Bassus. Each of these distinctive thematic units is known as a point of imitation. Successive points of imitation and cadences of varying weight help articulate the individual sections even while moving the whole work forward.

The work does not consist entirely of points of imitation using all four voices, however. Like most Renaissance composers, Josquin is careful to provide textural variety. He differentiates each unit of the text—an opening salutation to the Virgin, five strophes in praise of the Virgin, and a closing petition, a brief prayer invoking the protection of the Virgin—through a series of contrasting textures that are sometimes imitative and sometimes not. He also uses only two voices at certain junctures, at times playing off high against low registers. Josquin organizes *Ave Maria...virgo serena* around the structure of its text. Each strophe has its own thematic material, and each varies from the others in terms of texture, cadences, and the number of voices. The opening and closing sections feature a symmetrical use of all four voices. The five interior strophes, as we have seen, move fluidly between imitative counterpoint and a more chordal texture. The texts of the first and second strophes are closely linked—both begin with the same two words (*Ave cuius...*)—and Josquin gives them appropriately similar settings.

THE STRUCTURE OF JOSQUIN'S *AVE MARIA...VIRGO SERENA*

Text section	Measure number	Texture	Liturgical significance of text
Salutation *Ave Maria, gratia plena*	1–30	Pervading imitation; four voices together only at the very end	A greeting to the Virgin Mary
Strophe 1 *Ave cuius conceptio*	31–54	High vs. low, followed by full chordal texture	Celebrates the Immaculate Conception of the Virgin Mary (December 8)
Strophe 2 *Ave cuius nativitas*	55–77	High vs. low, followed by full imitative texture	Celebrates the birth of Christ to Mary (December 25)
Strophe 3 *Ave pia humilitas*	78–93	High vs. low, non-imitative	Celebrates the archangel Gabriel's announcement to Mary that she will give birth to Christ (March 25)
Strophe 4 *Ave vera virginitas*	94–110	Fully voiced, note-against-note counterpoint	Celebrates the presentation of the infant Jesus in the Temple of Jerusalem 40 days after his birth (February 2)
Strophe 5 *Ave praeclara omnibus*	111–142	Four voices, pervading imitation	Celebrates the ascension of Mary into heaven (August 15)
Petition *O Mater Dei*	143–155	Four voices, note-against-note, long rhythmic values	A prayer to the Virgin Mary

The cadential structure of each individual unit is carefully calibrated. The Saluation and first strophe both end with relatively weak cadences on the interval of a third that overlap rhythmically into the following section. Cadences at the end of strophes 2–4 have no rhythmic overlap but are at the unison. The penultimate cadence, at the end of Strophe 5, is fairly strong, on the interval of a fifth, followed by a rest. The strongest of all cadences—a fifth over a sustained series of held breves—is reserved for the very end of the motet (see diagram on page 123 of the textbook).

34 Se la face ay pale (ca. 1435)

Guillaume Du Fay

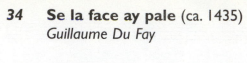

p. 127

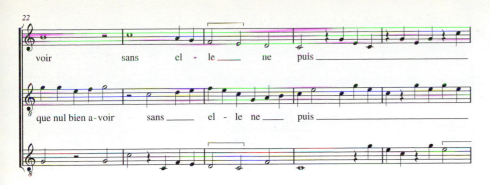

voir sans el - le ne puis
que nul bien a-voir sans el - le ne puis

C'est la plus reale | It is the most regal bearing
Qu'on puist regarder | One could ever see,
De s'amoure leiale | From loyal love
Ne me puis guarder | I cannot defend myself;
Fol sui de agarder | Foolish would I be
Ne faire devoir | to look upon her
D'amours recevoir | Without wanting to receive love
Fors d'elle, je cuij | except from her, I think;
Se ne veil douloir | If I did not want to be sad,
Sans elle ne puis | Without her I cannot be happy.

Judging by its circulation in contemporary manuscripts, Du Fay's ballade *Se la face ay pale* was one of the most popular songs of its time. The tenor line of the ballade would provide the cantus firmus of Du Fay's later *Missa Se la face ay pale* (Anthology 1/#35).

Performance notes: The cantus in this recording is doubled by a recorder, while the tenor is doubled by a kortholt, a double-reed woodwind. The contratenor line is performed on a viol.

Se la face ay pale | If my face is pale,
La cause est amer | the cause is love,
C'est la principale | That is the principal reason,
Et tant m'est amer | And to love is so bitter
Amer, qu'en l'amer | that I want to throw myself
Me voudroye voir | into the sea;
Or scet bien de voir | Now, she knows well,
La belle à qui suis | The lady whom I serve,
Que nul bien avoir | that without her
Sans elle ne puis | I cannot be happy.

Se ay pesante malle | If I have a heavy load
De dueil a porter | of sorrow to bear,
Ceste amour est male | It is love that is so hard
Pour moy de porter | for me to bear;
Car soy deporter | For to enjoy oneself
Ne veult devouloir | Is something she does not allow,
Fors qu'a son vouloir | But that one
Obeisse, et puis | obeys her will,
Qu'elle a tel pooir | Because she has such power,
Sans elle ne puis | Without her I cannot be happy.

Missa Se la face ay pale: Gloria

(ca. 1450)

Guillaume Du Fay

CD2　　Track 34

p. 127

II. GLORIA IN EXCELCIS DEO

Canon: Tenor ter dicitur. Primo quaelibet figura crescit in triplo, secundo in duplo, tertio ut jacet.

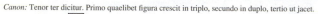

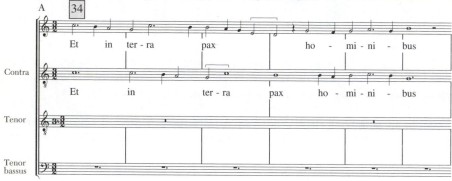

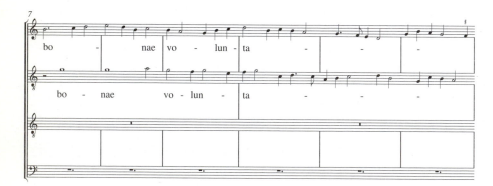

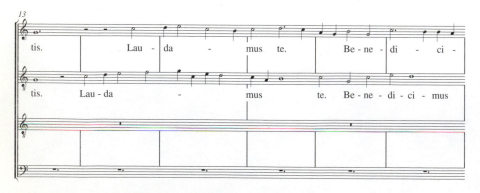

Du Fay's *Missa Se la face ay pale* is the first Mass setting by any composer to be based on a cantus firmus from a secular source, in this instance, the tenor of Du Fay's own ballade *Se la face ay pale* (Anthology 1/#34). It is also the first Mass setting in which the tenor—the line carrying the cantus firmus—is no longer the lowest voice. This second feature is of particular importance, for with the lowest voice no longer bound to the cantus firmus, composers were free to exercise a wider range of vertical sonorities—what we now think of as harmony.

The cantus firmus appears repeatedly throughout the Mass and is absent only in a few internal sections of certain movements. Du Fay wrote a verbal canon (meaning "rule" or "law") at the beginning of each movement of the Mass to indicate the rhythmic value of the cantus firmus in that movement. At the beginning of the Gloria, we read (in translation from the original Latin): "The tenor is stated three times. The first time it grows by three, the second by two, the third as set down." In other words, the tenor is sung three times in succession within the Gloria, the first time at three times the value of the notated original, the second time at twice the value (beginning with the text "Et in terra pax"), the third time at the original of the notated value (beginning with the text "Qui tollis"). (For an overview of the cantus firmus's distribution through the entire Mass, see the Textbook, p. 130.)

Performance notes: The cantus voices in this recording are doubled by a recorder, the contratenor voices by a viol. The tenor voices are doubled by a sackbut (a forerunner of the trombone), the bass voices by a rankett (also known as a racket), a small double-reed woodwind (for an illustration of this instrument, see p. 155 of the Textbook).

36 Missa prolationum: Kyrie I
(last quarter of 15th century)
Johannes Ockeghem (c. 1420–1496)

CD2   Track 40

p. 128

Ockeghem's "Mass of the Prolations" reflects the fascination of many composers of the late 15th century with complex compositional artifice. In this Mass, Ockeghem notates only two of the work's four voices; the other two are derived from them through a series of mensuration canons. Thus, the superius and contratenor sing exactly the same pitches, but in different mensurations ("prolations"), the equivalent of modern-day time signatures. The tenor and bassus, in turn, sing their own identical pitches, but in two contrasting mensurations different yet again from those in the superius and contratenor. Thus whenever all four voices are present, so too are all four of the basic mensurations. Throughout, the upper voices are in imperfect (duple) prolation, the lower voices in perfect (triple) prolation. In the first Kyrie, given here, the two upper voices share exactly the same sequence of pitches, but the superius line presents them in the equivalent of today's 2/4 while the contratenor moves in the equivalent of 3/4. The two lower voices, which share an altogether different melodic line, move in the equivalent of modern-day compound duple and compound triple meter (6/8 and 9/8, respectively).

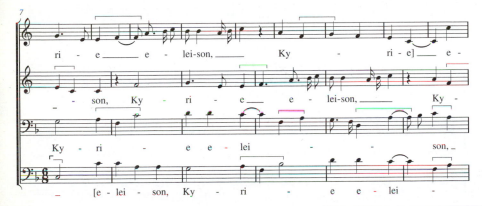

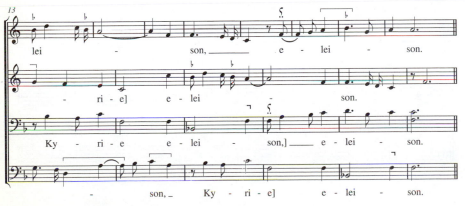

37 Fortuna desperata (ca. 1473–1478)

Antoine Busnois (?) (ca. 1430–1492)

CD2 Track 41

p. 135

Fortuna desperata

Fortuna desperata,
Iniqua e maledecta,
Che, de tal dona electa,
La fama ai denegrata.
  Fortuna desperata.

O morte dispiatata,
Inimica e crudele,
Che, d'alto più che stelle,
Tu l'hai cusì abassata.
  F.d.

Meschina e despietata,
Ben piangere posso may,
Et desiro finire
Li mei guay.

Hopeless fortune,
Unjust and cursed,
Who has defamed the reputation
Of so distinguished a lady.
  Hopeless fortune.

O pitiless death,
Hostile and cruel,
Who has thus lowered one
Who was higher than the stars.
  Hopeless fortune.

Wretched and pitiless,
Well can I cry now,
And I desire to end
My woes.

The authorship of this song is much disputed. Only one contemporary source attributes it to Busnois; most manuscript indicate no composer's name at all. In any event, this was the most popular Italian song of the entire 15th century. It was transmitted in dozens of different sources in the decades after 1470. The song also provided the basis for some 35 known re-workings: some of these add an additional voice, while others replace one or more voices of the original. Still other composers, including Josquin, used all three voices of the song as the basis for a setting of the Mass Ordinary (see Anthology 1/#38).

38   Missa Fortuna desperata: Kyrie and Agnus Dei (ca. 1500?)

Josquin des Prez

CD2   Track 42

p. 135

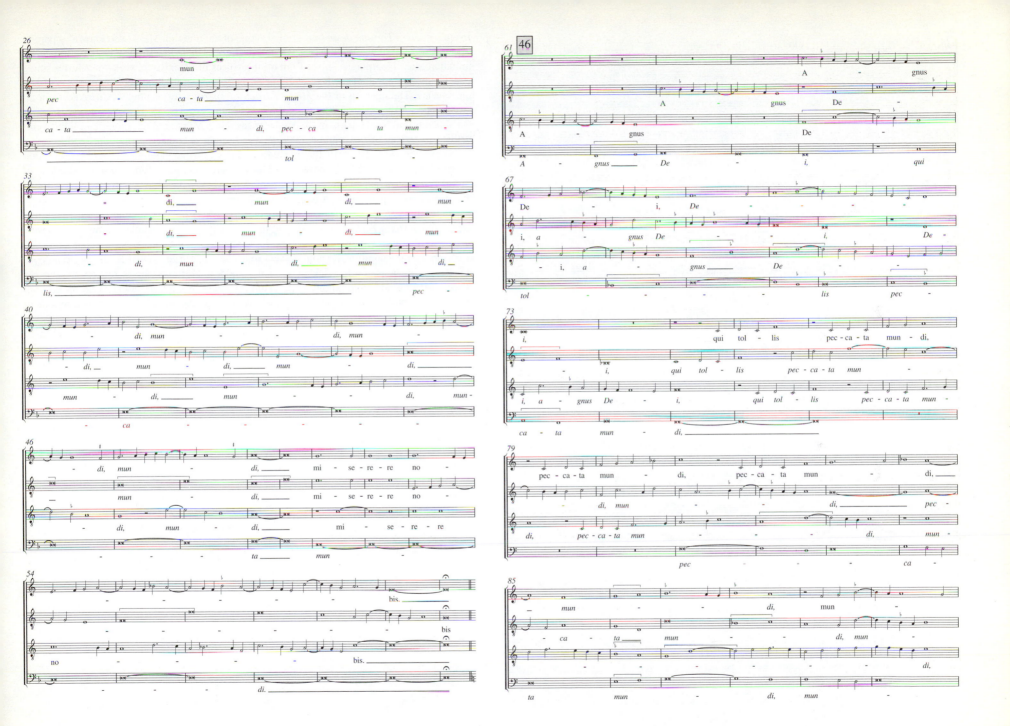

Josquin's *Missa Fortuna desperata* is an example of an imitation Mass (also known as parody Mass). Unlike a cantus firmus Mass, which uses only a single line from an existing source, an imitation Mass incorporates most if not all the voices of an existing work—not just a single voice—into the fabric of the new work, or at the very least into the opening sections of key movements. The opening of the *Missa Fortuna desperata,* for example, is derived from all three voices of the chanson *Fortuna desperata* (Anthology 1/#37). The opening measures of the superius and bassus parts in the Kyrie of Josquin's Mass are little more than lightly embellished versions of the original chanson. Yet Josquin also makes important modifications to the existing work. He shifts the music from duple to triple meter and reworks the rhythm of the tenor voice to make it move at a slower speed—that is, to function more like a strict cantus firmus. The added fourth voice in Josquin's work—the altus—also takes the tenor of the original as its point of departure.

Josquin carries the idea of reworking multiple voices a step further in subsequent movements of the *Missa Fortuna desperata.* In the Agnus Dei I, for example, he moves the inversion (melodic mirror image) of the superius of the chanson to the bass line and augments it (increases the length of the note values) fourfold. This bizarre twist is almost certainly a musical commentary on the fickleness of the goddess Fortuna, who is forever turning her wheel, bringing down the mighty and raising the lowly in a never-ending cycle. In keeping with this symbolism, the original tenor melody, having been turned upside down, returns in its original form in the bass line of the final Agnus Dei.

Josquin des Prez

CD2   Track 47

p. 135

The technique of paraphrase involves borrowing an existing melodic idea from a different work but elaborating it freely in most or all the voices of a new work. In the *Missa Pange lingua*, Josquin's last Mass, written sometime after 1513, all four voices use melodic material derived from the plainchant hymn of the same name (Anthology No. 4) but often in highly embellished form, with substantial interpolations between pitches. In the opening Kyrie, the composer distributes the six phrases of the plainchant hymn across a series of corresponding points of imitation (see table below). The texture is almost entirely homogeneous: no one voice stands out rhythmically or motivically. Later movements of the Mass do not adhere so closely to the structure of the hymn; at times, in fact, the plainchant is abandoned, but it returns in its entirety in the final Agnus Dei.

DISTRIBUTION OF PHRASES FROM THE PLAINCHANT HYMN *PANGE LINGUA* IN THE KYRIE OF JOSQUIN'S *MISSA PANGE LINGUA*	
Phrase of plainchant	**Measure of Kyrie**
1 *Pange lingua...*	1
2 *Corporis mysterium...*	9
3 *Sanguinisque...*	17 (transposed); 25 (original pitch)
4 *Quem in mundi...*	35
5 *Fructus ventris...*	53
6 *Rex effudit...*	61

The motet *Absalon, fili mi* ("Absalom, my son"), ascribed to Josquin but possibly by Pierre de la Rue (ca. 1452–1518), illustrates the expressive power of the motet and at the same time reminds us of just how many questions remain to be answered about much of Renaissance music. The text is pieced together from three separate Biblical passages, each of which deals with a father's lament on the death of his son: 2 Samuel 18:33, in which King David mourns the death of Absalom; Job 7:16, in which Job mourns the death of his son; and Genesis 37:35, in which Jacob mourns the death of Joseph.

The motivation behind this patchwork text is uncertain. Some scholars believe it was written in response to the murder of Juan Borja, Duke of Gandía and eldest son of Pope Alexander VI, in June of 1497. Other scholars have pointed to the death of Emperor Maximilian I's son Philip the Fair in 1506. Still other candidates include the English princes Arthur (son of Henry VII) and Henry (son of Henry VIII), both of whom died in infancy in the early years of the 16th century.

The distribution of the voices and their notation, at least in the earliest surviving source of this work, are striking: the upper two voices carry a sign of two flats; the tenor, three; and the bass, four. All four voices, moreover, occupy an extremely low range, in keeping with the textual theme of lamentation. The bass, which in vocal literature rarely descends below the F that lies an octave-and-a-half below middle C, hits the E♭ below it many times and eventually descends to D♭ and even the B♭ below that, a full fifth below what is normally the lowest note of the range. Scholars have debated this notation for many years without reaching a consensus about what it means or how the music should be performed. It may be that the work was sung in transposition at a higher pitch. One later version of *Absalon* (from the mid-16th century) transposes the work upward by a ninth (which makes the uppermost voice difficult to sing). But if the work was meant to be transposed, why was it notated in such a low range in the first place? Surely this had something to do with the text's theme of loss and mourning. The bass hits its lowest note at the very end of the piece, on the word *plorans* ("weeping"), concluding a line set to the words *non vivam ultra, sed descendam in infernum plorans* ("Let me live no longer but descend into hell, weeping"). In an early instance of word painting—the use of musical elements to imitate the meaning of a specific passage of a text—the pain and depths of hell are represented by an unusual and unusually low pitch. Still other commentators have pointed out that the concept of fixed pitch did not exist in Josquin's time—a low F in Milan was not necessarily the same as a low F in Rome—have suggested that the notation is effectively an instruction to the performers to sing the music as low as they possibly can.

The notation of *Absalom fili mi* also raises the vexing issue of *musica ficta* (see Focus: *Musica ficta* Textbook p. 141). As a look at specific passages reveals, it is one thing to learn the conventions of *ficta*, quite another to apply them to a network of polyphonic voices in which changes in one melodic line frequently affect other lines as well. Consider, for example, the explicitly notated D♭ in the tenor in m. 58. This requires a flattened A in the superius to avoid an augmented fifth, which in turn demands another flattened A in the altus later in the same measure to avoid a cross-relation (the simultaneous or nearly simultaneous sounding of two pitches a half-step apart) between the A♭ in the superius and the notated A♮ in the altus. The A in the altus should remain unflattened, however, at the end of m. 59 to provide a half-step move to the cadential B♭ that follows. Matters get even more convoluted as the work progresses, as for example with the cascading consequences of the notated G♭ in m. 66 and in m. 83.

Performance notes: Like most modern recordings, the version here transposes the music to a more singable range—in this case, up a fourth, beginning on E♭ rather than B♭.

Absalon, fili mi
quis det ut moriar pro te
fili mi, Absalon?
Non viam ultra
sed descendam in infernum plorans.

Absalom, my son
Would that I had died instead of you,
My son, Absalom?
Let me live no longer,
But descend into hell, weeping.

41 Adieu ces bons vins de Lannoys

(ca. 1425–ca. 1450)

Guillaume Du Fay

CD2 Track 53

p. 142

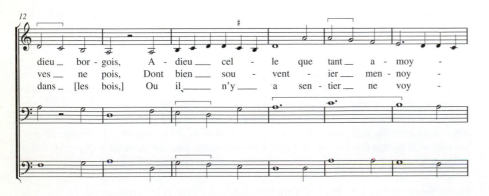

Adieu ces bons vins de Lannoys,	Farewell these good wines of Lannoys,
Adieu dames, adieu borgois,	Farewell ladies, farewell citizens,
Adieu celle que tant amoye,	Farewell she whom I so loved,
Adieu toute playsante joye,	Farewell every pleasing joy,
Adieu tous compaignons galois.	Farewell all my gallant companions.

Je m'en vois tout arquant des nois,
Car je ne truis feves ne pois,
Dont bien souvent entier mennoye.
Adieu ces bons vins de Lannoys,
Adieu dames, adieu borgois,
Adieu celle que tant amoye,

De moy seres, par plusieurs fois
Regretés par dedans les bois,
Ou il n'y a sentier ne voye;
Puis ne scaray que faire doye,
Se je ne crie a haute vois.

Adieu ces bons vins de Lannoys,
Adieu dames, adieu borgois,
Adieu celle que tant amoye,
Adieu toute playsante joye,
Adieu tous compaignons galois.

I am going away aiming my bow at nuts,
For I find neither beans nor peas,
Of which very often I bore a load.
Farewell these good wines of Lannoys,
Farewell ladies, farewell citizens,
Farewell she whom I so loved.

By me you will be very often
Missed, as I go through the woods,
Where there is no path or way;
Then I shall not know what to do,
If I do not cry out aloud.

Farewell these good wines of Lannoys,
Farewell ladies, farewell citizens,
Farewell she whom I so loved,
Farewell every pleasing joy,
Farewell all my gallant companions.

Du Fay's rondeau *Adieu ces bons vins de Lannoys* ("Farewell These Good Wines of Lannoys") illustrates the composer's early style and is typical of many chansons written between around 1425 and 1450. It opens and closes with brief untexted passages that were likely performed instrumentally. Only the uppermost line, the superius, is texted in the sources, and the tenor and contratenor were probably performed on instruments. Indeed, many Renaissance sources transmit chansons with no text at all, suggesting that this repertory might well have been performed at times entirely on instruments, with no singing at all. The three voices in this particular chanson move in more or less the same rhythms throughout, with little syncopation. The tenor and the superius are the structural voices, providing all necessary consonances at openings and cadences. The contratenor is a filler voice: it cannot substitute for either the superius or the tenor to provide needed points of consonance. And in contrast the other two voices, which are characterized by conjunct motion, the contratenor features several octave leaps.

42 De tous biens plaine (ca. 1470)

Hayne van Ghizeghem (ca. 1445–1485)

CD3   Track 1

p. 143

De tous biens plaine est ma maistresse,
Chacun lui doit tribut d'onneur.
Car assouvye est en valeur
Autant que jamais fut deesse.

En la veant j'ay tel leesse
Que c'est paradis en mon cuer.
De tous biens plaine est ma maistresse,
Chacun lui doit tribut d'onneur.

Je n'ay cure d'autre richesse
Si non d'estre son serviteur,
Et pource qu'il n'est choix milleur
En mon mot porteray sans cesse:

De tous biens plaine est ma maistresse,
Chacun lui doit tribut d'onneur.
Car assouvye est en valeur
Autant que jamais fut deesse.

Source. Laborde, fol. 62v.

My mistress is full of all good virtue,
Everyone owes her honorable tribute.
For she is accomplished in merit
As much as a goddess ever was.

When I see her I have such cheer
That paradise is in my heart.
My mistress is full of all good virtue,
Everyone owes her honorable tribute.

I have no care for other riches
Except to be her servant,
And because there is no better choice,
I carry as my unceasing motto:

My mistress is full of all good virtue,
Everyone owes her honorable tribute.
For she is accomplished in merit
As much as a goddess ever was.

Hayne van Ghizighem's *De tous biens plaine* ("Of all good things") represents the chanson style of the generation that came after Du Fay. Again, the options for performance range from three texted voices to entirely instrumental. And as before, the tenor and superius provide the essential pitches for all cadences, with the contratenor acting as a "filler" voice. But in contrast to Du Fay's rondeau *Adieu ces bons vins de Lannoys* (Anthology 1/#41), the melodic lines in Hayne's work are longer and more fluid, and there is a greater sense of rhythmic interplay among the voices.

Performance notes: The ensemble of three viols creates a homogeneous sound of matched instruments which vary only in their range. Other performance options include juxtaposing entirely contrasting instruments, creating an effect in which the distinctiveness of the individual voices is more clearly articulated.

43 Hélas, que pourra devenir (late 1480s)
Heinrich Isaac (ca. 1450–1517)

CD3   Track 3

p. 144

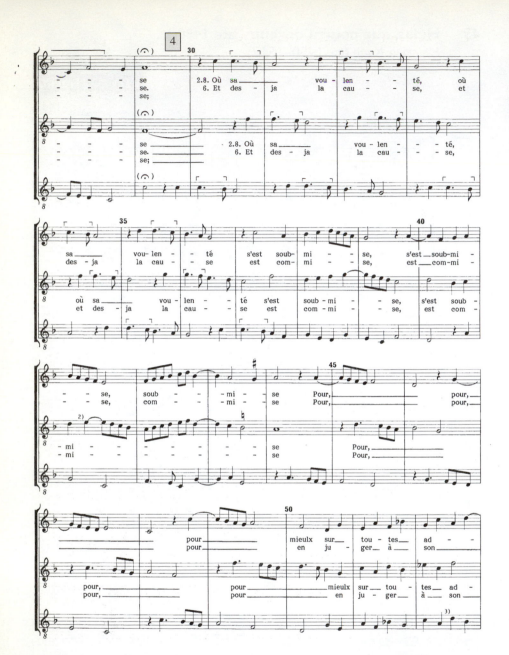

1) This note, present in all other sources, is missing in Florence 229.

2) Flat in Formschneider 1538⁹ *Trium vocum carmina* and Petrucci 1501 *Odhecaton*. On problems of *musica ficta* in this and the following two measures, see Atlas, *Cappella Guilia* 1:177.

3) Orig.: C semibreve. Emendation follows all other sources.

4) Orig.: D. Emendation follows all other sources.

Helas, que pourra devenir,	Alas, what can happen
Mon cueur, s'il ne peut parvenir	to my heart, if it cannot achieve
A celle haultaine entreprise.	that high enterprise
Où sa voulenté, s'est soubmise,	to which its will has been subjugated,
Pour mieuix sur toutes advenir?	above all else in the future?
C'est chois sans ailleurs revenir:	It is a choice without the possibility of return,
Eslicte pour temps advenir,	chosen for the future;
Avoir plaisance à sa de vise.	to have delight for its device.
Helas, . . .	Alas, etc.
Or est contraint pour l'advenir,	My future of my heart is constrained,
Car Desir l'a faict convenir,	For desire has made it appear
Qui l'a mis hors de sa franchise;	And put it beyond any sanctuary:
Et desja la cause, est commise,	And already the case is being tried,
Pour en juger à son plaisir.	For desire to judge as it pleases.
Helas, . . .	Alas, etc.

Isaac's *Helas, que pourra devenir* reflects the growing importance of pervading imitation in the chanson in the late 15th century. This three-voiced rondeau consists of four clearly articulated sections, each of which begins with a point of imitation and ends with a cadence:

Section	I	II	III	IV
Starting measure	1	18	30	44
Initial order of entry	CT, T, S	S, CT	CT, S, T	CT, S, T
Cadence on	C (unison)	F, C (fifth)	A (unison, S and T)	F (unison)

S=Superius, T=Tenor, CT=Contratenor

The paratactic structure used here—successive points of imitation, with each section presenting new thematic material—would become the predominant form of all chansons for the next hundred years or more. Within each section, all voices share the same ideas and participate equally in the polyphonic fabric.

Performance notes: In this instrumental performance of a chanson, the musicians have chosen instruments that emphasize the contrast among the three voices: recorder (superius), lute (tenor), and viol (contratenor).

44 Hor venduto ho la speranza
(ca. 1500–1504)
Marchetto Cara (ca. 1470–1525)

CD3   Track 5

p. 147

Hor vendu _ t'ho la   spe ran _ za   Che si ca _

_ ra   la   com _ pra _ i   E se ben ne ho per _ so as _ sa i

Pa _ ti _ en _ tia   ché gli è u _ san _ za.   Pa _ tien _ tia   che   gli è u _ san _ za.

Ogni mer _ ce vol ven _ tu _ ra,   Io fu'in que _ sta ven _ tu _ ra _ to
Forsi mo' por _ rò più cu _ ra   In ogni al _ tro mio mer _ ca _ to.

89

Ogni de - bit' ho pa - ga - to E an cor cre - di - to m'a - van - za.

ut supra

Hor vendut'ho la speranza	I have just sold hope
Che sì cara la camprai	For which I paid so dearly,
E se ben ne ho perso assai	And if thereby I lost badly
Patientia che gli è usanza.	Well—too bad, that's the way it goes.
Ogni merce vol ventura,	Every market is risky
Io fu' in questa venturato	And in this venture I was unlucky;
Forsi mo porrò più cura	I shall learn to be more prudent
In ogni altro mio mercato.	In all my other dealings.
Ogni debito ho pagato	I have paid off all my debts
E ancor credito m'avanza.	And I have credit to spare.
Hor vendut'ho la speranza . . .	I have just sold hope . . .
Se col credito che ho anchora	If with that credit I still have
Più mi acade far contratto	I should make another contract,
Da speranza sempre in fora	I shall always exclude hope
D'ogni cosa ver a patto:	From every new agreement;
Stato è 'l mal mio per un tratto	For a while it was my bad luck
Più appetito che ignoranza.	To have more ambition than sense.
Hor vendut'ho la speranza . . .	I have just sold hope . . .
O insensati ciechi amanti	O silly blind lovers.
Voi che sempre stati sete	You who are such
Di speranza gran mercanti	Great merchants of hope.
Al consiglio mio attendete	Now listen to my counsel:
In speranza non spendete	Do not trade in hope
Ché di inganno è propria stanza.	For its value is always false.
Hor vendut'ho la speranza . . .	I have just sold hope . . .
Questi falsi desleali	Those false deceitful smiles,
Risi lachryme parole	Honeyed words and tender glances
Dolci sguardi son sensali	Are negotiators
De chi speme vender suole.	For those who wish to sell.
Hor ne compri mo chi vole	Now you can buy some if you wish,
Ch'io per me compro costanza.	I, for my part, shall buy constancy.
Hor vendut'ho la speranza . . .	I have just sold hope . . .

—Translations from Peggy Forsyth,
©1984, London

Harmonic progressions in the frottola are often simple. In modern terminology, the genre makes frequent use of patterns like I–IV–V–I. The music could be performed entirely vocally, entirely by instruments, or by any of various combinations of voices and instruments. Many frottole were arranged for solo voice and lute, or for keyboard alone, for frottole were in high demand. The Venetian publisher Petrucci produced no fewer than eleven books of them between 1504 and 1514—a rate of roughly one a year.

The frottola was cultivated with greatest intensity by Italian-born composers, most notably Bartolomeo Tromboncino (ca. 1470–ca. 1535) and Marchetto Cara (ca. 1470–1525). Both were active in the northern Italian city of Mantua. Cara's *Hor venduto ho la speranza* appeared in the first book of frottole published by Petrucci in 1504 in a four-voice version and then later in a version for solo voice and lute in 1509, also published by Petrucci. The lute part of this later version, which is the one that appears in the anthology, is essentially polyphonic, in two voices.

Performance notes: Rather than sing each strophe relentlessly as written, the ensemble here takes a more creative approach to performance, beginning with a solo lute version of the refrain, followed a reiteration of the refrain by the voice with the full ensemble of lute, viols, cornetto, and drum. The individual strophes then proceed, with the return of the refrain sometimes sung, sometimes played. This kind of informal approach to the notated score is still evident in popular song of more recent times.

45 El grillo (ca. 1500–1505)

Josquin des Prez (?)

CD3 Track 6

p. 149

El grillo,	The cricket,
el grillo è buon cantore,	The cricket is a good singer
Che tienne longo verso,	He can sing very long
Dalle beve grillo canta	He sings all the time,
dalle, dalle, beve, beve, grillo, grillo, canta.	all the time.

| El grillo, | The cricket, |
| el grillo è buon cantore. | The cricket is a good singer. |

| Ma non fa come gli altri uccelli, | But he doesn't act like the birds. |

Come li han cantato un poco,	If they've sung a little bit
Van' de fatto in altro loco	They go somewhere else
	The cricket remains where he is

| Sempre el grillo sta pur saldo, | |

| Quando la maggior è'l caldo | If the month of May is warm |
| Al' hor canta sol per amore. | Because he sings out of love. |

The very title of *El grillo* ("The Cricket"), attributed to Josquin, tells us that we are far from the realm of courtly love in which the poetry of the chanson usually dwells. The musical style of this brief piece also contrasts sharply with that of contemporary chansons. *El grillo* is predominantly chordal in texture, occasionally antiphonal (in the back-and-forth between high and low voices in m. 11–14), and not at all imitative. Its authorship, however, is unclear. In the only contemporary source in which it appears—Petrucci's third book of frottole, published in Venice in 1505—it is ascribed to "Josquin d'Ascanio." This may or may not be Josquin des Prez; recent research suggests that it may have been the "other" Josquin in the service of Cardinal Ascanio Sforza of Milan from 1459–1498. Whoever wrote the piece had a wonderful ear for translating animal sounds into music, however.

46 **Tant que vivray** (ca. 1520–1528)
Claudin de Sermisy (ca. 1490–1562)

CD3 Track 9

p. 159

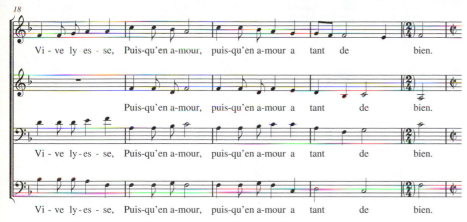

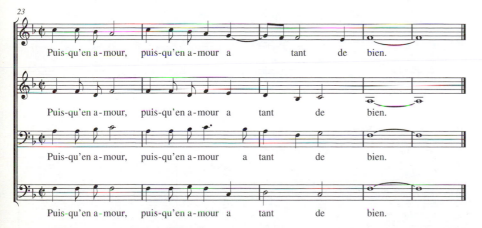

Tant que vivray en aage florissant
Je serviray d'amours le roy puissant
En faictz, en ditz, en chansons et accordz;
Par plusieurs jours m'a tenu languissant,
Et puis après ma fait resjoyssant,
Car j'ay l'amour de la belle au gents corps;

Son alliance, c'est ma fiance
Son cœur est mien, le mien est sien,
Fy de tristesse, vive liesse
Puisqu'en amours a tant de biens.

Quand je la veux servir et honorer
Quand par esprit veux son nom decorer
Quand je la voie et visite souvent
Ses envieux non font que murmurer,
Mais notre amour n'en saurer moins durer,
Autant ou plus en emporte le vent.
Malgré envie toute ma vie
Je serviray et chanterer
C'est la première, c'est la dernière,
Que j'ay servie et serviray.

As long as I live in my prime,
I shall serve the mighty king of Love
in deeds, in words, in songs, in harmonies.
That king made me languish a while;
but afterwards he made me rejoice,
since now I have the love of the sweetbodied
      beauty.

In her friendship is my trust,
her heart is mine, mine hers.
Away with sadness, long live gladness!—
since there are so many good things in love.

When I seek to serve and honor her,
when I seek to adorn her name with my words,
when I see and visit her—
her enviers only gossip.
But our love doesn't last any less long for that;
the wind carries their gossip and more away.
Despite their envy, I shall serve her
And sing of her all my life.
She is the first, she is the last
whom I have served and shall serve.

—Translation by Lawrence Rosenwald

Tant que vivray ("As long as I live") is a typical Parisian chanson. First published in 1528, it provided fodder for dozens of subsequent arrangements and reworkings (some with new texts) and was still being printed in anthologies more than 100 years later. Sermisy's chanson is modest in dimension, with a lyrical melody that lies squarely in the uppermost voice. The text is conventional and unpretentious, a love song in praise first of love itself, and then of the beloved. The rhythms and cadences of the music largely mirror those of the text, with one syllable per note except for a few discrete melismas toward the very ends of the phrases, as in m. 10. Except for a hint of imitation on the words *Son cueur est mien, le mien est sien* ("Her heart is mine, mine is hers") in m. 14–16, the text is declaimed in a predominantly chordal fashion.

Il bianco e dolce cigno (ca. 1535–1539)

Jacob Arcadelt (ca. 1505–1568)

CD3   Track 11

p. 161

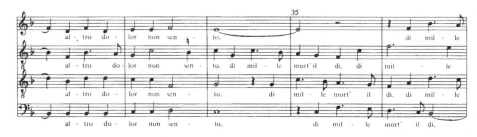

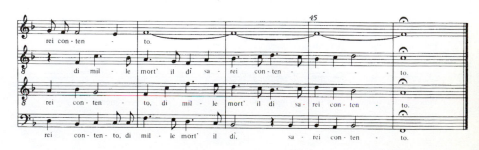

Il bianco e dolce cigno
cantando more et io
piangendo giung' al fin del viver mio.
Stran' e diversa sorte,
ch'ei more sconsolato
et io moro beato.
Morte che nel morire
m'empie di gioia tutto e di desire.
Se nel morir' altro dolor non sento
di mille mort' il dì sarei contento.

The white and gentle swan
dies singing, and I,
weeping, approach the end of my life.
Strange and diverse fates,
that he dies disconsolate
and I die happy.
Death, that in the [act of] dying
fills me wholly with joy and desire.
If in dying I feel no other pain
I would be content to die a thousand times a day.

With its clear declamation, modest dimensions, limited use of word-painting, and predominantly chordal texture, Arcadelt's *Il bianco e dolce cigno* ("The White and Gentle Swan") exemplifies the early madrigal. The text plays on two poetic conceits. One is the legend that swans, otherwise mute, sing just before they die. The other is a pun on the word death, used in one sense literally and in another as a euphemism (popular among Renaissance poets) for sexual climax. The poem's narrator contrasts the literal death of the swan, who sings yet is disconsolate, with his own desire for a euphemistic death "a thousand times a day." "Death," he explains, "fills me wholly with joy and desire."

Aracdelt's setting of this poem is at once tasteful and graphic. His music is more rhythmically supple than that of the typical frottola and he attends to the projection of individual words—the unexpected inflection on *piagendo* ("weeping") in m. 6–7, for example—without diverting the flow of the music as a whole. Toward the very end, however, on the words *di mille mort' il dì*, ("a thousand deaths a day"), he introduces a suggestively rapid-fire imitative counterpoint that resolves chordally on the words *sarei contento* ("would make me happy").

p. 161

48 **Da le belle contrade d'oriente** (1566)

Cipriano de Rore (1516–1565)

CD3 Track 13

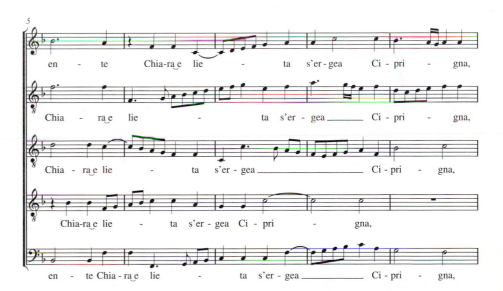

■ No. 48 de Rore: *Da le belle contrade d'oriente*

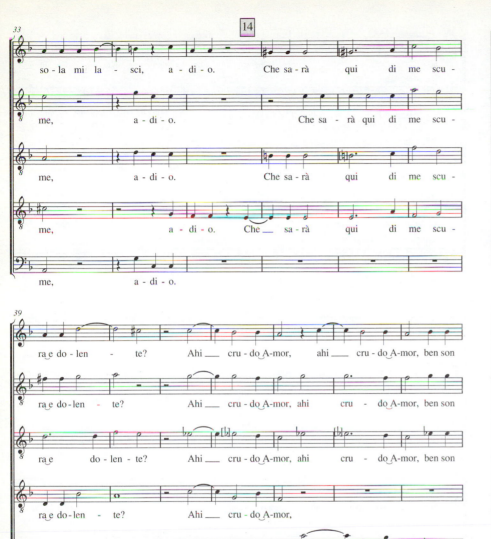

Da le belle contrade d'oriente	From the fair region of the East
Chiara e lieta s'ergea Ciprigna, et io	bright and joyful arose the morning star, and I
Fruiva in braccio al divin idol mio	in the embrace of my divine idol enjoyed
Quel piacer che non cape humana mente;	that pleasure which surpasses human understanding
Quando sentii dopo un sospir ardente:	when I heard, after an ardent sigh,
"Speranza del mio cor, dolce desio,	"Hope of my heart, sweet desire,
Te'n vai, haime, sola mi lasci, adio.	You go, alas! You leave me alone! Farewell!
Che sarà qui di me scura e dolente?	What will become of me here, gloomy and sad?
Ahi crudo Amor, ben son dubiose e corte	Alas, cruel love, how false and brief
Le tue dolcezze, poi ch'ancor ti godi.	are your pleasures, for while I yet enjoy you,
Che l'estremo piacer finisca in pianto."	the ecstasy ends in tears."
Nè potendo dir più, cinseme forte,	Unable to say more, she embraced me tightly,
Iterando gl'amplessi in tanti nodi,	repeating her embraces in more entwinings,
Che giamai ne fer più l'edra o l'acanto.	than ever ivy or acanthus made.

Cipriano de Rore's *Da le belle contrade d'oriente* ("From the fair region of the east") exemplifies the stylistic changes that distinguish the midcentury madrigal from earlier manifestations of the genre. The part-writing is more imitative and less chordal, and with five voices, the texture is fuller. By the 1560s, five voices had become the norm for madrigals, although works for four and even three voices continued to appear through the end of the century.

The text of Rore's madrigal, by an unknown poet, draws on the age-old image of two lovers parting at dawn. The young man describes himself as musing contentedly in the arms of his beloved when she cries out in anguish over his impending departure. She then embraces him even more tightly, so that they become entwined like ivy and acanthus vines. Rore creates a distinctive musical profile for each line or pair of lines of this text, using melodic material with more internal contrasts than did Arcadelt. Rore also devotes more attention to individual words and phrases. He articulates the anxiety in the beloved's words *sola me lasci* ("you are leaving me alone")—and mimics their meaning—by setting them in a passage that the cantus (superius) voice sings entirely alone for a full m. (33). He conveys the meaning of the phrase *iterando gl'amplessi* ("repeating her embraces") with many repetitions (from m. 62 onward). And he captures the image of acanthus entwining itself around ivy by setting the word *edra* ("ivy") to relatively slow notes and *acanto* ("acanthus") to a sinuously rapid melisma (m. 72–81).

It is easy to see why almost forty years later Claudio Monteverdi (see Textbook, Chapter 8) would point specifically to this composition (among others) in defending an aesthetic in which the "harmony obeys [the] words exactly." Monteverdi considered Rore one of the true founders of what he called "modern music" precisely because of the way he shaped his compositions around the text at hand.

49 Morir non può il mio cuore (1566)

Maddalena Casulana (ca. 1544–after 1583)

CD3   Track 16

p. 164

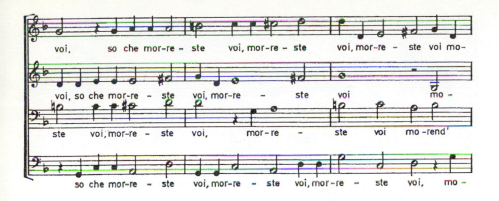

Morir non può il mio cuore,
Ucciderlo vorrei, poi che ve piace;
Ma trar non si può fuore
Dal petto vostr'ove gran tempo giace.
Et uccidendol'io come desio,
So che morreste voi morend'anch'io.

My heart cannot die,
I would like to kill it, for it would please you;
But it cannot be dragged
From your breast, where it has long lain.
And in slaying it, as I desire,
I know that you would die when I die, too.

Maddalena Casulana's *Morir non può il mio cuore* ("My heart cannot die") is another representative midcentury madrigal that also happens to be among the earliest printed vocal works by a professional woman composer. The poetic text plays on the idea of a lover "owning" the heart of his or her beloved. But the relationship here has obviously gone sour, and the imagery is quite violent. The narrator would like to drive a stake through his (or her) own heart, since it causes so much pain, "but it cannot be dragged out from your breast where it has lain for so long." The narrator also recognizes that to commit suicide would also kill the beloved. Whether this is a good thing or not remains wonderfully ambiguous.

Casulana's music projects the despairing tone of this poem in measured but effective terms. The music is sometimes contrapuntal (as in m. 1–3), sometimes chordal (as in m. 4–5). The rising chromatic progression at the end of the text on the line *so che morreste voi* ("I know that you would die"), beginning at m. 15 and repeated at m. 21, is particularly effective. The major third of the final cadence conveys the idea of death as a means of achieving peace.

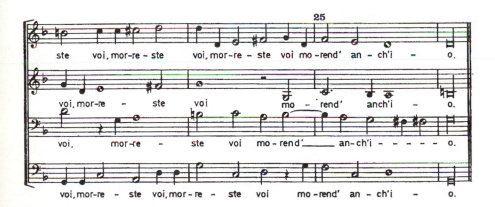

50 Solo e pensoso (ca. 1595–1599)
Luca Marenzio (1553 or 1554–1599)

CD3 Track 18
p. 164

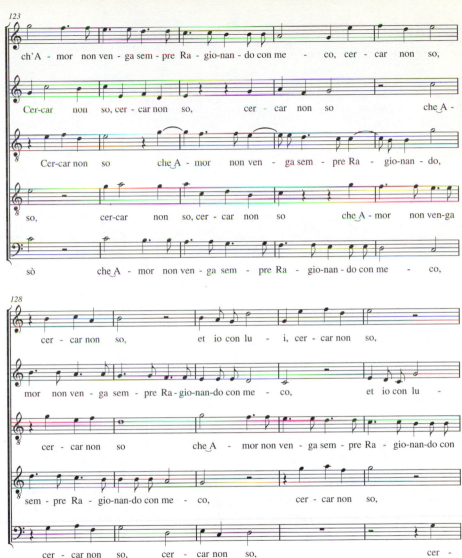

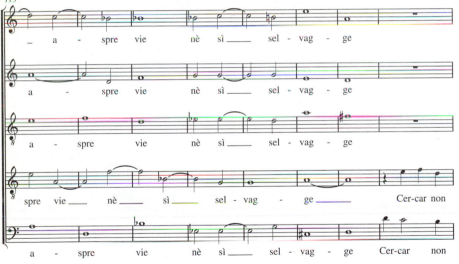

No. 50 Marenzio: *Solo e pensoso* ▣ 107

et io con lu - i, et io_con lu-i, et io con lu - i.

i, cer-car non so et io con lu - i.

me - co, et io con lu - i, et io con lu - i.

et io con lu - i, et io con lu - i, et io con lu-i.

car non so et io con lu - i, et io con lu - i.

Italian text	English translation	Starting measure	Textual emphasis and musical effect
Solo e pensoso i più deserti campi	Alone and pensive through the most deserted fields	1	Solitude and contemplation, conveyed by the isolation and extraordinary chromaticism of the uppermost voice
vo misurando a passi tardi e lenti,	I go with measured steps, dragging and slow	9	Slow steps, conveyed by long note values
e gl'occhi porto per fuggir intenti	And my eyes intently watch in order to flee	25	Running, conveyed by points of temporally close imitation
dove vestiggio human l'arena stampi.	From any spot where the trace of man the sand imprints.	33	A fixed spot, conveyed by relatively static melody and rhythm
Altro schermo non trovo che me scampi	No other defense do I find to escape	44	Escape, conveyed by the rapid imitative figure on "scampi" ("escape")
dal manifesto accorger de le genti,	From the plain knowledge of people,	56	Commonplace people and knowledge, conveyed by a relatively undistinctive passage, stated only once
perché ne gl'atti d'allegrezza spenti	Because in my actions, of joy devoid	63	The absence of joy, conveyed by a thinner texture of mostly three voices
di fuor si legge com'io dentr'avampi.	From without one may read how I blaze within	66	The contrast between external calm and inward agitation, conveyed by the juxtaposition of slow and rapid rhythms

WORD PAINTING IN MARENZIO'S SOLO E PENSOSO, PART I

In the later decades of the 16th century, madrigal composers took word-painting to greater extremes than ever before. Marenzio's *Solo e pensoso* ("Alone and pondering"), set to a text by Petrarch, illustrates the lengths to which composers were willing to go to capture the meaning and emotion of a text. The opening measure is harmonically extraordinary, moving from the outline of a G major triad to one on E major, with a spectacularly exposed octave leap in the alto that reverses the motion of the previously steady downward skips. The piece proceeds to unfold in an even more bizarre fashion. The whole notes in the uppermost line that progress form G to G♯ in m. 1 turn out to be the beginning of a long chromatic ascent that will span a ninth (to A in m. 15) and then descend chromatically back down a fourth by m. 22.

Paratactic in form like almost every other madrigal of its time, Marenzio's *Solo e pensoso* uses musical means to emphasize key points in each line of the text. The table here spells out how this works for the first part of the madrigal. The second part of the madrigal—by this time it was common for madrigals to have multiple parts—continues in this same vein.

Seconda parte
Sì ch'io mi cred' homai che monti e piagge
e fiumi e selve sappian di che tempre
sia la mia vita, ch'é celata altrui,
ma pur sì aspre vie né si selvagge
cercar non so ch'Amor non venga sempre
ragionando con meco, et io con lui.

—Petrarch

Part Two
Yet I believe that hills and vales,
Rivers and forests know of my life and
What is hidden from others.
For no matter how arduous and wild a path
I seek, Amor always appears
Speaking to me, and I with him.

51   T'amo mia vita (ca. 1590?)

Luzzasco Luzzaschi (1545–1607)

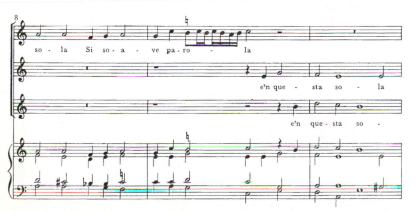

"T'amo mia vita," la mia cara vita
dolcemente me dice; e in questa sola
si soave parola
Par mi trasformi lietamente il core.
O voce di dolcezza e di diletto.
Prendila tosta Amore,
stampala nel mio petto,
spiri dunque per lei l'anima mia.
"T'amo mia vita," la mia vita sia.

"I love you my life," my dearest life
softly tells me; and with these
such gentle words
my heart is joyfully transformed.
O voice of sweetness and delight.
Take it soon, Love,
stamp it upon my breast
so that I may breathe only for her.
"I love you my life," be my life.

T'amo mia vita ("I love you, my life"), by Luzzasco Luzzaschi (1545–1607), illustrates another growing trend in the madrigal toward the end of the 16th century: the increasing importance of virtuosity. The florid embellishments in each of the three voices seem for the most part unconnected to the text at hand. They cannot be considered word-painting, for a similar figure serves for a wide variety of individual words. The same cadential gesture, for example, appears on *parola* ("word"), *amore* ("love"), *mia* ("mine"), *core* ("heart"), and *signore* ("lady").

Although not published until 1601, the work almost certainly dates from the 1590s, if not earlier. It is part of a larger collection of "Madrigals for One, Two, or Three Sopranos" written expressly for the celebrated "Three Ladies of Ferrara," a group of extraordinarily talented singers whose performances were something of a legend throughout musical Europe. Luzzaschi's published score includes a fully written-out harpsichord accompaniment that doubles the structural pitches of the vocal parts and adds independent pitches of its own as well. By the end of the Renaissance, composers were exploring the possibilities of integrating voices and instruments to an unprecedented degree.

52 Matona mia cara (ca. 1575–1581)
Orlande de Lassus (1530 or 1532–1594)

CD3   Track 26

p. 166

■   No. 52 Lassus: *Matona mia cara*

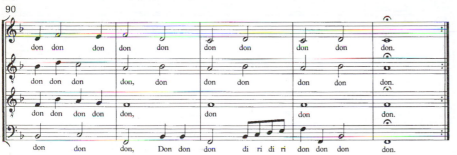

Matona, mia cara,
Mi follere canzon,
Cantar sotto finestra,
Lantze buon compagnon,
Don don don, di ri di ri don don don don,
Don don don, di ri di ri don don don don.

O my good lady,
I want to sing a song
Below your window
Lancer good companion
Don don don . . .

Ti prego m'as coltare,
Che mi cantar de don,
E mi ti foler bene,
Come greco e capon,
Don don don . . .

I beg you listen to me,
Because I sing good,
And I want you,
Like a Greek wants his capon.
Don don don . . .

Com' andar alle cazze,
Cazze, cazzar con le falcon,
Mi ti portar beccazze
Grasse come rognon.
Don don don . . .

When I go to the hunting,
To the hunting with the falcon,
I bring you a woodcock
So fat as a kidney.
Don don don . . .

Si mi non saper dire
Tante belle rason,
Petrarcha mi non saper,
Ne fonte d'Helicon.
Don don don . . .

I do not know how to say
The beautiful things;
Petrarch I do not know,
Nor the fount of Helicon,
Don don don . . .

Si ti mi foler bene,
Mi non esser poltron,
Mi ficcar tutta notte,
Urtar, urtar come monton,
Don don don . . .

But if you love me,
I am not a fool,
I make love all night,
Pushing like a ram.
Don don don . . .

Lassus's *Matona mia cara* ("My dear lady") offers a witty example of the *villanella,* a lighter type of polyphonic song in a homophonic style, often in dialect. This particular song is a *todesca,* a German soldier's song that like others of its kind pokes fun at the heavy accent of a German mercenary. In this instance, the German soldier is serenading a young woman in broken Italian. The text is difficult to translate into English because it derives much of its humor from the way the German accent mangles the Italian, such as the tendency to pronounce a "v" at the beginning of a word as if it were an "f." The text also lampoons the more universal tendency of all speakers struggling with a foreign language to limit themselves to the infinitive form of verbs, no matter what the context. Thus the opening line, translated into a correspondingly corrupted English, might read something like "My tear leddy, I vant make song under vindow…" And like many songs of this lighter variety, *Matona mia cara* is full of nonsense syllables that can be heard as either meaningless or suggestive, depending upon the listener's perspective ("Lancer makes good companion. Don, don, don, diri diri don…"). When Lassus's lancer pleads toward the end that he "knows no Petrarch," we recognize that we are dealing here with what might be called an anti-madrigal, one that intentionally adopts a lowbrow approach to its poetry. The music, too, is less intricate than what we find in the madrigals that Lassus otherwise wrote by the dozens. Yet *Matona mia cara,* and the hundreds of other works like it, are nonetheless marvelously compelling.

53 Zwischen Berg und tiefem Tal

(ca. 1530–1534)

Ludwig Senfl (ca. 1486–1542 or 1543)

Companion CD   Track 6

p. 167

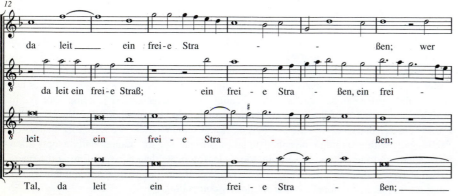

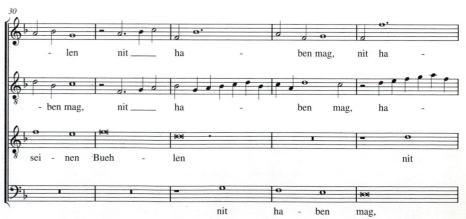

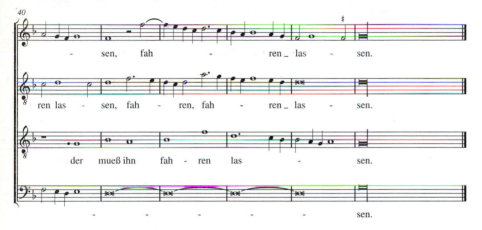

The most prominent varieties of song in 16th-century Germany were the *Lied* ("Song") and *Tenorlied* ("Tenor Song"). The *Tenorlied* was so called because it typically incorporated a well-known tune in the tenor or other voice, making it, in effect, a secular cantus firmus genre. In Ludwig Senfl's *Zwischen Berg und tiefem Tal* ("Between the mountain and the deep valley"), the popular melody lies in the slower-moving tenor. In this setting, the two upper and lower voices constitute contrasting units, with the discantus and altus moving at a faster speed than the tenor and bass.

Performance notes: Emphasizing the inherent contrast between the upper and lower voices, this performance presents the former on instruments (treble viol and lute), the latter with voices.

Zwischen Berg und tiefem Tal
Da leit ein freie Straßen.
Wer seinen Buehlen nit haben mag,
Der mueß ihn fahren lassen.

Fahr' hin, fahr' hin, du hast die Wahl,
ich kann mich dein wohl massen.
Im Jahr sind noch viel langer Tag,
Glück is in allen Gassen.

Between the mountain and the deep valley
There lies an open road.
Whoever doesn't want to keep his love
Must let that love go.

Go on, go on! You have the choice.
I can well tell what you're up to.
There's many a long day left in the year,
Good fortune can be found in every alley.

54 Silberweise (1513)

Hans Sachs (1494–1576)

Companion CD — Track 7

p. 169

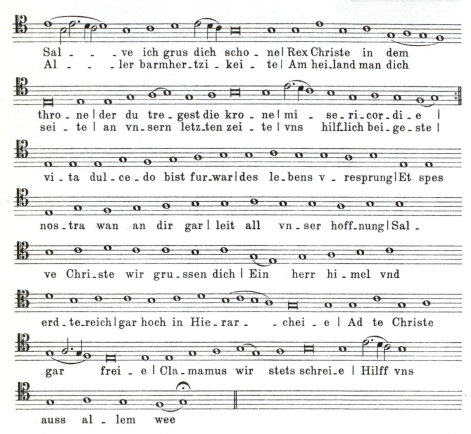

Sal — — ve ich grus dich scho — ne | Rex Christe in dem
Al — — ler barmher_tzi _ kei _ te | Am hei_land man dich

thro — ne | der du tre_gest die kro — ne | mi — se _ ri_cor_di _ e |
sei _ te | an vn_sern letz_ten zei _ te | vns hilf_lich bei_ge_ste |

vi _ ta dul_ce_do bist fur_war | des le_bens v _ resprung | Et spes

nos_tra wan an dir gar | leit all vn_ser hoff_nung | Sal _

ve Chri_ste wir gru_ssen dich | Ein herr hi_mel vnd

erd_te_reich | gar hoch in Hie_rar _ chei _ e | Ad te Christe

gar frei _ e | Cla_mamus wir stets schrei_e | Hilff vns

auss al _ lem wee

Salve ich grus dich schone / Hail! I greet you most fittingly.
Rex Christe in dem throne / O Christ, King on the throne,
der du tregest die krone / you who wear the crown,
misericordie / have mercy.

Aller barmhertzikeite / You of all mercy,
Am heiland man dich seite / you were proclaimed the savior.
an vnsern letzten zeite / In our ultimate days
vns hilflich beigeste / may you support us with your help!

vita dulcedo / Life and sweetness,
bist furwar des lebens vresprung / you are indeed the source of life.
Et spes nostra / And also our hope,
wan an dir gar leit all vnser hoffnung / for in you lies all of our hope.

Salve Christe wir grussen dich / Hail, O Christ, we greet you,
Ein herr himel vnd erdtereich / one Lord in the kingdom of heaven and earth,
gar hoch in Hierarcheie / most high in the celestial hierarchy.
Ad te Christe gar freie / To you, O Christ, most willingly we cry,
Clamamus wir stets schreie / continually we cry.
Hilff vns auss allem wee / Deliver us from our misery.

—Translation by Salvatore Calomino

Hans Sachs was a cobbler in 16th-century Nuremberg (in the southern part of present-day Germany) who belonged to the guild of *Meistersinger* ("Master Singers"). Its members were not professional musicians but rather tradesmen and craftsmen who formed societies and schools throughout Germany to foster the cultivation of music, poetry, and singing. The guilds were governed by an elaborate system of rules and ranks, and held competitions on a regular basis. Judges kept constant vigil against the violation of established norms. (Richard Wagner would make such a competition the centerpiece of his 1868 opera *Die Meistersinger von Nürnberg.*) The songs were often written in bar form (AAB) in emulation of the medieval *Minnelieder* (see Anthology 1/#8) and were performed by voice alone, with no accompaniment. Despite the rigid rules that governed them, many of the melodies from this repertory are memorable. Among them is Hans Sachs's *Silberweise* ("Silver Melody"), set to the words *Salve, ich grus dich* ("Hail, I greet you"). Some scholars have speculated that this melody was the model for the roughly contemporary melody of Martin Luther's most famous chorale, *Ein feste Burg ist unser Gott* (see the tenor line of Anthology 1/#58). More likely, however, the two works emerged from a common fund of German popular song. The text of the song presents a mish-mash of Latin and German.

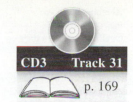

CD3   Track 31

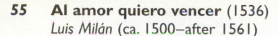

p. 169

A. Molto Lento

1. Al a—mor quie—ro ven—cer mas quien po—dra.
4. Quien tu—vies—se tal po—der mas quien po—dra. Qu'e—lla con su

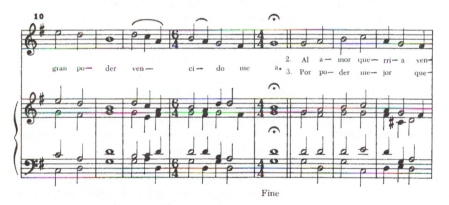

gran po—der ven—ci—do me a.
2. Al a—mor quer—ri—a ven
3. Por po—der me—jor que—

Fine

cer y con bien ser del ven—ci—do.
rer pa—ra ser me—jor que—ri—do.

D.C. al Fine

B. Allegro Moderato

1. Al a—mor quie—ro ven—cer mas quien po—
4. Quien tu—vies—se tal po—der mas quien po—

dra.
dra.

Qu'e—lla con su gran po—

der ven—ci— do me ha.

Fine

117

D.C. al Fine

Al amor quiero vencer
mas quien podrá?
Quella con su gran poder
vencido me ha.
Al amor querria vencer
y con bien ser del vencido,
por poder mejor querer,
para ser mejor querido.
Quien tuviesse tal poder,
mas quien podrá?
Quella con su gran poder
vencido me ha.

I wish to conquer Love
But how can it be done?
She has overcome me
with her great power.
I wish to overcome Love
and to be overcome,
To love better
And be better loved.
Oh! to have such power!
But whoever could?
She has overcome me
with her great power.

—Translation by Nicki Kennedy

The principal genre of Spanish song in the Renaissance was the *villancico*. The term was first used in the late 15th century to identify a poetic form equivalent to the French virelai (AbbaA). The Spanish composer Luis Milán published twelve *villancicos* in his *El Maestro* (Valencia, 1536), a large collection of works for solo vihuela—a guitar-like instrument with five to seven courses of gut strings tuned in the same manner as a lute—and for voice and vihuela. Within this collection, Milán presents two different versions of *Al amor quiero vencer* ("I want to conquer love"). In the first of these (Anthology 1/#55A), notated in simple, note-against-note fashion, Milán asks the singer to embellish his or her part. In the second (Anthology 1/#55B), the vihulea line is written out in a more elaborate form, and here the composer asks the instrumentalist *not* to embellish. In either fashion, the texture of this and other villancicos in Milán's collection is similar to that of the frottola: the uppermost voice dominates while the lower voices fill out the polyphonic framework.

El Maestro is important not only as the first collection of printed music for the vihuela, but also as the first publication of any kind to indicate performance tempos. Milán uses markings in Italian that range from *Molto Lento* to *Molto Allegro*.

Performance notes: This performance intermingles the two versions A and B. The singer and vihuela player both embellish the A version considerably, creating, in effect, a series of variations on a theme.

Thomas Morley (1557–1602)

CD3   Track 33

p. 169

The Italian madrigal was transplanted to England first through manuscripts in the 1560s and then in a series of publications. The first of these, *Musica Transalpina* ("Music from Across the Alps"), published in 1588, was an anthology of 57 late-16th-century Italian madrigals with texts translated into English. The most notable among the composers represented were Ferrabosco, Marenzio, Palestrina, and de Monte. The English, at the time, were in the midst of an infatuation with things Italian. Shakespeare, for example, wrote a number of plays in the 1590s that are set in Italy, including *The Taming of the Shrew, The Two Gentlemen of Verona, Romeo and Juliet,* and *The Merchant of Venice.*

In 1597, the English composer Thomas Morley (1557–1602) complained that the Italian fad was preventing his compatriots from appreciating the work of English composers. He expressed disgust with "the new-fangled opinions of our countrymen who will highly esteem whatsoever cometh from beyond the seas (and specially from Italy) be it never so simple, condemning that which is done at home though it be never so excellent."

Morley, though, had an axe to grind—or more precisely, music to sell. He had already established himself as a composer of English madrigals and was eager to see the public taste move away from Italian music. He also conveniently avoided mentioning that he had based a number of his madrigals on Italian models. What's more, he adopted anglicized versions of the Italian terms *canzonetti* and *balletti* for his own lighter, dance-inspired madrigals. The madrigal *Now is the Month of Maying* is from the collection of 1595. It is almost entirely chordal in texture, very much in the style of Lasso's *Matona mia cara*. And perhaps almost as bawdy: the "barley break" in the last line refers to an old English game of mixed-sex tag in which the "losing" couple often wound up kissing.

57 Come, Heavy Sleep (ca. 1590–1597)
John Dowland (1563–1626)

CD3 Track 34

p. 171

2. Come, shadow of my end, and shape of rest,
   Allied to death, child to this black-faced night,
   Come thou and charm these rebels in my breast,
   Whose waking fancies doth my mind affright.
   O come, sweet sleep, come or I die for ever;
   Come ere my last sleep come, or come never.

The lute song is essentially a strophic madrigal notated for lute and any combination of one or more voices. It flourished in England at the end of the 16th and beginning of the 17th centuries, and its chief proponent was the composer John Dowland. In practice, the uppermost voice is consistently the most melodic, though this should not exclude other arrangements that distribute voices and instruments among any of various combinations of parts. Dowland's setting of *Come, Heavy Sleep* plays on the perennial image of sleep as "the image of true death" both in its poetry and music. The long, languid arch of the cantus line conveys an almost palpable sense of fatigue in its measured rhythms and repeated downward progressions.

A note on the edition: This edition transmits the original tablature notation for lute. What look like staff lines actually correspond to the strings ("courses") of the lute. The letters indicate which finger is to be depressed on which string, and what look like the flags of eighth-, sixteenth-, and thirty-second- notes indicate the rhythms; the indicated rhythm prevails until a different one appears. Tablature continues as a notational system today in music for the guitar, ukelele, and similar plucked instruments.

p. 173

58 Ein feste Burg ist unser Gott (1551)
Johann Walter (1496–1570)

CD3 Track 36

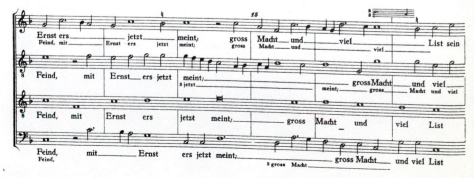

Ein feste Burg ist unser Gott,
ein gute Wehr und Waffen.
Er hilft uns frei aus aller Not,
die uns jetzt hat betroffen.
Der alt böse Feind,
mit Ernst ers jetzt meint;
gross Macht und viel List
sein grausam Rüstung ist;
auf Erd is nicht seins Gleichen.

A mighty fortress is our God,
A trusty shield and weapon;
He helps us free from ev'ry need
That hath us now o'ertaken.
The old evil foe
Now means deadly woe:
Deep guile and great might
are his dread arms in fight,
On earth is not his equal.

Many of the earliest Protestant chorales were derived from existing melodies, both liturgical and secular. Still other chorales were newly composed to new texts, including Martin Luther's *Ein feste Burg ist unser Gott* ("A Mighty Fortress is Our God"). Luther himself wrote the melody and adapted the text from Psalm 46 ("God is our refuge and our strength…"). The melody bears significant points of similarity to the Hans Sachs's *Silberweise* (Anthology 1/#54); whether or not Luther consciously modeled the tune on this source remains unclear.

Originally intended to be sung in unison by a congregation, chorale melodies soon began to be harmonized in increasingly sophisticated polyphonic settings. Johann Walter's setting of *Ein feste Burg ist unser Gott,* published in 1551, looks very much like a contemporary *Tenorlied,* with the principal melody in the tenor, surrounded by three other voices that move at a somewhat faster speed. The setting is well within reach of a moderately proficient choir. Walter (1496–1570) was the most prominent of the first generation of composers who wrote specifically for the Protestant liturgy.

Performance notes: A work like Walter's polyphonic setting of *Ein feste Burg ist unser Gott* could just as easily be performed on instruments as sung. The performance here is on a set of recorders (soprano, alto, tenor, bass). The slower-moving chorale melody is distinctly audible on the tenor recorder.

59　Verily, Verily I Say Unto You (ca. 1580?)
Thomas Tallis (ca. 1505–1585)

CD3　Track 38

p. 174

St. John 6, vv. 53-56.

■ No. 59 Tallis: *Verily, Verily I Say Unto You*

In England, the Reformation was driven by the monarchy, beginning with Henry VIII (1491–1547, reigned 1509–1547). With the publication of the first *Book of Common Prayer* in 1549, English began to replace Latin as the language of the liturgy, but the Communion Service continued to follow the basic outline of the Mass. This permitted musicians to maintain their existing repertory by converting the texts of existing Mass settings and motets into English.

Not surprisingly, composers soon took up the challenge and opportunity to write motets in the English language. These works, which eventually came to be known as anthems, took two forms, full and verse. The full anthem is for chorus throughout. The verse anthem alternates choral passages with passages for solo voice and instrumental accompaniment.

The most outstanding composers of anthems during the 16th century were Christopher Tye (1500–1573), Thomas Tallis (1505–1585), and William Byrd (1542–1623). Tallis's *Verily, verily I say unto You* exemplifies the earliest full anthems. The declamation is almost entirely chordal except for a few cadences (m. 11, 17–18) and a bit of word-painting on the rising figure that sets the phrase "…and I will raise him up" (m. 19–20).

Performance notes: Any conductor of Renaissance polyphony must face the question of how to perform the higher voice ranges of soprano and alto. Some groups assign the parts to women, others to adult males who sing in falsetto, still others to boys. There are merits and drawbacks to each solution, and much depends on the repertory in question. The Tallis Scholars, heard here, use women's voices. The group's conductor, Peter Phillips, has argued that even the most talented boy singers cannot match the high level of a professional adult singer. Those who object to this approach in this repertory do so on the grounds that women would not have been allowed to sing in church choirs in Tallis's lifetime. For an alternative approach, using boys' voices, listen to the recording of Byrd's *Sing Joyfully Unto God* (Anthology 1/#60).

60   Sing Joyfully Unto God (ca. 1590–1623)
William Byrd (ca. 1540–1623)

CD3   Track 40

p. 175

1-2: S1, S2 & A2 begin G♯m G♯m, B♭m B♭m, & E♭m E♭m, respectively, in Ni2; this version might possibly represent Byrd's original opening.

© Copyright 1983 by Stainer & Bell Ltd.

■ No. 60 Byrd: *Sing Joyfully Unto God*

No. 60 Byrd: *Sing Joyfully Unto God*

The English anthem became increasingly elaborate over the course of the 16th century, as witnessed by Byrd's *Sing Joyfully unto God*. It features the six-voice texture so characteristic of choral music in the late 16th century. In many respects, the work resembles a sacred madrigal for chorus. It is paratactic in form and through-composed with discrete but unmistakable instances of word-painting. Note the rising figure on "Sing joyfully" in m. 1, for example, the long note values and octave leaps on "Sing loud" at m. 10, and the triadic, fanfare-like figure to the words "Blow the trumpet" at m. 30.

Performance notes: This recording, by the Salisbury Cathedral Choir, uses boys' voices to perform the soprano and alto parts. Boys choirs have long been an important part of English choral culture, and for many listeners, the characteristically transparent texture of the sound is inescapably associated with this repertory.

61 Missa Papae Marcelli: Credo
(ca. 1565–1567)

Giovanni Pierluigi da Palestrina
(1525 or 1526–1594)

CD3   Track 43

p. 176

No. 61 Palestrina: *Missa Papae Marcelli*   131

The Council of Trent met in three sessions (1545–1547, 1551–1552, 1562–1563) in Trento (Trent), in what is now northern Italy, to formulate doctrines of faith, revise the liturgy, and generally purge the Roman Catholic church of various practices that had accrued over many centuries. In the realm of music, the Council eliminated a number of plainchants that had been added to the liturgy since medieval times (such as the Sequence on which Josquin had based the opening of his *Ave Maria...virgo serena;* see Textbook, Chapter 4). The Council further declared that the function of sacred music was to serve the text, and that the text should be clear and intelligible to listeners.

Legend has it that Palestrina's *Missa Papae Marcelli* ("Mass for Pope Marcellus") convinced the Council of Trent not to ban polyphony altogether. The story is appealing but untrue. However, participants at the Council might very well have pointed to the straightforward and nonvirtuosic text setting in at least some of Palestrina's Masses in their defense of polyphony. Through his careful control of dissonance and largely syllabic setting of text, Palestrina was able to present the Mass Ordinary in a manner that was both textually intelligible and musically satisfying. Words at beginnings of phrases stand out with special clarity, but Palestrina introduces musical variety and relieves the mostly chordal declamation of the text with discrete melismas from time to time.

Performance notes: The performance begins with the vocal soloist intoning the opening words of the Credo: *Credo in unum Deum* ("I believe in one God"). Palestrina, like many of his contemporaries, never set these words to music, assuming that during the ritual of the Mass, the celebrant would sing these words before the entrance of the chorus with the subsequent text of the Credo ("...the Father almighty").

62 Diferencias sobre el canto de la Dama le demanda (ca. 1540–1566?)

Antonio de Cabezón (ca. 1510–1566)

CD3   Track 49

p. 178

Cabezón's "Variations on the Song 'The Lady Demands It'" takes as its theme the popular melody known in France as *Belle, qui tient ma vie* ("Beautiful one, who holds my life"). Cabezón presents the melody in the uppermost voice, then takes it through a series of five variations. Typically for keyboard music of the mid-16th century, the register remains fairly narrow throughout, the melody is never far from the surface, and the technical demands on the player are relatively modest. Cabezón's ability to weave new figures around this theme and change its rhythmic profile allow him to create a set of variations that build in intensity to the very end.

Francesco Spinacino (fl. early 16th century)

CD3 **Track 52**

p. 179

In Italian, *ricercare* means "to research, to seek out," and the ricercar of the early 16th century is a freely composed work that "seeks out" a particular mode or thematic idea. The typical ricercar of this era is full of runs and passagework. Francesco Spinacino's Ricercar, from the first book of his *Intabolatura de lauto* ("Lute Intabulations"), published by Petrucci in 1507, has all the hallmarks of improvisation: the dramatic pause after the opening stroke, the gradual accumulation of speed, and the eventual move from passagework to more tangible thematic ideas (beginning at m. 20) all create a sense of generative energy, a trajectory that moves from obscurity to focus, from generalities to specifics.

64 Ricercar del duodecimo tuono
(ca. 1589)

Andrea Gabrieli (1532 or 1533–1585)

CD3   Track 55

p. 179

Canto

Alto

Tenore

Basso

No. 64 Gabrieli: *Ricercar del duodecimo tuono*   139

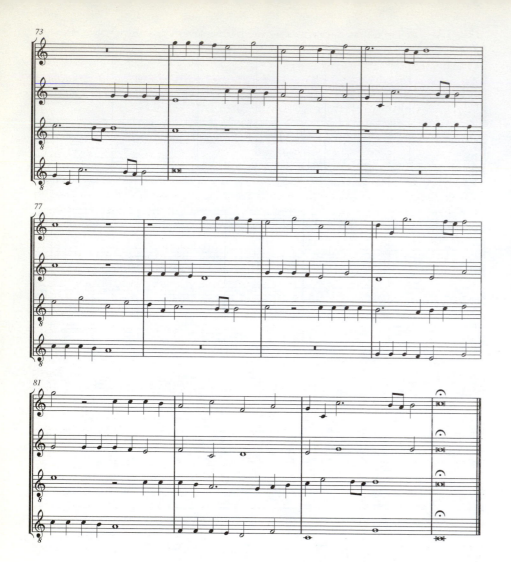

By the middle of the 16th century the genre of the ricercar had become primarily imitative; the sense of "seeking out" was now being applied to the exploration of the contrapuntal possibilities inherent in a series of themes. The *Ricercar del duodecimo tuono* by Andrea Gabrieli stands squarely in the tradition of the polyphonic ricercar. The *duodecimo tuono* ("twelfth tone") of the title corresponds to the Ionian mode on C, which happens to be the equivalent of the modern-day major scale. The work can be performed by any combination of appropriate instruments with the needed ranges—strings, winds, brass. The writing here is not idiomatic to any particular instrument or for that matter to instruments at all; with an appropriately underlaid text, the parts could just as easily be sung. The practice of writing in a manner unique to a specific instrument is something that would not emerge until the 17th century, and even then only gradually.

Performance notes: The group performing here, "His Majestys Sagbutts and Cornetts," takes its memorable name from a group of the same name founded in 1516. The sackbut, as the instrument is more commonly known, was a forerunner of the trombone. Its tone is more focused than its modern counterpart, however, which makes it suitable for doubling voices in the performance of vocal music. The cornetto, heard here in the upper two voices, also produces a less aggressive sound with a softer edge than its descendant, the trumpet.

65 La morisque (ca. 1551)
Tielman Susato (ca. 1500–ca. 1561)

Companion CD · Track 8 · p. 181

La morisque

The quantity of sources that preserve dance music increases dramatically over the course of the 16th century. Tielman Susato's *Het derde musyck boexken* ("Third Little Book of Music") includes many of the kinds of dances that were popular in the late Renaissance. Each of these dances has its own distinctive steps, meter, tempo, and musical character. The *morisque* or *moresca* is a dance in duple meter in which the dancers blacken their faces and attach bells to their legs, ostensibly to resemble the "Moors" of Spain and North Africa.

Whatever their differences, all of these dances are built on the principle of periodic phrase structure—that is, they consist of many modular units of equal length. This structure derives from the basic function of social dance, which by its very nature consists of a pre-scribed pattern of steps that are repeated over and over again. The pavane, the waltz, the cha cha, the tango, the fox-trot, square dancing, line dancing: no matter what the era or repertory, all of these dances require participants to execute a basic step—a modular unit—and repeat it many times. It is only natural that the music for this kind of dancing should rest on a corre-spondingly modular musical construction, with small units of equal size combining to make a larger whole.

In Susato's *La Morisque*, for example, the phrasing falls very clearly into a 4 + 4 pat-tern that corresponds harmonically to what we would today think of as tonic moving to dom-inant (m. 1–4), followed by four measures that remain in the tonic. These smaller units of periodic phrase structure are based on a combination of melodic, harmonic, and rhythmic elements. Phrases that move from tonic to dominant (I–V) are called antecedent phrases (antecedent meaning "to come before"), while phrases that move from the dominant back to the tonic (V–I) are called consequent phrases (consequent meaning "to follow as a result of something that has come before"). In the simplest kind of periodic phrase structure, a four-measure antecedent phrase is followed by a four-measure consequent phrase. This larger eight-measure unit, in turn, can be juxtaposed with another unit of eight measures (4 + 4), as in Susato's *La Morisque*.

Dance music abounds in repetition, and in performance, the individual reprises—the larger sections to be repeated—can be played as often as desired. Two reprises together con-stitute a binary form. Binary form represents one of the earliest instances of syntactic form, in which a central idea is presented and varied over the course of an entire movement, in con-trast to paratactic form, in which each new section presents an essentially new idea. Binary form takes its name from the fact that it always consists of two reprises, that is, sections to be repeated ("reprised"). Binary form provides the basis for a great many dance types and would eventually be incorporated into instrumental music not written expressly for dancing. During the 18th century, in fact, binary form would provide the structural basis for sonata form.

Susato promised his audiences that these dances "could be played quite delightfully and easily on all musical instruments," and his claim goes beyond mere salesmanship. The lines are so straightforward that they could in fact just as easily be sung. But as in the case of Andrea Gabrieli's *Ricercar* (Anthology 1/#64), no distinctively instrumental idiom is evident here, or even some 60 years later in the instrumental dances of Michael Praetorius (Anthology 1/#66).

Performance notes: The upper line in this performance is played on a flageolet, a recorder with only four holes for the fingers and two for the thumbs. The accompanying instruments are drums, tambourine, and a small reed organ (regal), which plays a drone bass in the fash-ion of a bagpipe.

CD3 Track 59 p. 181

Praetorius's *Terpsichore* is a collection of more than 300 four- and five-part harmonizations of dance tunes popular in France at the end of the Renaissance. The melodies were transmitted to him by a French dancing master employed at a German court near the town where Praetorius lived. Like almost all dance music, the melodies consist of units of four, six, or eight measures, with much repetition. The bourrée (also spelled bouree) is lively, flowing dance in duple meter; its melodies characteristically begin with a prominent upbeat into the first measure. The volta (volte) is a vigorous "turning" dance (*voltare* means "to turn" in Italian), often in compound duple meter. Praetorius leaves matters of instrumentation to the discretion and resources of the performers.

Performance notes: At the end of the Bourrée, the performers in this recording repeat the opening binary unit. Although not indicated in the score, this kind of repetition would have been taken for granted by most performers of Praetorius' time. Literal repeats are quite common in dance music, and musicians often repeated large sections at will in order to fill up the necessary amount of time for dancing. This particular dance, moreover, calls for a return to the opening key—what we would today think of as G Major, as opposed to the G minor with which the notated music ends.

67 Prophetiae Sibyllarum: Prologue
(ca. 1550–1552)
Orlande de Lassus

CD4 Track 1
p. 185

The Prologue to Orlande de Lassus's *Prophetiae sibyllarum* offers a good example of musical mannerism. The Sibylline Prophecies of the title are the work of 2nd-century authors apocryphally attributed to the legendary Sibyls, ancient Greek prophetesses. The texts, which purport to foretell the birth of Christ, were accepted as genuine by Saint Augustine and other early Christian thinkers, giving the Sibyls a status equal to that of Old Testament prophets. Michelangelo painted five of the Sibyls onto the ceiling of the Sistine Chapel in the Vatican in 1508–1512. The Prologue, whose text may have been written by Lassus himself, reads (in translation): "Polyphonic songs which you hear with a chromatic tenor / these are they, in which our twice-six sibyls once sang with fearless mouth the secrets of salvation." Lassus responds immediately to the idea of "chromaticism" with a series of jarring progressions. Within the opening nine measures, he uses all twelve chromatic pitches and builds triads on ten different roots. The piece is in Mixolydian mode on G; in modern terminology, the work might be said to begin on IV (C major) and move through harmonies as remote as B major (V/vi), which in turn swerves to C♯ minor, E♭ major, and B major before finally cadencing in the "tonic" at the end of the first line of text (m. 9). If we eliminate m. 4, we can see the progression V/VI–VI. But m. 4 is there, and it forces us into an astonishing detour through C♯ minor (♯iv). In the final eight measures, the music shifts back and forth between E and E♭ before finally cadencing on G.

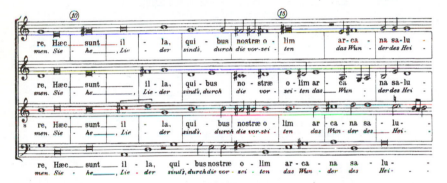

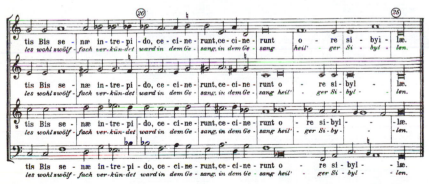

Carmina chromatico quae audis modulata
  tenore
Haec sunt illa quibus nostrae olim arcana salutis
Bis senae intrepido cecinerunt ore Sybillae.

These are songs which proceed chromatically.
They are the poems in which the twelve
Sibyls, one after the other, once sang the hidden
mysteries of our salvation.

68 Cum essem parvulus (ca. 1579)

Orlande de Lassus

CD4   Track 2

p. 188

Prima pars
Cum essem parvulus,
loquebar ut parvulus,
sapiebam ut parvulus,
cogitam ut parvulus.
Quando autem factus sum vir,
evacuavi quae erant parvuli.

Videmus nunc per speculum in aenigmate,
tunc autem facie ad faciem.

Seconda pars
Nunc cognosco ex parte,
tunc autem cognoscam sicut
et cognitus sum.

Nunc autem manent fides, spes, caritas,
tria haec, maior autem horum
est caritas.

Part One
When I was a child,
I spoke as a child,
I understood as a child,
I thought as a child;
but when I became a man,
I put away childish things.

We see now a riddle through a mirror
[King James: As through a glass darkly],
But then face to face.

Part Two
Now I know in part,
but then I shall know even as also
I am known.

And now abideth faith, hope, love,
these three; but the greatest of these
is love.

I Corinthians 13:11–13

The text of Lassus's *Cum essem parvulus* is Saint Paul's famous declaration from I Corinthians 13:11 ("When I was a child, I spoke as a child"). Lassus sets the opening words in the two uppermost voices; in the late 16th century these would almost invariably have been sung by boys, thereby reinforcing the meaning of the words through their sonority. *Loquebar*, in turn—"I spoke"—is intoned by the four lower voices. The effect evokes the idea of memory: the narrator is now a man, as this single word in a lower voices emphasizes. The last phrase of the opening statement—*ut parvulus* ("as a child")—returns to the boys' voices. The next verb, *sapiebam* ("I thought"), is again given to the men, "as a child" to the boys. And so on. The turning point comes with the words *quando autem factus sum vir* ("but when I became a man"). The first words of this phrase are intoned by the men alone, but on the words *factus sum vir* ("became a man") all the voices enter. The effect is striking. Even if we did not understand a word of the text, we would have a sense of having arrived at a fullness of sound here, a goal. And at the end of the text, when we are presented with the promise of seeing God face to face, the music, appropriately enough, moves from fragmented counterpoint (on the word *aenigmate*—"in riddles") to simple note-against-note counterpoint.

69 Dunque fra torbid' onde from Il Canto d'Arione (1589)

Giacopo Peri (1561–1633)

CD4 Track 6 p. 209

Arione

Dunque fra torbide onde
Gli ultimi miei sospir manderà fuore,
Ecco gentil con tuoi suavi accenti:
Raddoppia i miei tormenti;
Ahi, lacrime, ahi dolore,
Ahi morte troppo acerba e troppo dura,
Ma deh, chi,
O di Terra o di Cielo
S'a torto io mi querelo:
E s'a ragion mi doglio;
Movetevi a pietà del mio cordoglio.

Arion

Thus over troubled waters
I shall exhale my final sighs.
Gentle Echo, with your tender accents,
Redouble my torments,
O tears, O pains!
O death, too bitter and too hard!
Oh, who on the Earth or in the Sky
Would accuse me
Of a wrongful complaint?
And if I grieve with reason,
Have pity on me in my grief.

Peri's *Dunque fra torbid' onde* ("Thus over troubled waters") was part of the elaborate musical and dramatic festivities staged at the 1589 Florentine wedding of Ferdinando de' Medici, Grand Duke of Tuscany, to Christine de Lorraine, Princess of France. It draws on Greek mythology in depicting the poet Arion, who is about to be thrown into the sea by pirates. Arion sings a lament so moving that Apollo summons a dolphin to rescue him and carry him to shore. The aria *Dunque fra torbid' onde* is scored for four stringed instruments and three solo voice parts. Arion's line is labeled *parte principale* because it is clearly more important than the other two voices, which echo in response (*riposta*) to Arion's melody and words. All three voices stand out from the instrumental accompaniment by virtue of their rhythmic freedom and melodic virtuosity. In this respect, we can see Peri moving toward a texture that is homophonic—consisting, that is, of a principal melodic line with subordinate accompanying voices. Homophony is particularly well suited to the clear projection of a text in the principal melodic voice. Yet the instrumental accompaniment here consists of four-part counterpoint, and on closer inspection, it turns out that the tenor, the principal singing voice, adheres in its outline to the tenor voice of the instrumental ensemble. Even though the tenor's line is elaborately embellished, it functions structurally within the framework of traditional four-part polyphony.

No. 69 Peri: *Dunque fra torbid' onde*   ■ 151

Sfogava con le stelle (1602)

Giulio Caccini (1545–1618)

vo-stro au-reo sem- bian-te Pie- to- sa sì, pie-to- sa sì, co-

me me fa- - tea- man- te, co- me me fa-

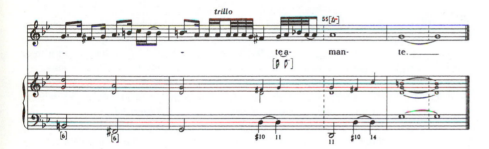

trillo

tea- man- te.

Monody opened up important new possibilities of performance in the early Baroque era. The soloist was now free to embellish at will, without rhythmic or motivic regard for any other melodic line. Ornamentation and pure flights of fancy unthinkable in polyphonic textures were now suddenly a very real option. All of this could help give the music an air of spontaneity in performance—what Caccini called *sprezzatura,* a certain freedom in the pace and manner of delivery, a kind of noble disregard for the meter and rhythm.

Caccini's monody *Sfogava con le stelle* ("He vented to the stars") from *Le nuove musiche* of 1602 illustrates the new practice vividly. The music, following the text, divides into two parts: the first (m. 1–11) is presented from the perspective of a narrator, who sets the scene of a lover venting his grief to the stars. The second (m. 12–57) presents the words of the lover himself, calling on the stars to convince his beloved to return his affections. The rhythms of the opening are slow and measured, and its pitches are confined to a limited range. But once the lover himself begins to declaim *O immagini belle Dell'dol mio ch'adoro* ("Oh, beautiful images of the one I adore…"), the music rises in pitch, velocity, and intensity. Caccini emphasizes key words either by long notes (*adoro*—"adore"—m. 15–16) or by rapid passagework (*ardori*—"passions"—m. 29–30). The vocal line throughout the second half gives the impression of spontaneity, as if the singer is thinking up the words on the spot: the pace of delivery is never predictable. The underlay follows the rhythms of a person speaking, at times slow or even hesitant, at other times rushing forward in a torrent.

Sfogava con le stelle	He vented to the stars
Un inferno d'amore	An inferno of love
Sotto notturno cielo il suo dolore,	Under the night sky, grieving,
E dicea fisso in loro:	Saying to them:
O immagini belle	"O lovely images
Dell'idol mio ch'adoro,	Of my adored one,
Si come a me mostrate,	Just as you reveal to me,
Mentre così splendete,	By shining so brightly,
La sua rara beltate,	Her rare beauty,
Così mostraste a lei,	Show to her as well
Mentre cotanto ardete,	My intense passion,
I vivi ardori miei.	My burning love.
La fareste co'l vostro aureo sembiante	Make her, with your golden gleam,
Pietosa sì, come me fate amante.	Pity me, as you have made me love her."

71 Al fonte, al prato (1609)
Giacopo Peri (1561–1633)

Companion CD — Track 9

p. 213

[1] Al fon-te, al pra-to, Al bo-sco, al-l'om-bra, Al fre-sco fia-to

Che'l cal-do sgom-bra, Pa-stor cor-re-te Cia-scun ch'ha se-te,

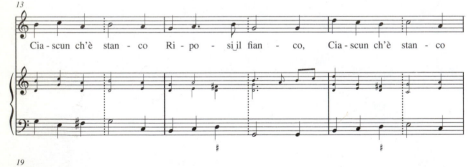

Cia-scun ch'è stan-co Ri-po-si il fian-co, Cia-scun ch'è stan-co

Ri-po-si il fian-co.

Ritornello

Al fonte, al prato, Al bosco, all'ombra,
Al fresco fiato Che'l caldo sgombra,
Pastor correte Ciascun ch'ha sete,
Ciascun ch'è stanco Riposi il fianco.

Fugga la noia, Fugga 'l dolore,
Sol riso e gioia, Sol caro Amore
Nosco soggiorni Ne' liete giorni,
Ne' s'oda mai Querele o lai.

Ma dolce canto Di vaghi uccelli,
Per verde manto Degli arboscelli,
Risuoni sempre Con nuovi tempre,
Mentre ch'all'onde Ecco risponde.

E mentre alletta, Quanto più puote,
La cicaletta, Con roche note,
Il sonno dolce Che 'l caldo molce,
E noi pian piano Con lei cantiamo.

(To the spring, to the meadow, to the glade, to the shade, to the fresh breeze that lessens the heat, hasten each shepherd who is thirsty; he who is weary, let him rest.

Away with boredom, away with sorrow! Let only laughter, joy, and welcome Cupid be our companions in these happy days; let there never be heard complaints or laments.

Let only the sweet song of the charming birds with new timbres sound forever through the green mantle of the trees, while Echo answers the streams.

And while the grasshopper, as best it can, charms with chirping tones the sweet sleep that soothes the heat, with it let us softly sing.)

Peri's *Al fonte, al prato* follows a rhythmic pattern identical to that of a great many dances of the time, its spirit similar to that of the contemporary frottola. The work is constructed on a series of four-measure units (m. 1–4, 5–8, 9–12, 13–16, 17–20). The first, fourth and fifth of these units end on what we nowadays consider the tonic harmony (I) while the second and third finish on IV and V, respectively (again, using modern-day terminology). This pattern—establishing the tonic, moving away from it, and returning to it at the end—would become basic to a great deal of music written over the ensuing decades and centuries.

Al fonte, al prato concludes with a four-measure instrumental phrase labelled ritornello, literally a "brief return," an idea that recurs repeatedly over the course of a work or movement and contrasts either in its instrumentation or theme with the other ideas of the work. Here, the instrumental ritornello separates the end of each vocal strophe from the beginning of the next.

Performance notes: The continuo group in this performance consists of a guitar, harp, and *lirone* or *lira da gamba,* a fretted instrument with two drone strings, held and played in a manner similar to a viola da gamba. The instrumentalists interpose their own version of the complete melody—not just the ritornello—between the second and third strophes of the song.

Cruda Amarilli (ca. 1598–1605)

Claudio Monteverdi (1567–1643)

CD4   Track 11

p. 221

Cruda Amarilli
che col nome ancora
d'amar, ahi lassa, amaramente insegni;
Amarilli, del candido ligustro
più candida e più bella,
ma dell'aspido sordo
e più sorda e più fera e più fugace,
poi che col dir t'offendo,
i' mi morrò tacendo.

         —B. Guarini

Cruel Amaryllis,
who with your name still
Teaches us, alas, a bitter lesson of love;
Amaryllis, whiter and more beautiful
Than the white privet blossom,
But also more stealthy than the adder
More stealthy, and wilder, and more elusive,
If in saying this I offend you
I shall go to my death in silence.

Commentary on next page

Monteverdi never claimed to have created the *seconda prattica* or "new practice." To the contrary: he identified two madrigalists of the mid-16th century—Cipriano de Rore and Adrian Willaert—as the originators this style, on the grounds that both composers had gone out of their way to make their music project the essence of the words being sung. The most serious public dispute about the *seconda prattica* in fact did not center on any collection of monodies, but rather on certain polyphonic madrigals that would later be published in Monteverdi's Fifth Book of Madrigals. The Italian composer and theorist Giovanni Maria Artusi (ca. 1540–1613) attacked Monteverdi's treatment of dissonance in these works as unacceptable, spelling out his objections in considerable detail in a pamphlet issued in 1600 entitled *L'Artusi, ovvero delle imperfettioni della moderna musica* ("The Artusi; or, On the Imperfections of Modern Music"). Artusi knew these madrigals through manuscript copies—Book 5 would not actually be published for another five years—and he took particular exception to Monteverdi's five-voiced *Cruda Amarilli* ("Cruel Amaryllis"). Artusi chastised the composer for having violated the precepts of counterpoint as set down by Zarlino. He objected to Monteverdi's practice of repeating suspended notes and of descending after a sharpened tone and rising after a flattened one, pointing specifically to the vertical dissonances in m. 12–14 of *Cruda Amarilli*. He disapproved of the cross-relations between G-F♯ and F♮ in this passage, as well as the unprepared dissonant entry of the A in the highest voice in m. 14 against the G in the bass. He also criticized the work for having more cadences in the twelfth mode (C plagal) than in the seventh mode (G authentic), the mode of its opening and closing.

Monteverdi replied with a brief manifesto of his own when his Fifth Book of Madrigals was finally published in 1605 (see Textbook, p. 221). The set opens quite pointedly with *Cruda Amarilli,* the very madrigal Artusi had attacked so sharply. Two years later the composer's brother, Giulio Cesare Monteverdi (1573–ca. 1630), offered an extended gloss on this brief statement, and while this additional commentary may not have been written by Claudio himself, it was surely approved by him. In this gloss, Giulio Cesare Monteverdi argues that in the *seconda prattica* "the oration is the mistress of the harmony"—that is, that the delivery of the words, the manner of the oration, dictates the nature of the music, and not vice versa. He goes on to point out that Artusi, in his critique of *Cruda Amarilli,* had paid no attention whatsoever to the madrigal's words, "as though they had nothing to do with the music." And he reiterated Claudio Monteverdi's promise to weigh in with a longer statement justifying the *seconda prattica*. But this work never appeared—Claudio seems to have been too busy writing new music.

The Artusi-Monteverdi controversy exposes the fundamental differences in outlook between advocates of the "old" and the "new" practice. Artusi, representing the traditional approach, looks first and foremost at the construction of the music, whereas Monteverdi justifies the use of unconventional musical techniques with the assertion that words demand them.

73   T'amo mia vita (ca. 1598–1605)
Monteverdi

p. 222

Monteverdi's setting of *T'amo mia vita,* published in 1605, exhibits striking differences with Luzasscho Luzasschi's setting of the same text issued only four years earlier (Anthology 1/#51). Thanks to the use of the solo voice, Monteverdi is able to distinguish quite clearly between the narrator's memory of the words he has heard from his beloved ("I love you, my life") and his own injunction to the god of love, Amor, to imprint these words on his heart. The madrigal begins with the remembered words themselves, sung by a solo soprano (representing the beloved's voice) and supported by basso continuo. Only with the entrance of the three lower (men's) voices do we realize that the opening line is a quotation, a memory. The effect is quite dramatic, with the contrasting perspectives represented by contrasting sonorities. When the memory returns in m. 9, it is not only the words that come back (*T'amo mia vita*), but also the beloved's voice as well, for this line is consistently given to the soprano alone in the first half of Monteverdi's setting.

Beginning in m. 40, after the narrator implores the god of love to imprint them on his heart and let his "soul breathe through them alone," Monteverdi incorporates the remembered words into the full texture of all six voices. The soprano sings exactly the same pitches as at the beginning, but her words and the sound of her voice have now been integrated into the body of the whole. Monteverdi projects the text "Let 'I love you, my life,' be my whole life" by folding the falling motive associated with the remembered words into the full texture of the music. Because it is a concertato madrigal—a work for voice and instruments that function both together and independently of one another—Monteverdi can distinguish solo passages from polyphonic ones and capture the drama of the poetry in a way that Luzasschi's wholly polyphonic setting cannot.

"T'amo mia vita," la mia cara vita
dolcemente me dice; e in questa sola
si soave parola
Par mi trasformi lietamente il core.
O voce di dolcezza e di diletto.
Prendila tosta Amore,
stampala nel mio petto,
spiri dunque per lei l'anima mia.
"T'amo mia vita," la mia vita sia.

"I love you my life," my dearest life
softly tells me; and with these
such gentle words
my heart is joyfully transformed.
O voice of sweetness and delight.
Take it soon, Love,
stamp it upon my breast
so that I may breathe only for her.
"I love you my life," be my life.

(ca. 1630)

Monteverdi

CD4 Track 17
p. 224

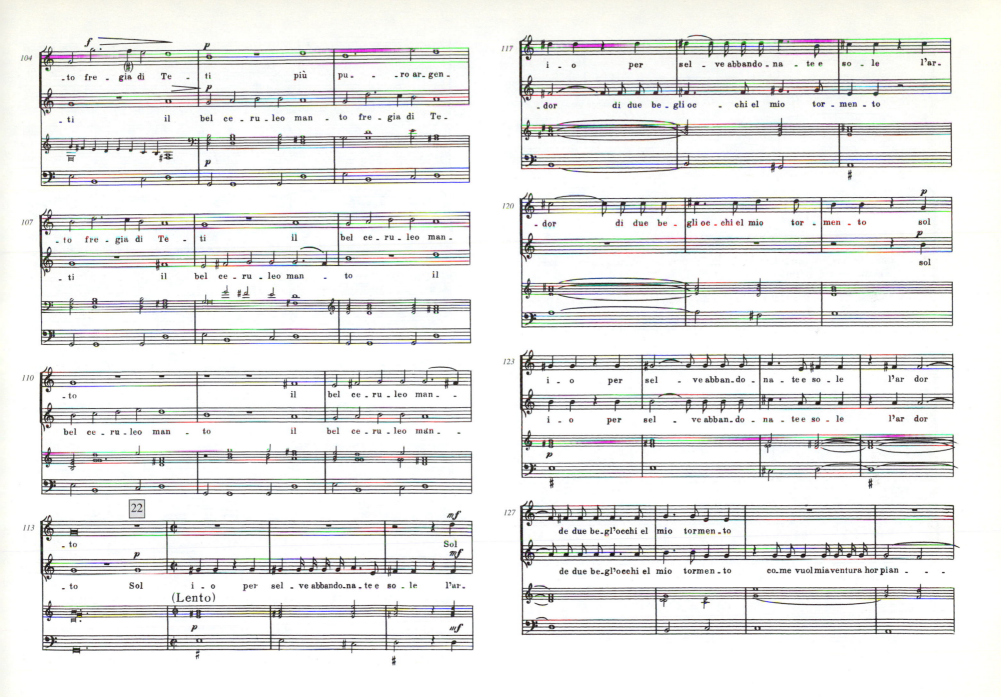

No. 74 Monteverdi: *Zefiro torna e di soavi accenti*   ■   **165**

Zefiro torna e di soavi accenti
L'aer fa grato e'l piè discioglie a l'onde,

E mormorando tra le verdi fronde
Fa danzar al bel suon su'l prato i fiori,
Inghirlandato il crin Fillide e Clori
Note temprando amor care e gioconde
E da monti e da valli ime e profonde
Raddopian l'armonia gli antri canori.
Sorge più vaga in ciel l'aurora e'l sole

Sparge più luci d'or, più puro argento
Fregia di Teti il bel ceruleo manto.
Sol io per selve abbandonate e sole
L'ardor di due begli occhi e'l mio tormento.
Come vuol mia ventura hor piango, hor canto.

—Ottavio Rinuccini

The west wind returns and with soft accents
makes the air gentle and releases swift-footed
    waves,
and murmuring among the green branches
makes the flowers dance at its lovely sound
and curls round the hair of Phyllis and Clori,
love giving rise to fond and joyful song,
and from mountains and valleys low and deep,
the sonorous caves reecho the music.
The dawn rises more lovely in the sky, and the
    sun
scatters more golden rays, and a purer silver
decorates Teti's beautiful sky blue coat.
Only I in the lonely, deserted forest—
the fire of two bright eyes is my torment.
As my fortune wills, I weep, then sing.

Monteverdi's *Zefiro torna e di soavi accenti* ("The west wind returns and with soft accents"), for two tenors and basso continuo, illustrates just how musically elaborate the concertato madrigal had become by the early 1630s. Most of the work rests upon a ground bass, a short phrase repeated over and over again in the lowest voice. This particular bass pattern, complete in two-and-half measures in modern transcription, shares no thematic material with the upper voices but instead provides a structural framework that allows the voices above it to unfold freely, without regard to their harmonic underpinnings. The ground bass also provides continuity at those moments when neither of the two tenors is singing (m. 54, 56, 58, 66, etc.). Without the basso continuo, such pauses would simply not be feasible.

The first eleven of the poem's fourteen lines are full of pastoral clichés. A gentle wind (the zephyr) blows from the west, branches murmur in the gentle breeze, nymphs dance, the sun rises in a sky of deep blue. The repeating bass reinforces the static nature of this pastoral perfection. Everything is constant and unchanging. So constant and so unchanging, in fact, that something must be about to happen. And it does. In the twelfth line, the poem shifts abruptly to the first person when the narrator says "I alone stand solitary in the lonely forest / The ardor of two beautiful eyes is my torment." The ground bass suddenly breaks off here (m. 113) and the music slows down through a change in mensuration: a breve in the opening section now equals a half note. For the last line of the poem ("As my fate wills it, I sometimes weep, sometimes sing"), Monteverdi forcefully juxtaposes the contrast between joy and sorrow, setting the final statement of the word *piango* ("weep") on a suspension with a jarring dissonance (m. 143–144) whose resolution ushers in the final return of the ground bass with the word *canto* ("I sing").

75 **Lasciatemi qui solo** (1618)
Francesca Caccini (1587–ca. 1640)

CD4   Track 25
p. 226

Lasciatemi qui solo (author unknown; last line of each stanza echoes a line from Rinuccini's lament for the title character in *L'Arianna*, 1608)

Lasciatemi qui solo	Leave me here alone.
Tornate augelli al nido	Return, birds, to your nest
Mentre l'anim'e'l duolo	While I breathe out my spirit
Spiro su questo lido.	and sorrow on this beach.
Altri meco non vòglio	I want no other with me
Ch'un freddo scoglio e'l mio	But a cold rock and my fatal
fatal martire.	suffering.
Lasciatemi morire.	Let me die.
Dolcissime sirene,	Sweetest sirens,
Ch'en si pietoso canto	Who in such piteous song
Radollcite mie pene	Sweeten my pains
Fate soave il pianto	(And) make gentle weeping,
Movete il nuoto altronde	Move your swimming elsewhere.
Togliete all'onde i crudi	Remove from the waves cruel
sdegni e l'ire	scorn and angers.
Lasciatemi morire.	Let me die.
Placidissimi venti	Most placid winds,
Tornate al vostro speco	Return to your cave.
Sol miei duri lamenti	Only my harsh laments
Chieggio che restin meco.	Do I ask to remain with me.
Vostri sospir non chiamo	I call not on your sighs.
Solingo bramò i miei dolor	Solitary, I long for my sorrow
finire.	to end.
Lasciatemi morire.	Let me die.
Felicissimi amanti	Happiest lovers,
Tornate al bel diletto	Return to sweet delight.
Fere occh'o notanti	Fierce, observant eyes,
Fuggiti'il mesto aspetto	Flee this sad sight.
Sol dolcezza di morte	Only the sweetness of death
Apra la porte all'ultimo	Opens the door to the ultimate
languire.	pleasure.
Lasciatemi morire.	Let me die.
Avarissimi lumi	Greediest of eyes
Che su'l morir versate	That shed over my death
Amarissimi fiumi	The bitterest of streams,
Tard'è vostra pietate.	Your pity is late.
Già mi sento mancare	Already I feel faint.
O luci avar'e tarde al mio	O greedy eyes, you come too
conforto.	late to comfort me.
Già sono e sangu'e smorto.	I am already both bleeding and dying.
	—Translation by Suzanne Cusick

Variation was an important structural device in a great deal of early Baroque music. This is particularly evident in Francesca Caccini's stophic monody *Lasciatemi qui solo* ("Leave me in solitude here"). The text is a lament—once again, a lover has been abandoned—that progresses from sorrow to death. The music's basic structural unit is the nine-measure pattern stated at the outset by the bass. Reinforcing the process of psychological transformation described in the text, Caccini subtly varies both the bass line and the melody in each strophe (m. 1–9, 10–19, 20–29, and 30–39, and 40–49) but maintains exactly the same music for the relentless refrain of *lasciatemi morire* ("let me die"). At the very end, however, the longed-for death is now imminent (*Già sono e sangu'e smorto*: "Already I am bloodless and pale," m. 47–48), and the slight change in the melodic line is full of meaning.

Tradimento! (1659)
Barbara Strozzi (1619–1677)

CD4 Track 30 · p. 226

Tradimento! Tradimento!

Amore e la Speranza
voglion farmi prigioniero,
e a tal segno il mal s'avanza
ch'ho scoperto ch'il Pensiero
dice d'esserne contento.

Tradimento! Tradimento!

La Speranza per legarmi
a gran cose mi lusinga.
S'io le credo, avvien che stringa
lacci sol da incatenarmi.
Mio core all'armi, all'armi!

S'incontri l'infida!
Si prenda, s'uccida!
Sù presto, è periglioso ogni momento!
Tradimento! Tradimento!
—Giovanni Tani

Betrayal! Betrayal!

Love and Hope
Want to make me their prisoner,
And my sickness is so advanced
That I realize I am happy
Just thinking of it.

Betrayal! Betrayal!

Hope, to bind me,
Entices me with great things.
The more I believe what she says,
The tighter she ties the knots that imprison me
To arms, my heart! To arms!

Against the unfaithful one!
Take her and kill her!
Hurry, every moment is dangerous!
Betrayal! Betrayal!

Tradimento! ("Betrayal!"), an arietta for soprano and continuo by Barbara Strozzi, illustrates one of the most important of all formal innovations of the Baroque, the ritornello principle. A *ritornello* (the word means "small return" in Italian) is an opening musical idea that returns at several points over the course of a work, usually after contrasting material of some kind. Composers used the ritornello principle to establish a framework of both repetition and variation, and it appears in a great many genres of the Baroque era, vocal as well as instrumental. It would later take on special importance in the genre of the concerto.

The ritornello in Strozzi's *Tradimento!*—the exclamation "Betrayal!" and the agitated theme associated with it—is both textual and musical. In these recurring outbursts, the scorned lover swears to kill the object of her (or his?) wrath. The ritornello sections offset more inward and less violent reflections: "My sickness has advanced so / That I have discovered that the thought of being [a prisoner of love] makes me contented." But these contrasting emotions are always driven out by thoughts of revenge in the guise of the ritornello ("Betrayal!").

Strozzi's ritornello captures the physical energy of the scorned lover's fury with rapid-fire repeated notes. This technique, developed by Monteverdi for evoking a mood of bellicose agitation or anger, was known as the *genere concitato*—the "agitated" or "war-like" manner. The flurry of repeated notes outlining a triad that opens *Tradimento*—and recurs with each statement of the ritornello between strophes and at the end—sounds almost like a trumpet fanfare, rousing troops for battle.

Etienne Moulinié (ca. 1600–after 1669)

CD4   Track 34

p. 228

[♩=84]

En- fin la beau- té que j'a- do- re Me fait cognoistre en son re- tour,

1.

tour,   Qu'el- le veut que

2.

(1) ♪ dans la tablature.

je voye en- co- re Ces yeux pour qui je meurs pour—qui je meurs d'a-

mour.   Mais puis que je re- voy—la beau- té qui m'en- fla-

me,   Sor- tez mes des- plai- sirs, hos- tez vous de mon a- me.

Enfin la beauté que j'adore
Me fait cognoistre en son retour,
Qu'elle veut que je voye encore
Ces yeux pour qui je meurs d'amour.
Mais puis que je revoy la beauté qui m'enflame,

Sortez mes desplaisirs, hostez vous de mon ame.

Le ciel voyant que son absence
M'oste tout mon contentement,
Octroye à ma persévérance
La fin de mon cruel tourment.
Mais puis que je revoy . . .

Mes maux changés vous en délices,
Mon cœur, arretes vos douleurs,
Amour bannissez mes supplices,
Mes yeux ne versez plus de pleurs.
Et puis que je revoy.

At last the beauty I worship
Lets me know upon her return
That she still wishes me to see
Those eyes for which I die of love.
But since I see again the beauty which
    consumes me,
Be gone, troubles, leave my soul.

Heaven, seeing that her absence
Deprives me of my happiness,
Grants, because of my perseverance,
The end of my cruel torment.
But since I see . . .

My wounds, turn yourselves into delights.
My heart, stop your aching.
Love, banish my tortures.
Eyes, shed no more tears.
And since I see . . .

—Translation by Ellen Hargis and Candice Smith

The most important repertory of secular song in early 17th-century France centers on the *air de cour* ("courtly air"). Like the madrigal, the *air de cour* was at first polyphonic but eventually evolved into the favored vehicle for solo voice and lute accompaniment. The first published set of this genre appeared in 1571. It includes arrangements of earlier four-part compositions as well as new works in the style of the *voix de ville* (simple strophic verse set to chordal accompaniments). Étienne Moulinié's *Enfin la beauté que j'adore* ("At last, the beauty whom I adore"), published in 1624, resembles many similar *airs de cour* in its fluid, syllabic declamation of text, and its harmonic simplicity and melodic grace, avoiding overt displays of virtuosity. Moulinié (ca. 1600–after 1669) served for many years as director of music to Gaston d'Orleans, Louis XIV's younger brother, and he was one of many French composers of the early 17th century to cultivate the *air de cour,* along with Pierre Guédron (ca. 1570–ca. 1620) and Antoine Boësset (1586–1643).

78 Orfeo, Act II, excerpt (1607)
Monteverdi

CD4 Track 36 — p. 230

Fu sonato questo ritornello di dentro da cinque viole da braccio, un contrabasso, due Clavicembani e tre chitaroni.

Ritornello

(Allegro, ma non troppo)

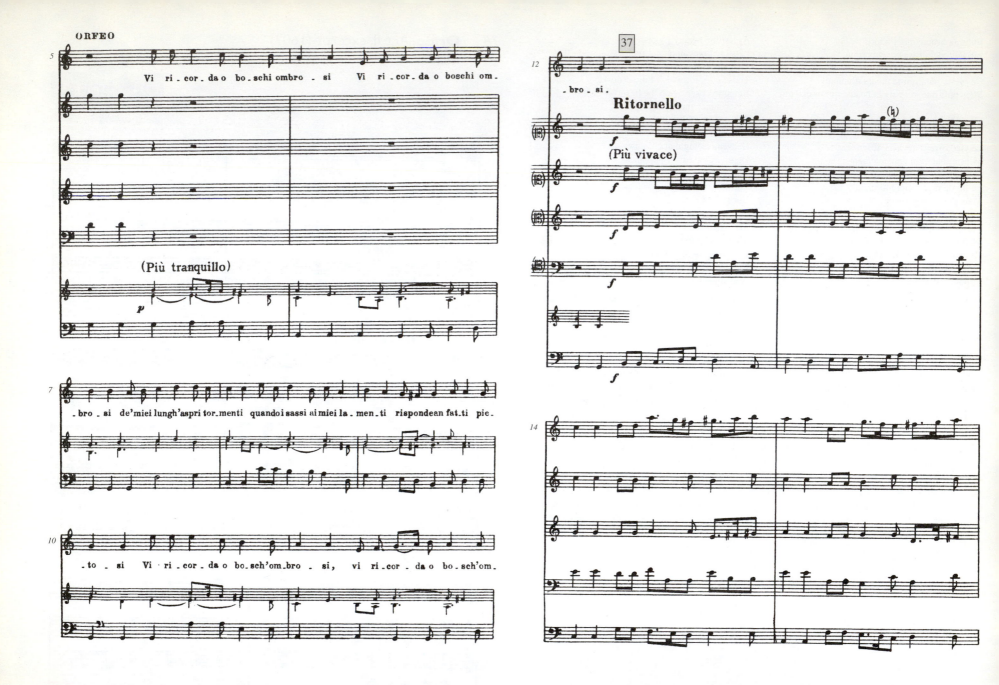

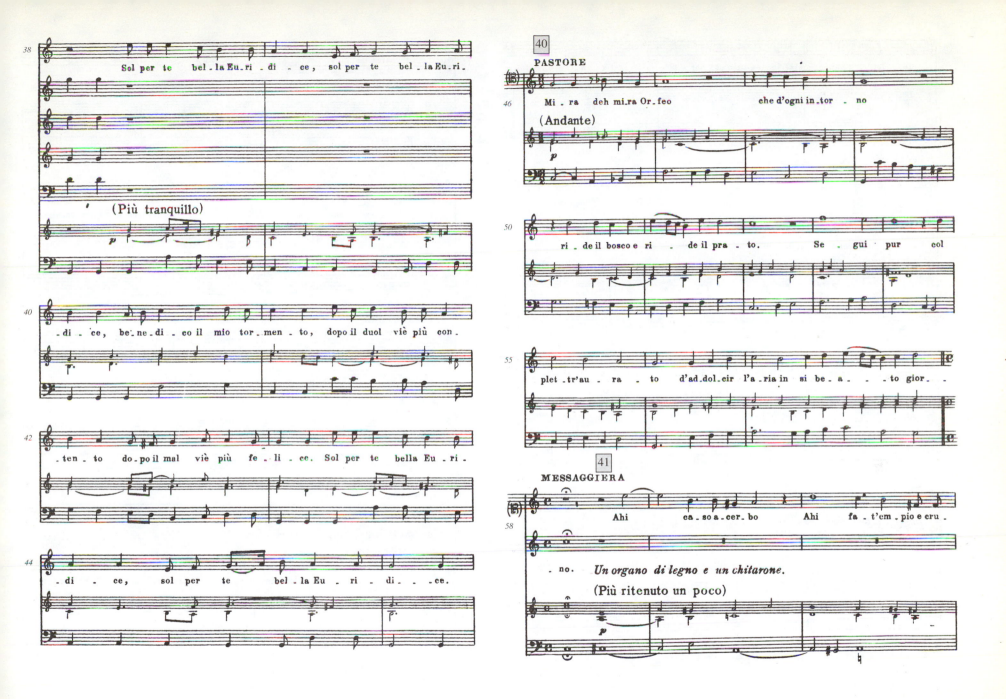

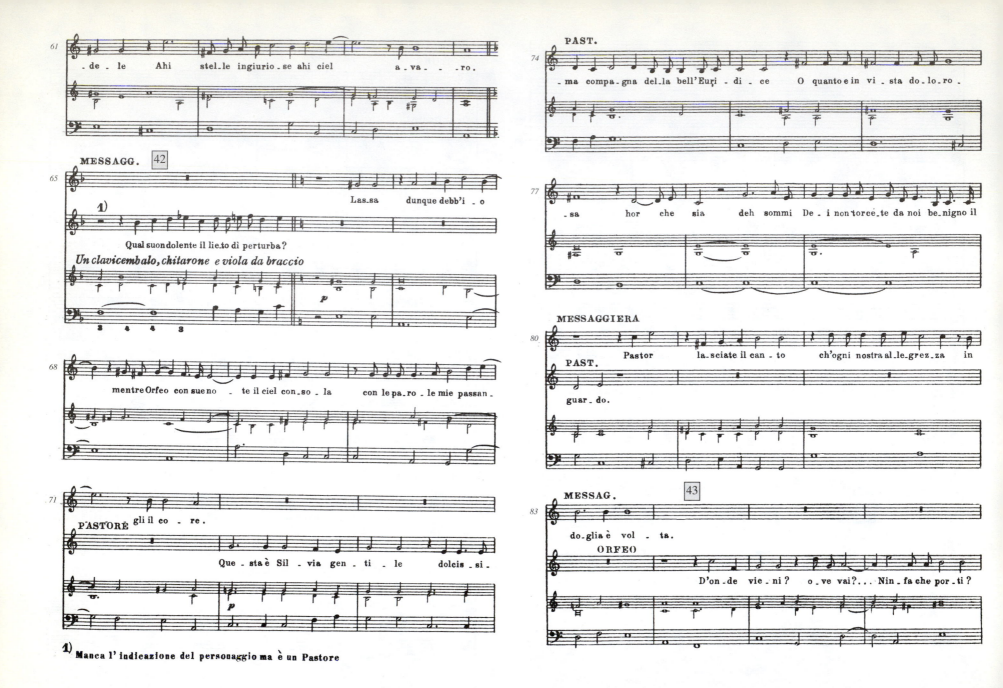

ORPHEUS

Vi ricorda, o boschi ombrosi
de'miei lungh'aspri tormenti,
quando i sassi ai miei lamenti
rispondean fatti pietosi?

Dite, all'hor non vi sembrai
più d'ogn'altro sconsolato?
Or fortuna ha stil cangiato
et ha volto in festa i guai.

Vissi già mesto e dolente,
Or gioisco, e quegli affanni
che sofferti ho per tant'anni
fan più caro il ben presente.

Sol per te bella Euridice,
benedico il mio tormento;
dopo il duol vie più contento
dopo il mal viè più felice.

FIRST SHEPHERD

Mira, deh mira, Orfeo
che d'ogni intorno
ride il bosco e ride il prato.
Segui pur col plettr'aurato
d'addolcir l'aria in si beato giorno.

MESSENGER

Ahi caso acerbo
Ahi fat'empio e crudele.
Ahi stelle ingiuriose,
ahi ciel avaro.

FIRST SHEPHERD

Qual suon dolente il lieto di perturba?

MESSENGER

Lassa! dunque debb'io mentre
Orfeo con sue note il ciel consola,
con le parole mie passangli il core?

THIRD SHEPHERD

Questa è Silvia gentile,
dolcissima compagna della bell'Euridice.
O quanto è in vista dolorosa!
Or che sia? Deh, sommi Dei,
Non torcete da noi benigno il guardo.

ORPHEUS

Woodland groves do ye remember,
all my cruel bitter torments,
when the rocks heard my lamenting
and in pity gave me answer?

Come reply, more broken hearted,
did ye e'er behold a lover?
Now has fortune tuned her lute strings
and has turned to joy my sorrow!

I was full of grief and sorrow,
but rejoice now in my gladness.
By so many years of sighing
is my joy today perfected.

In thy favours, fair Eurydice,
do I bless my bitter torments.
After grief is joy thrice hallow'd,
after evil good thrice blessed.

FIRST SHEPHERD

Marvel, yea marvel, Orpheus,
that all around thee
laughs the forest, laugh the meadows!
Haste thee then with plectrum of gold
to soothe the zephyrs of this blessed morning.

MESSENGER

Ah bitter sorrow!
Ah fate cruel and impious!
Ah stars of ill designing!
ah heav'n voracious!

FIRST SHEPHERD

What cries of mourning disturb this our gladness?

MESSENGER

Ah me! Wherefore must I now
while with song all the heav'n Orpheus rejoiceth
with cruel tidings rend his heart asunder?

THIRD SHEPHERD

This is Sylvia most gentle,
the sweetest of the comrades of the fair Eurydice.
Heavy her eyes with sorrow!
Whate'er her news turn not from us,
O gods in heaven above your kind regarding.

MESSENGER
Pastor, lasciate il canto,
ch'ogni nostra allegrezza in doglia è volta.

ORPHEUS
D'onde vieni? ove vai? . . .
Ninfa che porti?

MESSENGER
A te ne vengo, Orfeo,
messaggera infelice,
di caso più infelice e più funesto:
la tua bella Euridice. . .

ORPHEUS
Ohimè che odo?

MESSENGER
La tua diletta sposa è morta.

ORPHEUS
Ohimè!

MESSENGER
In un fiorito prato
con l'altre sue compagne
giva cogliendo fiori
per farne una ghirlanda a le sue chiome,
quand'angue insidioso,
ch'era fra l'erbe ascoso,
le punse un piè con velenoso dente.
Ed ecco immantinente
scolorirsi il bel viso e nei suoi lumi
sparir que lampi, ond'ella al sol fea scorno.
All'hor noi tutte
sbigottite e meste
le fummo intorno, richiamar tentando

gli spirti in lei smarriti
con l'onda fresca e con possenti carmi,
ma nulla valse, ahi lassa,
ch'ella i languidi lumi alquanto aprendo,
e te chiamando, Orfeo,
Dopo un grave sospiro,
spirò fra queste braccia; ed io rimasi
piena il cor di pietade e di spavento.

MESSENGER
Fair youth, have done with singing,
For today our rejoicing is turned to mourning.

ORPHEUS
Whence dost thou come? Whither go?
Nymph, tell thy tidings!

MESSENGER
To thee, Orpheus, I come,
cruel tidings I bear thee:
a tragedy of horror dark and grievous;
For thy lovely Eurydice. . .

ORPHEUS
Alas, what hear I?

MESSENGER
Thy well beloved bride is dead.

ORPHEUS
Woe's me!

MESSENGER
As through the meads she wandered
with three of her companions
gathering woodland blossoms,
Wherewith to wreath a garland for her tresses,
A treacherous serpent,
which in the grass was lurking,
Within her buried his envenom'd fangs.
And lo!
the wine-red hue of life deserts her fair visage,
and from her eyes banisheth that lustre
which made the sun ashamed,
and we, our horror and dismay withstanding,
around her stood and with cool water bathing
  her forehead,
strove to recall the ebbing spirit,
and loudly heav'n invoked,
but all in vain, ah sorrow!
For then her languid eyes
a little opening she cried upon thee
"Orpheus, my Orpheus!"
With a last deep sigh
within these arms she perish'd,
and I remained of pity and terror
a victim spellbound.

FIRST SHEPHERD
Ahi caso acerbo
ahi fat'empio e crudele.
Ahi stelle ingiuriose,
ahi ciel avaro.

SECOND SHEPHERD
A l'amara novella
rassembral'infelice un muto sasso
che per troppo dolor non può dolersi.

FIRST SHEPHERD
Ahi ben havrebbe
un cor di tigre o d'orsa
chi non sentisse del tuo mal pietate,
privo d'ogni tuo ben, misero amante.

ORPHEUS
Tu se' morta, mia vita, ed io respiro?

Tu se' da me partita

per mai più, non tornare, ed io rimango?
No, che se i versi alçuna cosa ponno,

n'andrò sicuro a più profondi abissi;
e intenerito il cor del Re de l'ombre,
meco trarrotti a riveder le stelle,

O, se ciò negherammi empio destino,
rimarrò teco in compagnia di morte,
Addio terra, cielo
e sole, addio.

CHORUS OF NYMPHS AND SHEPHERDS
Ahi caso acerbo, ahi fat'empio e crudele,
Ahi stelle ingiuriose, ahi cielo avaro.
Non si fidi uom mortale
Di ben caduco e frale,
che tosto fugge, e spesso
a gran salita
il precipizio è presso.

FIRST SHEPHERD
Ah bitter sorrow!
Ah fate cruel and impious!
Ah stars of ill designing!
Ah heav'n voracious!

SECOND SHEPHERD
At these tidings so grievous
he all unhappy stands like a rock in silence.
Grief so bitter as his no tongue can utter.

FIRST SHEPHERD
Ah, he must have a heart of bear or tiger
who would not pity feel for thy affliction,
of ev'ry joy bereft, star crossed lover!

ORPHEUS
Thou art dead, art dead my life,
and I am living?
Thou now from me art sever'd,
sever'd from me now forever.
Thou mayest return never and I shall remain?
No, No!
If there still lies virtue in my singing,
I will go down to the most deep abysses,
I will soften the heart of the king of shadows,
and I will bring thee once more to see the star
  light,
or if destiny impious this denies me,
I will remain there with thee in death abiding.
Farewell earth, farewell sky,
and Sun, farewell.

CHORUS OF NYMPHS AND SHEPHERDS
Ah bitter sorrow! Ah fate cruel and impious!
Ah stars of ill designing! Ah heav'n voracious!
Bring not thy gifts O mortal,
to Fortune's transient portal;
Soon will thy goddes frustrate thee
Wheree'er thou climbest,
Lo! yawning gulfs await thee.

Having established the new style of recitative, composers now faced the challenge of integrating this manner of singing into a work that was both musically and dramatically satisfying. Claudio Monteverdi's *Orfeo* of 1607 is generally acknowledged to be the first opera to have achieved this goal. It was certainly not the first opera (as it is sometimes mistakenly called), but it was the first to gain critical acclaim. Part of its appeal lies in its keen sense of dramatic pacing, as illustrated in this extended excerpt from Act II.

Orfeo takes as its subject the most celebrated musician of ancient myth, Orpheus, whose music was so powerful that it persuaded the gods of the underworld to release Euridyce from the realm of the dead. All of Act I and the first half of Act II of *Orfeo* are very much in the pastoral spirit, depicting an idyllic world of shepherds and shepherdesses, a world without care or sorrow. Orpheus himself gives expression to this untainted state in his "Vi ricorda," a strophic aria written in a manner reminiscent of the frottola, alternating between duple and triple meters within the compound meter of 6/8. The whole is introduced by a ritornello, which reappears before every strophe.

With the entrance of the Messenger bearing news of Euridice's death (*Ahi caso acerbo*), the mood shifts suddenly. The unprepared dissonance on the middle syllable of *acerbo* ("harsh") is particularly grating. Orpheus is stunned, but Monteverdi resists depicting this with a sudden outpouring of grief, opting instead for the utterly simple but all the more moving exclamation on two long notes (*Ohimè*). The messenger's narrative illustrates the declamatory powers of the new monodic style splendidly, climbing to a registral high when it quotes Euridice's dying word: *Orfeo*.

Monteverdi also makes effective use of instrumentation here, contrasting the brightness of the strings in *Vi ricorda,* for example, from the hushed, dark sound of the *organo di legno* (a small organ with wooden pipes), which makes its first appearance with the Messenger at m. 58. The announcement of death has a distinctive sound.

Performance notes: The ensemble in this recording alters each return of the ritornello in some way, adding recorders (which play melodic embellishments) at m. 12, reducing the dynamics to *piano* in m. 23 (the dynamic markings in the score are the editor's interpretation and not in the original), and adding melodic embellishments in the violin parts in m. 34. The intervening solo passages for *Orfeo,* in turn, alter the sound of the basso continuo, substituting a harp for the harpsichord at m. 27.

p. 233

Scena seconda
Ottone e due Soldati, che si risvegliano

Soldati di Nerone si svegliano, e da'patimenti sofferti in quella notte maledicono gl'amori di
Poppea, e di Nerone, e mormorano della corte.

Scene II
Otho and two soldiers

*Nero's soldiers awake; while complaining about the discomforts of the previous night, they curse
the love of Poppaea and Nero, and gossip about the court.*

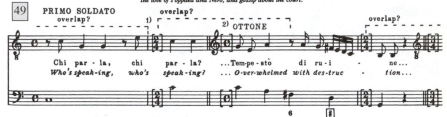

1) The irregular barring at the beginning of this scene would seem to indicate overlapping and interruption for the portrayal of the soldier's waking exclamations.
2) The two interrupted fragments of Ottone's parting speech which Monteverdi(?) overlapped into Scene ii are in *alto* clef in N and V, as is his entire part in Act III in V (see Preface).

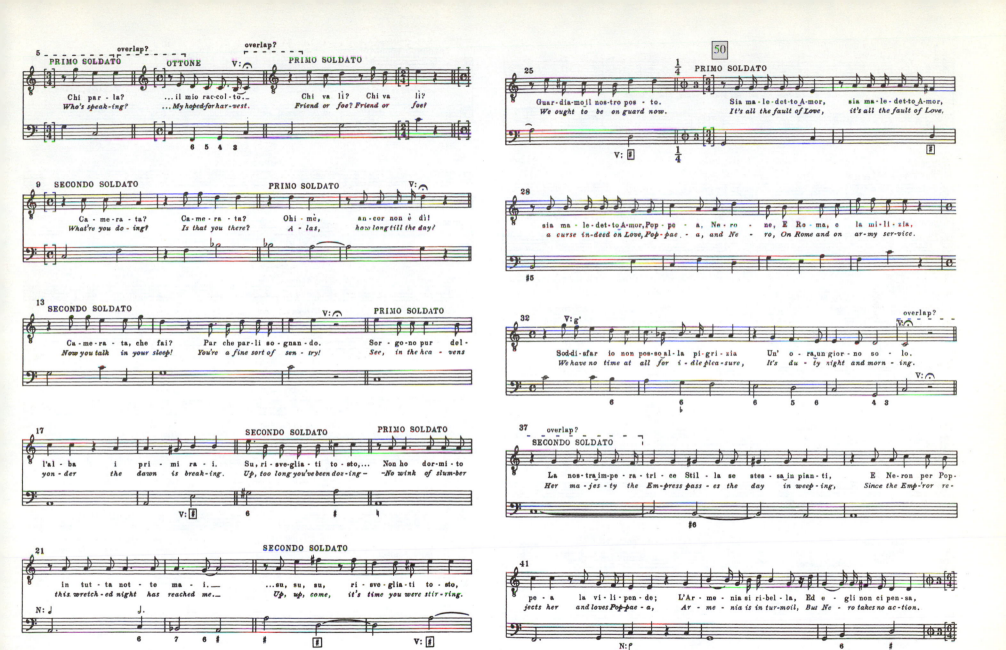

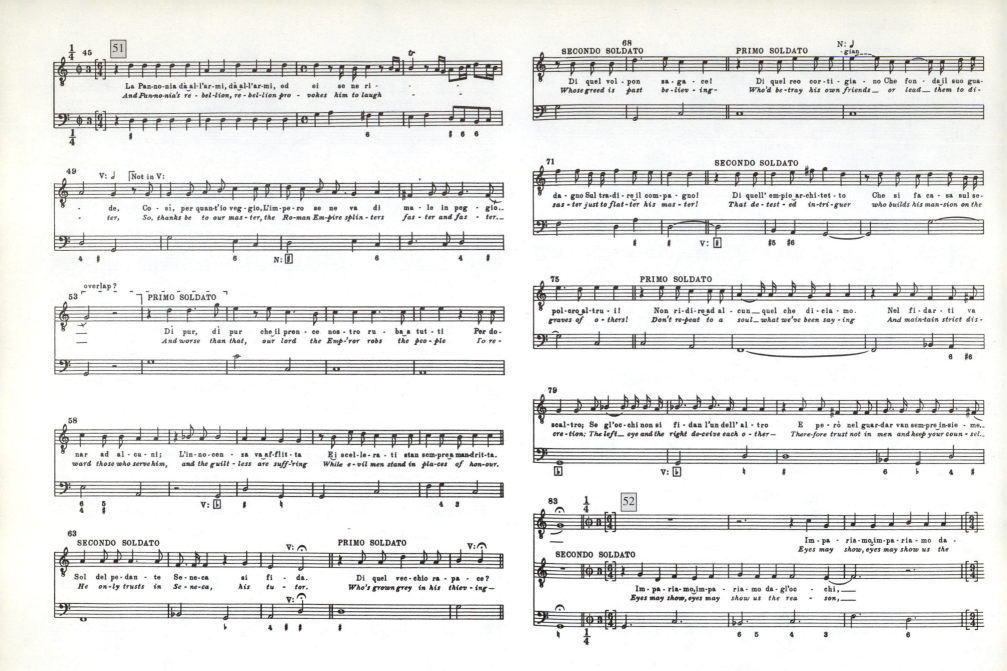

Scena terza

Poppea, Nerone

Poppea, e Nerone escono al far del giorno amorosamente abbracciati, prendendo commiato
l'uno dall'altro con tenerezze affettuose.

Scene III

Poppaea, Nero

Poppaea and Nero enter in the early morning light, fondly embracing, and bid farewell to one
another with tender caresses.

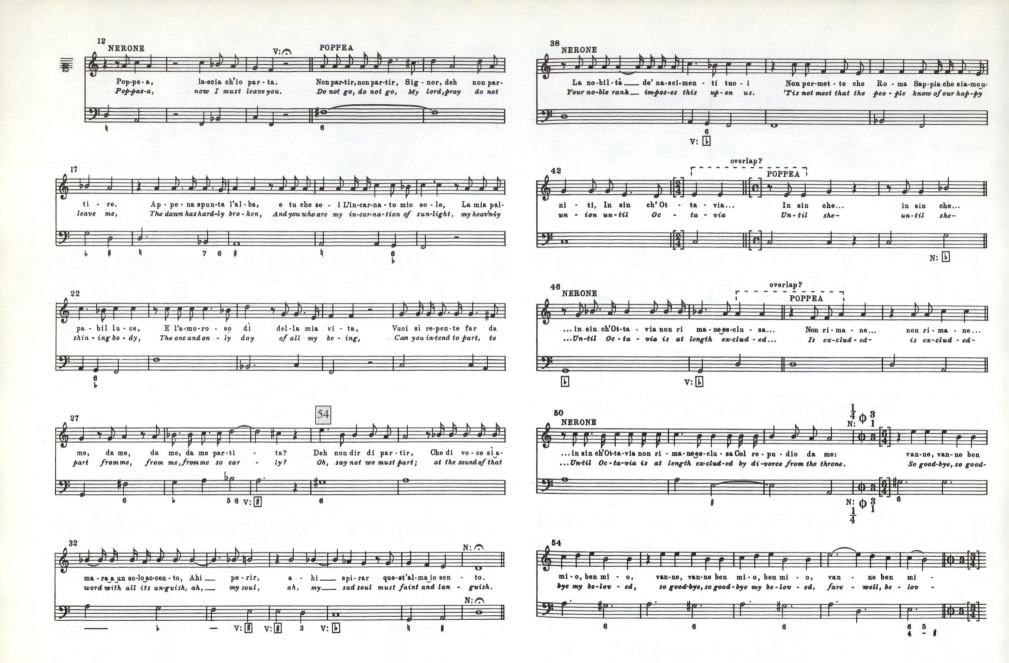

1) N: flat lacking   2) ♭ in both MSS
   V: ♯ (by mistake?)
3) Bass bars 136–149 in tenor clef in both N and V, although V mistakenly continues F clef.
4) c″ instead of d″ in both MSS.

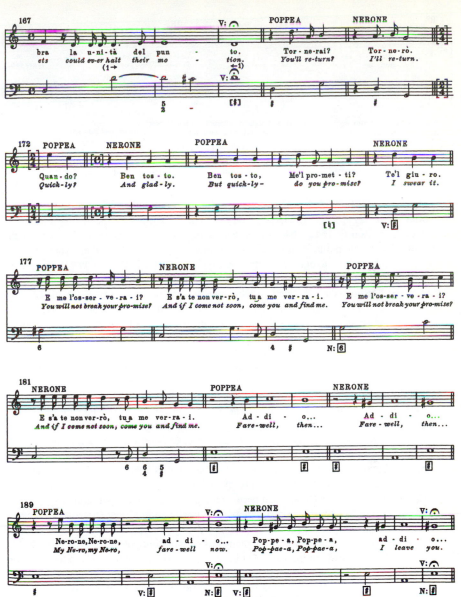

1) When Nerone is sung by a tenor, the d′, c♯′, and d′ must also be transposed down an octave.

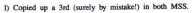

1) Copied up a 3rd (surely by mistake!) in both MSS.

N: Subito ch'há detto à Dio Poppea ben mio si fà il seguente Ritornello et poi segue scena 4ª
As soon as he has said 'Farewell Poppaea, I leave you', the ensuing Ritornello is performed, and then scene 4.

80 Singet dem Herren ein neues Lied, SWV 342 (1647)

Heinrich Schütz (1585–1672)

p. 234

A comparison of Monteverdi's *Orfeo,* written for the court of Mantua in 1607, and his *L'incoronazione di Poppea* ("The Coronation of Poppea"), written for the Teatro Grimano in Venice in the season of 1642–1643, illustrates the differences between courtly opera of the early 17th century and public opera of the mid-17th century. *Orfeo,* for all its stylistic variety, is serious from beginning to end, without an ounce of comic relief. *Poppea,* in contrast, mixes high seriousness with comic scenes. It also requires relatively little in the way of chorus and orchestra and has no scenes that call for elaborate sets or machinery. *Poppea'*s very human characters, drawn from history, contrast vividly with the mythic, allegorical characters in *Orfeo.* Nero, the Emperor of Rome, is married to Ottavia but hopelessly in love with Poppea, who in turn is married to Ottone. Smitten by his love for Poppea, Nero turns to putty in her hands. At Poppea's urging, he banishes her husband to exile, divorces his own wife, and puts to death the philosopher Seneca for the simple reason that his moralizing is inconvenient for her. Poppea is, in short, a close cousin to Lady Macbeth, a very realistic personality whose lust for power leads her to cut down everything in her path.

This is scarcely the kind of scenario one finds in courtly opera, in which the heroes and heroines are unfailingly strong and virtuous. But it is precisely the type of story that would have appealed to a broader, less aristocratic audience. Monteverdi was not writing for the lower classes, to be sure—that portion of the public could not afford tickets to the opera and probably would not have attended in any event—but he was writing for the lesser nobility, businessmen, bankers, and the huge influx of visiting dignitaries that came to Venice for Carnival season every year. Opera soon became a big business in its own right.

As in *Orfeo,* Monteverdi uses a variety of dramatic and musical strategies to create a story that is consistently fast-paced. The prologue to *Poppea* opens with a quarrel between Fortune (Fate) and Virtue, each of whom claims to be the more powerful. Love, a child-like cupid figure, intervenes to remind them that in spite of his small stature, he is in fact far more powerful than either Fate or Virtue, and he shows them the story of Poppea to prove his point.

As the curtain rises on Act I, Ottone arrives home late one night to find Nero's bodyguards at his door. Ottone's opening number flows seamlessly into a comic dialogue between the two guards; at the beginning of Scene 2, in fact, we hear the closing lines of Ottone's despair from Scene 1 as he hides himself in the shadows. This scene flows into an extended dialogue (Scene 3) between Nero and Poppea. The juxtaposition of serious and humorous, lyrical and declamatory is readily apparent in this sequence. The boundary between recitative and aria, which would become more pronounced in the opera of the later 17th and 18th centuries, is still quite fluid here.

■ No. 80 Schütz: *Singet dem Herren ein neues Lied*

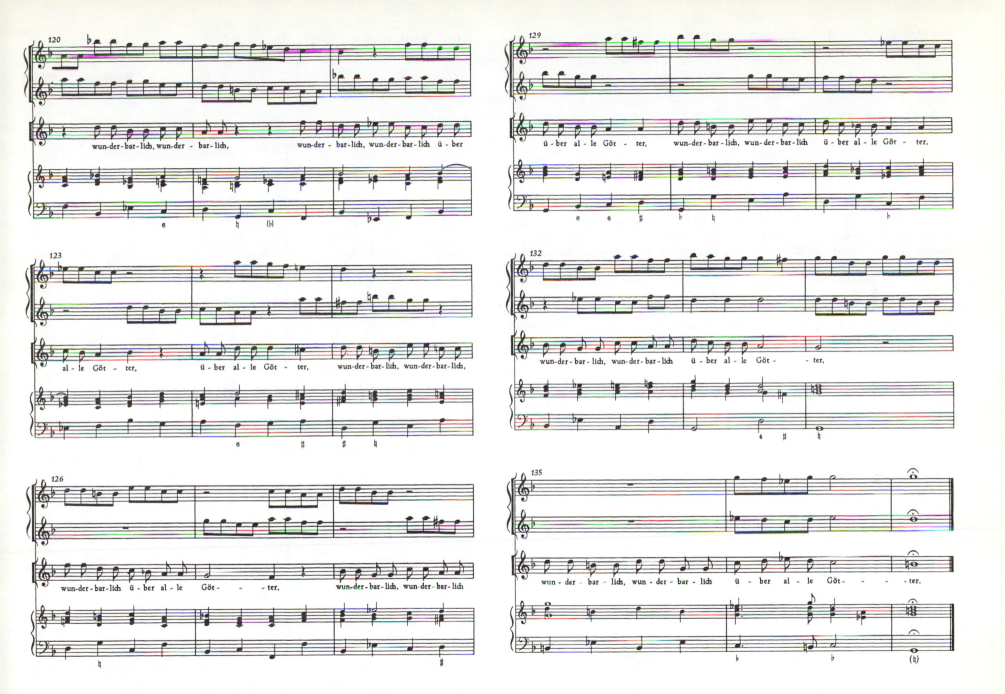

Singet dem Herren ein neues Lied,
singet dem Herren alle Welt.
Singet dem Herrn und lobet seinen Namen.
Prediget einen Tag am andern sein Heil.
Erzählet unter den Heiden seine Ehre,
unter allen Völkern seine Wunder.
Denn der Herr ist groß und hoch zu loben,
wunderbarlich über alle Götter.

O sing unto the Lord a new song:
sing unto the Lord all the earth.
Sing unto the Lord, bless his name;
shew forth his salvation from day to day.
Declare his glory among the heathen,
his wonders among all people.
For the Lord is great, and greatly to be praised:
For he is to be feared above all gods.

Psalm 96: 1–4

Composers applied the principles of the *seconda prattica* to sacred as well as secular music. Heinrich Schütz's *Singet dem Herren ein neues Lied* ("Sing Unto the Lord a New Song") owes much to the "new practice." Schütz may or may not have actually studied with Monteverdi in Venice, but he was certainly aware of the older composer's music.

The two solo violin lines of this work operate at times in counterpoint to the tenor solo, at times as an antiphonal "choir" of their own. Every verse or half-verse of the psalm text (Psalm 96: 1–4) is differentiated by a new musical idea, yet the individual sections are connected through a slow but steady increase in register, rhythmic motion, and melodic intensity. In a series of carefully graduated steps, the listener is moved from stasis to a state of spiritual ecstasy at the end.

Performance notes: The vocal soloist in this recording is a male soprano (sometimes call a "sopranist"), who sings falsetto in the soprano range. The idea behind this kind of performance is to try to recapture at least some semblance of the vocal qualities of the castrato (see Textbook, p. 248), combining the range of the soprano with the physical power of the male voice.

81 Saul, was verfolgst du mich?
SWV 415 (1650)
Schütz

CD5   Track 1

p. 236

© Copyright 1969 by Hänssler-Verlag, Stuttgart-Hohenheim
Alle Rechte vorbehalten / All rights reserved

Herausgeber: Günter Graulich
Generalbaßaussetzung: Paul Horn
English text by Derek McCulloch

198

No. 81 Schütz: *Saul, was verfolgst du mich?* ■ 199

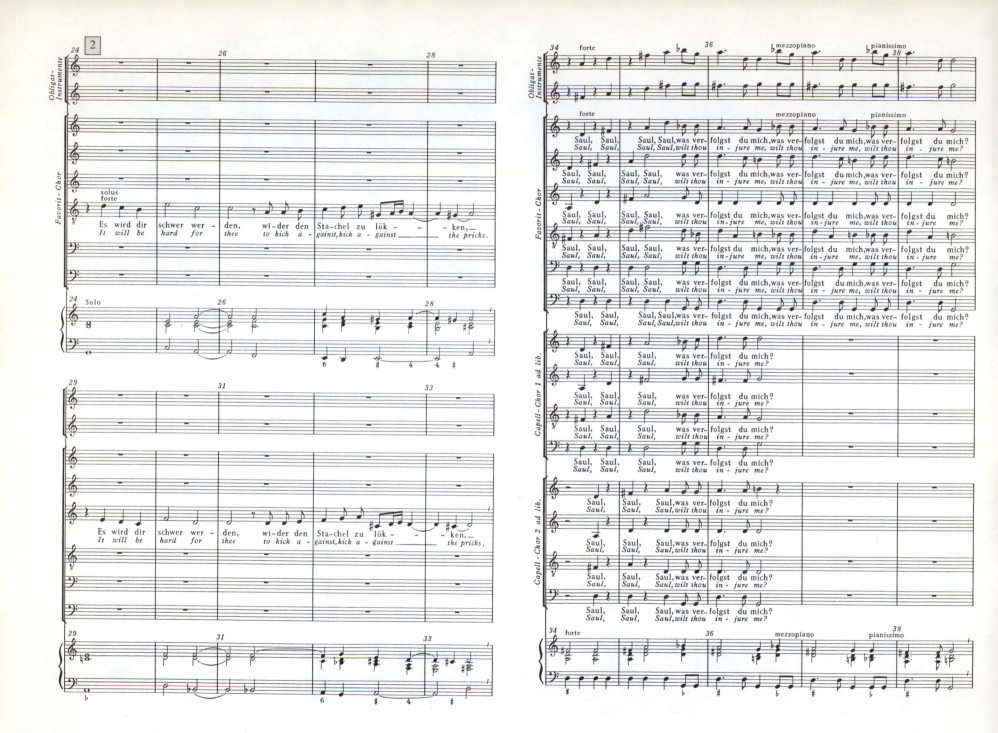

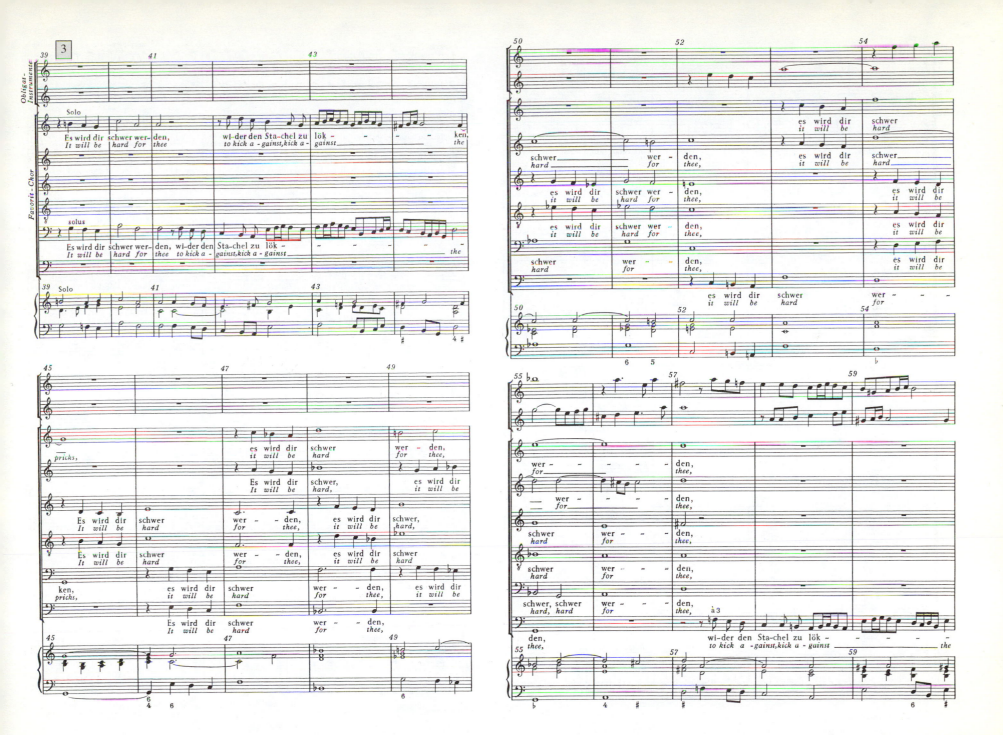

No. 81 Schütz: *Saul, was verfolgst du mich?* ■ **203**

Like Monteverdi, Schütz never abandoned the *prima prattica* entirely. On the contrary, he believed that training in *prima prattica* counterpoint was essential for aspiring composers. Still, even in a polychoral motet like *Saul, was verfolgst du mich?* he incorporates distinct traits of the *seconda prattica*. In a moment of high drama, Saul (later to become the Apostle Paul) is struck blind on the road to Damascus and hears the voice of God calling to him: "Saul, Saul, why dost thou persecute me?" The opening cry rises out of the low depths of the bass, punctuated by the basso continuo, eventually swelling into the combined voices of two four-part choirs, six soloists, and two additional lines for unspecified treble instruments (usually played by violins). The echo of the cry is not just softer but eerily different in timbre (m. 21–23). God's words to Saul continue with a series of lines distributed among the various vocal and instrumental forces. Solo passages alternate with choral and instrumental sections. The words rush ahead at times, hold back at others; certain of them (such as *löcken,* "to kick") are emphasized through the use of melisma, while others ("Saul") make their effect through simpler declamation. The cumulative effect is stunning as it captures the reverberations of God's words in Saul's mind at the very moment in which Saul is struck blind.

Performance notes: Schütz calls in the score for two violins "or their equivalent." In this recording, these parts are performed on the cornetto, a Renaissance forerunner of the trumpet. The continuo consists of organ, theorbo (a large lute with an extended neck), and violone (literally, a "large violin"), a forerunner of today's double bass.

82 Armide, Overture and Act II, Scene 5 (1686)
Jean-Baptiste Lully (1632–1687)

p. 239

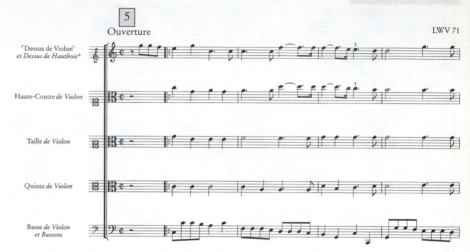

* See Introduction regarding instrumentation.

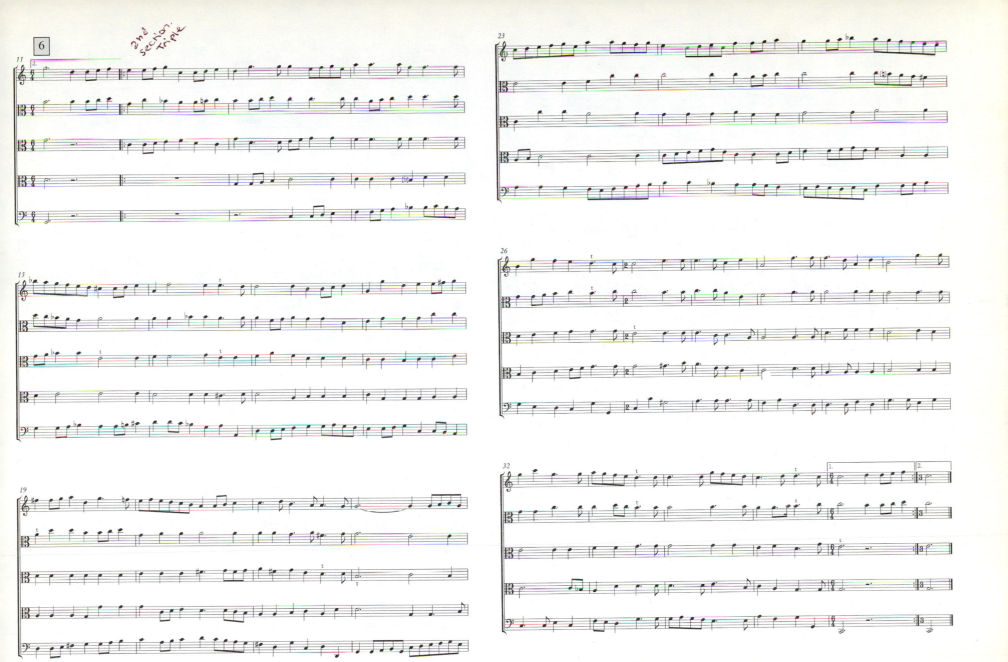

Scène 5

Renaud endormy, Armide

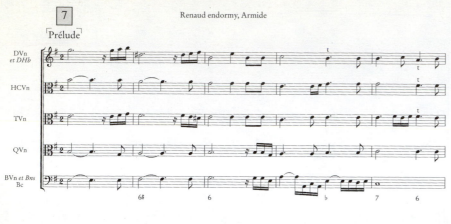

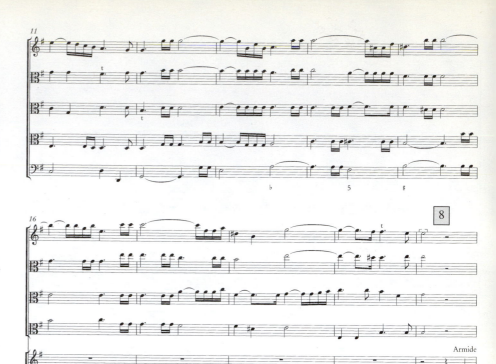

'Armide tenant un dard à la main'

-fin   il est en ma puis-san - ce,   Ce fa-tal En-ne-my,   ce su-per - be Vain-

- queur.   Le char-me du som - meil le li-vre à ma ven-gean - ce;   Je vais per-cer son in - vin-ci - ble

coeur.
Par luy tous mes cap-tifs sont sor-tis d'es-cla - va - ge; Qu'il é-prou - ve tou-te ma

'Armide va pour fraper Renaud, et ne peut executer le dessein qu'elle a de luy oster la vie.'

ra - ge.
Quel trou-ble me sai-sit?
qui me fait he - si - ter? Qu'est-ce qu'en sa fa - veur la pi - tié me veut

di - re? Fra-pons... Ciel! qui peut m'ar-re-ter? A-che-vons... je fre-mis! van-geons-nous... je soû-

- pi - re!
Est-ce ain-si que je doy me van-ger au-jour-d'huy! Ma co-le-re s'é-teint quand j'ap-pro - che de

luy.
Plus je le voy, plus ma ven-gean-ce* est vai - ne; Mon bras trem-blant se re-fu - se à ma hai - ne.
Ah!

- quel-le cru-au - té de luy ra-vir le jour! A ce jeu-ne He-ros tout ce - de sur la Ter - re.
Qui croi-

- roit qu'il fut né seu - le - ment pour la Guer - re?
Il sem - ble es-tre fait pour l'A - mour.
Ne puis - je me van-

- ger à moins qu'il ne pe - ris - se? Hé ne suf-fit-il pas que l'A-mour le pu - nis - se? Puis-qu'il n'a pû trou-

- ver mes yeux as-sez char-mant, Qu'il m'ai-me au moins par mes en-chan-te-ments, Que, s'il se peut, je le ha-

Prélude

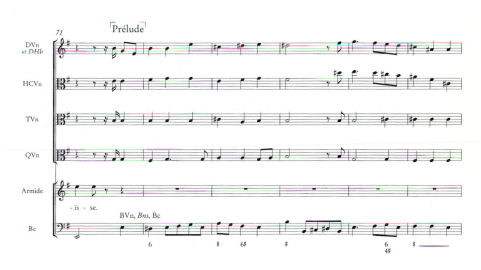

DVn
et DHb

HCVn

TVn

QVn

Armide
- ïs - se.

Bc
BVn, Bns, Bc

'Les Demons transformez en Zephirs, enlevent Renaud et Armide.'

ARMIDE

(tenant un dard à la main)

Enfin il est en ma puissance,
Ce fatal ennemi, ce superbe vainqueur.
Le charme du sommeil le livre à ma vengeance;

Je vais percer son invincible coeur.
Par lui tous mes captifs sont sortis d'esclavage;

Qu'il éprouve toute ma rage.
Quel trouble me saisit? qui me fait hésiter?
(Armide va pour frapper Renaud
et ne peut executer le dessein
qu'elle a de luy oster la vie)
Qu'est-ce qu'en sa faveur la pitié me veut dire?
Frappons . . . Ciel! qui peut m'arrêter?
Achevons . . . je frémis! vengeons-nous . . . je
    soupire!
Est-ce ainsi que je dois me venger aujourd'hui?
Ma colère s'éteint quand j'approche de lui.
Plus je le voi, plus ma vengeance est vaine;

Mon bras tremblant se refuse à ma haine.
Ah! quelle cruauté de lui ravir le jour!
A ce jeune héros tout cède sur la terre.

Qui croirait qu'il fut né seulement pour la
    guerre?
Il semble être fait pour l'Amour.
Ne puis-je me venger à moins qu'il ne périsse?
Hé! ne suffit-il pas que l'amour le punisse?

Puisqu'il n'a pu trouver mes yeux assez
    charmants,
Qu'il m'aime au moins par mes enchantements.
Que, s'il se peut, je le haïsse.

ARMIDE

(holding a spear in her hand)

Finally he is in my power,
this fatal enemy, this superb warrior.
The charm of sleep delivers him to my
    vengeance;
I will pierce his invincible heart.
Through him all my captives have escaped from
    slavery.
Let him feel all my anger.
What fear grips me? what makes me hesitate?
(Armide moves to strike Rinaldo
but cannot carry out her plan
to take his life)
What in his favor does pity want to tell me?
Let us strike . . . Heavens! Who can stop me?
Let us get on with it . . . I tremble! Let us
    avenge . . . I sigh!
Is it thus that I must avenge myself today?
My rage is extinguished when I approach him.
The more I see of him, the more my vengeance
    is ineffectual.
My trembling arm denies my hate.
Ah! What cruelty, to rob him of the light of day!
To this young hero everything on earth
    surrenders.
Who would believe that he was born only for
    war?
He seems to be made for love.
Could I not avenge myself unless he dies?
Oh, is it not enough that Love should punish
    him?
Since he could not find my eyes charming
    enough,
let him love me at least through my sorcery,
so that, if it's possible, I may hate him.

Venez, venez, seconder mes désirs,	Come, come support my desires,
Démons, transformez-vous en d'aimables zéphirs.	demons; transform yourselves into friendly zephyrs.
Je cède à ce vainqueur, la pitié me surmonte.	I give in to this conqueror; pity overwhelms me.
Cachez ma foiblesse et ma honte	Conceal my weakness and my shame
Dans les plus reculés déserts.	in the most remote desert.
Volez, volez, conduisez-nous au bout de l'univers.	Fly, fly, lead us to the end of the universe.
(Les demons transformez en Zephirs, enlevent Renaud et Armide)	(The demons are transformed in zephyrs, lifting up Rinaldo and Armida)

—Philippe Quinault

Lully and his librettist Philippe Quinault (1635–1688) drew on classical mythology and chivalric romances for subject matter for their operas, but the plots were widely understood as veiled commentaries (always favorable, of course) on recent events at court. The hero of any given opera was almost invariably understood to be an allegorical counterpart to Louis XIV. In *Armide,* the hero Renaud obeys the call of duty and spurns the enchantment of the sorceress for whom the opera is named.

The overture to *Armide* moves from a slow introduction with dotted rhythms to a fast imitative section. The dotted rhythms, associated with royalty, were an homage to the splendor of the king. This form eventually came to be known as the French overture and would be adopted by many composers—Italian and German as well as French—over subsequent decades.

In the widely admired scene toward the end of Act II of *Armide,* the sorceress Armida is about to kill the crusader-knight Renaud (Rinaldo), who is asleep under her spell. But she cannot bring herself to do the deed: she hates Renaud because he is indifferent to her beauty, yet she also loves him. The opera, based on Torquato Tasso's epic poem *Gerusalemme liberata* ("Jerusalem Liberated"), will end badly for Armida—Orlando's love for her, induced through spells, does not last—but for the moment, she is in complete command of everything but herself. The scene divides into two sections: (1) Armida's monologue and (2) a summons to her assisting demons. The opening monologue moves fluidly through a large quantity of text. The declamation here is more melodic than most Italian recitative. The opening thematic idea will in fact provide the basis for the more dance-like second part of this scene.

Performance notes: The notated rhythms are not observed strictly. This is in keeping with all that we know about performance practice in France during the Baroque era. Dotted values are exaggerated, with the longer notes made longer and the shorter ones shorter: dotted eighth notes followed by a sixteenth, for example, are performed like double-dotted eighths followed by a thirty-second note, as at the very beginning of the overture. This practice is known as *overdotting.* And runs notated in rhythms of equal value are not always performed in uniform rhythm; instead, some are lengthened while others are shortened to compensate. The eighth notes in the bass line throughout the overture's slow introduction, for example, are played in unequal time values. This practice, known by its French designation of *notes inégales* ("unequal notes"), is left to the discretion of the orchestra's leader. The sound of wind at the beginning of Act II, Scene 5, comes from a machine built specially for this purpose. Opera producers took great pride in special effects of all kind, including sound effects.

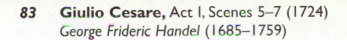

83   Giulio Cesare, Act I, Scenes 5–7 (1724)
George Frideric Handel (1685–1759)

CD5   Track 11
p. 244

Alma del gran Pompeo, che al cener suo d'in-tor-no in-vi-si-bil t'ag-gi-ri.

fur om-bra i tuoi tro-fe-i, ombra la tua gran-dez-za, e un'om-bra sei. Co-si ter-mi-na al

fi-ne il fa-sto u-ma-no. Je-ri chi vi-vo oc-cu-pò un mon-do in guerra, oggi ri-sol-to in polve un'ur-na

ser-ra. Tal di cia-scu-no (ahi lasso!) il prin-ci-pio è di terra, e il fi-ne è un sasso. Mi-se-ra

vi-ta! oh quan-to è fra il tuo sta-to! ti for-ma un soffio, e ti di-strugge un fia-to.

SCENA V	SCENE 5
CLEOPATRA	CLEOPATRA
Regni Cleopatra; ed al mio seggio intorno	Let Cleopatra reign, and around my throne
popolo adorator arabo e siro	Let the adoring peoples of Arabia and Syria
su questo crin la sacra benda adori:	Prostrate themselves before the sacred band that engirds my tresses.
sù, chi di voi, miei fidi,	Come, let those of you
ha petto e cor di sollevarmi al trono,	Who have the mind and heart to raise me upon the throne
giuri su questa destra eterna fede.	Swear eternal loyalty on my right hand.
NIRENO	NIRENUS
Reina, infausti eventi!	O Queen, ill-starred events!
CLEOPATRA	CLEOPATRA
Che fia? ché tardi?	What has happened? Why do you delay?
NIRENO	NIRENUS
Troncar fé Tolomeo	Ptolemy has
il capo . . .	beheaded . . .
CLEOPATRA	CLEOPATRA
Ohimè, di chi?	O heavens! Whom?
NIRENO	NIRENUS
Del gran Pompeo.	The great Pompey.
CLEOPATRA	CLEOPATRA
Stelle! Costui che apporta?	Gods in heaven! What news does this man bring?
NIRENO	NIRENUS
Per stabilirsi al soglio	To ascertain his throne he sent it,
a Cesare mandò fra doni involto . . .	Among other gifts, wrapped in a veil, to Caesar . . .
CLEOPATRA	CLEOPATRA
Che gli mandò?	What did he send?
NIRENO	NIRENUS
L'esanimato volto.	The lifeless head.
CLEOPATRA	CLEOPATRA
Sù, partite miei fidi; e tu qui resta.	Go, withdraw, my loyal subjects. You remain here.
Alle cesaree tende	I have resolved to betake
son risolta portarmi,	Myself to Caesar's camp,
e tu, Nireno, mi servirai di scorta.	And you, Nirenus, shall serve as my escort.
NIRENO	NIRENUS
Che dirà Tolomeo?	What will Ptolemy say?

CLEOPATRA
Non paventar: col guardo,
meglio ch'egli non fece
col capo di Pompeo,
Cesare obligherò.
Invano aspira al trono:
egli è il germano, e la regina io sono.

TOLOMEO
Tu di regnar pretendi,
donna superba e altera?

CLEOPATRA
Io ciò ch'è mio contendo; e la corona
dovuta alla mia fronte
giustamente pretendo.

TOLOMEO
Vanne, e torna omai, folle,
a qual di donna è l'uso:
di scettro invece, a trattar l'ago e il fuso.

CLEOPATRA
Anzi, tu pur, effeminato amante,
va' dell'età sui primi nati albori,
di regno invece, a coltivar gli amori!

    Non disperar, chi sa?
se al regno non l'avrai,
avrai sorte in amor.
    Mirando una beltà
in essa troverai
a consolar un cor.

SCENA VI

ACHILLA
Sire, signor!

TOLOMEO
    Achilla!
Come fu il capo tronco
da Cesare gradito?

ACHILLA
Sdegnò l'opra.

TOLOMEO
    Che sento?

CLEOPATRA
Have no fear. With a single look alone
I shall be able to compel Caesar
Better than he did
With the head of Pompey.
In vain he aspires to the throne:
He is my brother, and I am the queen.

PTOLOMY (enters)
You pretend to the throne,
Proud and presumptuous woman?

CLEOPATRA
I contest what is mine, and rightfully
Claim the crown
That belongs to my brow.

PTOLOMY
Get you gone and return, you madwoman,
To your proper place as a woman:
Wield the needle and the distaff instead of the
    sceptre.

CLEOPATRA
It is rather you, effeminate lover,
You, who are still in the dawn of your life,
To go and cultivate your loves instead of the
    kingdom!
    Do not despair: who knows,
But that you will have the luck in reigning
That you have in love.
    Gazing on your beauty
You find in it the way
To beguile a heart.
                    (Exits)

SCENE 6

ACHILLA
Sire! Lord!

PTOLOMY
    Achilla!
How did the severed head
Of Pompey please Caesar?

ACHILLA
He despised the deed.

PTOLOMY
    What do I hear?

ACHILLA
T'accusò d'inesperto e troppo ardito.

TOLOMEO
Tant' osa un vil romano?

ACHILLA
    Il mio consiglio
apprendi, o Tolomeo:
verrà Cesare in corte; in tua vendetta
cada costui, come cadé Pompeo.

TOLOMEO
Chi condurrà l'impresa?

ACHILLA
    Io ti prometto
darti estinto il superbo al regio piede,
se di Pompeo la moglie
in premio a me il tuo voler concede.

TOLOMEO
È costei tanto vaga?

ACHILLA
Lega col crine, e col bel volto impiaga.

TOLOMEO
Amico, il tuo consiglio è la mia stella.
Vanne, pensa e poi torna.

Muora Cesare, muora; e il capo altero

sia del mio piè sostegno.
Roma, oppressa da lui, libera vada,
e fermezza al mio regno
sia la morte di lui più che la spada.
    L'empio, sleale, indegno
vorria rapirmi il regno,
e disturbar così
la pace mia.
    Ma perda pur la vita,
prima che in me tradita
dall'avido suo cor
la fede sia.

ACHILLA
He accused you of misconduct and impudence.

PTOLOMY
A vile Roman has the effrontery?

ACHILLA
    Listen
To my advice, Ptolomy!
Caesar is coming to the court; let him fall victim
To your revenge as Pompey fell.

PTOLOMY
Who will undertake the business?

ACHILLA
    I promise
To lay the haughty corpse at your royal feet,
If in recompense you are willing
To grant me Pompey's wife.

PTOLOMY
Is she so desirable?

ACHILLA
She captivates one with her tresses and pierces
    one's heart with her fair face.

PTOLOMY
Friend, your counsel will be my guiding star:
Go, reflect and return.

Let Caesar die! Let him die! And his proud
    head
Sustain my footing. Let Rome,
Whom he oppresses, regain her freedom,
And his death, more than my sword,
Ascertain my rule.
    The infidel, traitor, villain
    Would rob me of my throne
    And thereby trouble
    My peace of mind.
    But rather let him lose his life
    Before my confidence
    Be betrayed
    By his avaricious heart!

SCENA VII

CESARE

Alma del gran Pompeo,
che al cener suo d'intorno
invisibil t'aggiri,
fur ombra i tuoi trofei,
ombra la tua grandezza, e un'ombra sei.

Così termina alfine il fasto umano.
Ieri chi vivo occupò un mondo in guerra,
oggi risolto in polve un'urna serra.

Tal di ciascuno, ahi lasso,
il principio è di terra e il fine è un sasso.
Misera vita, oh quanto è fral tuo stato!
Ti forma un soffio, e ti distrugge un fiato.

SCENE 7

CAESAR

Soul of great Pompey
That hovers invisible
About your ashes,
Your victories were but a shadow,
A shadow was your greatness, and you yourself
  are but a shadow.
To this end comes man's glory.
Yesterday he, who alive, engaged a world in war,
Is today dissolved into ash and is enclosed in an
  urn.
Such, alas, is the fate of everyone,
The beginning is earth, the end a stone.
Wretched life! O, how frail is your condition!
A sigh forms you, a breath destroys you.

Ptolomy (Tolomeo), co-ruler of Egypt with his sister, Cleopatra, is threatened by the arrival of the conquering Julius Ceaesar (Giulio Cesare). To appease Caesar, Ptolomy presents him with the severed head of Caesar's Roman rival, Pompey. But Caesar is disgusted by such barbarism and rejects the gift. In the *recitativo semplice*—"simple recitative," accompanied only by the basso continuo—that opens Act I, Scene 5, Cleopatra learns of these events from Nirenus (Nireno); her brother Ptolomy then enters the scene (m. 40), and they exchange rapid-fire barbs.

One of the structural conventions of opera seria is an underlying alternation of recitative and aria. Cleopatra's aria (*Non disperar*) sets itself off from the preceding recitative not only through its melody and orchestration, but also through its text: arias are typically written as poetic verse, not prose. Like so many arias in opera seria, this is a da capo aria, with the opening A section repeated (and embellished) after the conclusion of the contrasting B section.

Ptolomy, having discussed (in recitative) his plans with his aide Achilla, launches into his own da capo aria in Scene 6 (*L'empio, sleale, indegno*). This aria begins with an orchestral ritornello (Ritornello 1) that at once establishes the key, mood, and theme of the aria as a whole. The opening solo (Solo 1) reiterates the orchestral material in the same key, but now with words. The voice eventually carries the music from E♭ major to B♭ major (m. 32), and the new key signals the onset of Ritornello 2. This brief return of the instruments alone offers the singer the opportunity to catch his breath. The soloist reenters in m. 36 and guides the music through a variety of keys before finally bringing it to the dominant at m. 58. This half-cadence is a signal to orchestra and audience alike that the cadenza is about to begin. From the Italian word for "cadence," the cadenza is a truly soloistic moment, with no accompaniment of the orchestra at all; the soloist instead improvises (or at least gives the appearance of improvising), invariably with great virtuosity. Cadenzas are typically indicated in the score of an aria by a simple fermata sign, and the cadenza in the da capo performance of the A section was expected to be even more flamboyant than in the first. After this display of unaccompanied virtuosity, the second solo section concludes on the tonic (m. 61). At this point the third and final ritornello enters to bring this section of the aria—and on its return *da capo,* the entire aria—to closure in the tonic.

Handel, *Giulio Cesare*, Act I, *L'empio, sleale, indegno*; the A section.

	Rit. 1	Solo 1	Rit. 2	Solo 2	Cadenza	Rit. 3
Measure	1	12	32	36	58	61
Key	E♭ major	E♭ major	B♭ major	Unstable	V/E♭ major	E♭ major
Harmony	I		V		V/I	I

The ritornello principle is reinforced by the tonal structure: the A section begins and ends in the tonic, with a contrasting key in between. The B section, in C minor, beginning at the words *Mà perda pur la vita* is even briefer and consists of a single solo unit; there is no ritornello within this section. When considered within the context of the aria as a whole, however, this B section is framed by two ritornello passages: Ritornello 3 from the end of A, and Ritornello 1 from the da capo resumption of the aria's beginning. In a sense, then, the B section as a whole can be seen as a large Solo 3.

Handel, *Giulio Cesare*, Act I, *L'empio, sleale, indegno*: the structure of the whole in performance.

A					B	A (da capo)					
Rit. 1	Solo 1	Rit. 2	Solo 2	Rit. 3	Solo 3	Rit. 4	Solo 4	Rit. 5	Solo 5	Rit. 6	
I		V		I	vi	I		V		I	

The next scene is one of quiet contemplation. Julius Caesar is at the tomb of the murdered Pompey and reflects on the brevity of human life. Here, Handel uses *recitativo accompagnato,* that is, accompanied recitative, supported or punctuated by the full orchestra rather than the basso continuo alone. This type of recitative was used sparingly in opera seria and ususally reserved for moments of high emotion and drama.

Performance notes: In keeping with performance practices of Handel's time, both soloists in this recording embroider the A section of their respective arias with considerable embellishments. The soprano Barbara Schlick (Cleopatra) uses rapid figuration to display the agility of her voice and transposes the whole note B in m. 20 up an entire octave to display her impressive range. She goes on to interpolate a miniature cadenza at m. 35, slowing down the tempo for dramatic effect. The countertenor Derek Lee Ragin (Ptolomy) adds similar embellishments to the written score, even during the intitial performance of the aria's A section. The high outbursts show his voice to good advantange and are at the same time in keeping with the mood of outrage expressed by his character.

No. 83 Handel: *Giulio Cesare* ■ 215

Dido and Aeneas, Act I (excerpt) (1689)
Henry Purcell (1659–1695)

CD5   Track 23

p. 254

ACT I.

Scene.   *The Palace. Enter Dido, Belinda, and train.*

23 № **1.** SCENA and CHORUS.

Note: The harpsichord part here is the editor's realization of the basso continuo part.

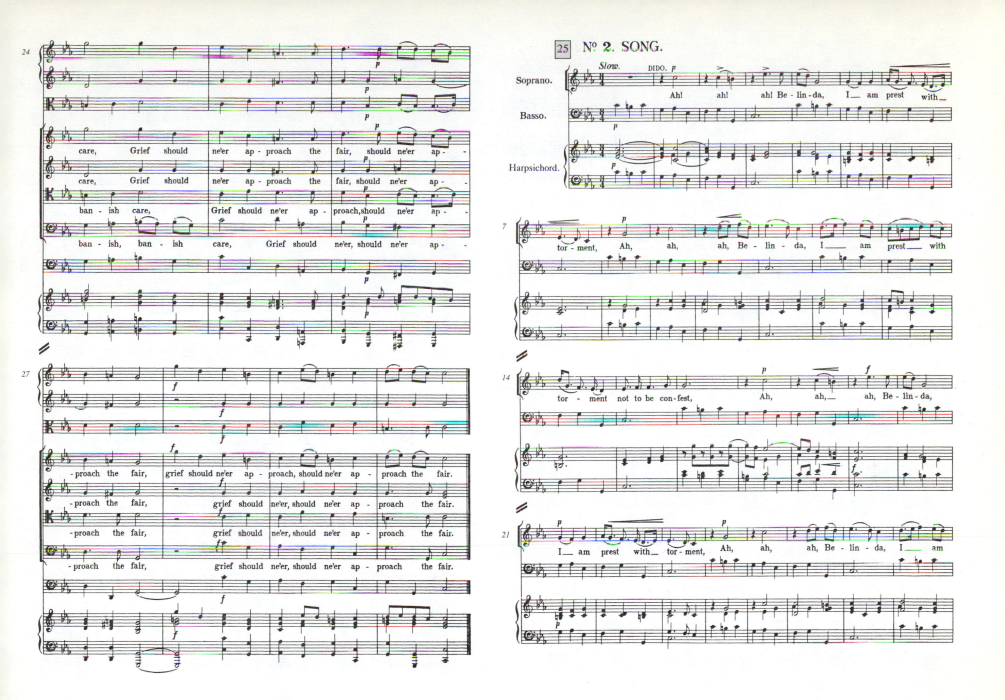

No. 2. SONG.

■ No. 84 Purcell: *Dido and Aeneas*

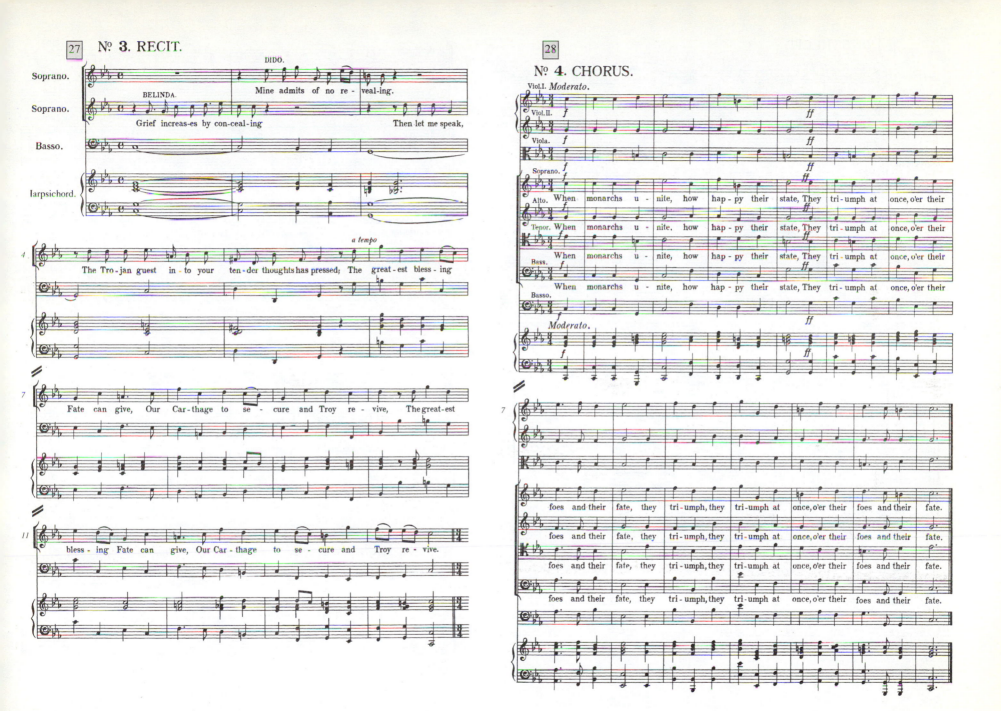

The origins and early performance history of Purcell's opera *Dido and Aeneas* remain shrouded in mystery. We know it was first performed by the students at a school for young ladies in Chelsea (west of London at the time), but the next known performance, in a drastically altered version, did not occur until 1700, and the earliest surviving musical sources date from well after the composer's death. *Dido and Aeneas* may have been suppressed for political reasons, either by Purcell himself or by the authorities, on the grounds of its potentially unflattering commentary on the dual reign of King William, a foreigner, and Queen Mary, daughter of Charles I. The plot, after all, deals with a foreign prince who promises to marry the Queen of Carthage, then reneges and abandons her, driving her to suicide.

The foreign prince is Aeneas, a refugee from fallen Troy, who is on his way to Italy with his companions to found the city of Rome in fulfillment of a promise from the gods. They land in Carthage, ruled by Queen Dido. Aeneas and Dido are smitten with one another. She, with great foreboding, knowing his destiny, lets herself be wooed. He pledges to abandon his promised Rome. But when a witch disguised as Mercury, the messenger of the gods, orders him to leave, he obeys and abandons Dido. She, disconsolate, dies, but not before singing an exquisite lament.

Purcell's opera owes much to the French tradition, beginning with the overture, a slow introduction followed by an imitative fast section. The singing moves rapidly and fluently, with a minimum of virtuosity and no *da capo* arias. Act I opens with a rapid sequence of brief numbers. Belinda, Dido's confidante, urges her mistress to shake off her grief, and the chorus echoes her thoughts in a kind of communal commentary. Dido makes her entrance with a lament over a ground bass, prefiguring her celebrated (but dramatically more static) lament at the very end of the opera. This brief number gives way to an exchange in simple recitative, in which Belinda forces Dido to confront her love of Aeneas. This exchange segues into a song extolling the virtues of a union between Carthage and Troy ("The greatest blessing…") which moves to a chorus ("When monarchs unite"). The recitative dialogue between Dido and Belinda resumes, leading in turn to a duet ("Fear no danger to ensue") and chorus.

Performance notes: This recording uses a variety of different instrumental combinations for the basso continuo: combinations of harpsichord, theorbo (a long-necked lute), bass violin (slightly larger than the modern-day cello), and, in the Duet and Chorus No. 6 ("Fear no danger to ensue"), guitars, a very popular instrument in Purcell's time. Thus, whereas the modern-day edition indicates simply "harpsichord," an imaginative performance like this one can invest the work with far more timbral variety.

85 The Beggar's Opera (excerpts) (1728)

John Gay (1685–1732) and *Johann Christoph Pepusch* (1667–1752)

Air 8. Grim King of the ghosts

POLLY Can Love be con-troul'd by ad-vice? Will Cu-pid our Mo-thers o-bey? Though my heart were as fro-zen as Ice, At his flame 'twould have melt-ed a-way. When he kist me so close-ly he prest, 'Twas so sweet that I must have com-ply'd: So I thought it both saf-est and best To mar-ry, for fear you should chide.

CUE: MACHEATH You see, Gentlemen, I am not a meer Court Friend, who professes every thing and will do nothing.

Air 44. Lillibulero

MACHEATH The modes of the Court so com-mon are grown, That a true friend can hard-ly be met; Friend-ship for in-terest is but a loan, Which they let out for what they can get. 'Tis true, you find Some friends so kind, Who'll give you good coun-sel them-selves to de-fend. In sor-row-ful dit-ty, They pro-mise, they pi-ty, But shift you for mo-ney, from friend to friend.

Air 51. Come, sweet lass

In 1728, the playwright John Gay achieved a rousing success with *The Beggar's Opera,* an English-language semi-opera that portrayed common criminals rather than mythological figures or historical heroes. Gay set his words to existing tunes and engaged the German-born Johann Christoph Pepusch (1667–1752) to provide the accompaniments. The arrangements are quite simple, and the dialogue is spoken rather than sung. As the Beggar explains at the outset: "I hope I may be forgiven, that I have not made my Opera throughout unnatural, like those in vogue; for I have no Recitative."

The original libretto of this ballad opera features 69 songs, of which 28 have been identified as English ballads, while another 23 derive from popular songs of Irish, Scottish, or French origin. *The Beggar's Opera* is full of political references that delighted contemporary audiences. Whereas the French overture was always understood to be in honor of the King, the overture to *The Beggar's Opera* quotes the song *Walpole, or the Happy Clown,* a ditty attacking Robert Walpole, prime minister of Great Britain at the time. *The Beggar's Opera* was an enormous commercial success and was soon being performed as far away as Charleston, South Carolina, and Williamsburg, Virginia; it is said to have been George Washington's favorite opera. It continued to be performed in one version or another at least once a year for the rest of the 18th century. The work took on new life in a German adaptation by Bertholt Brecht in 1928 entitled *Die Dreigroschenoper*—"The Three-Penny Opera"—with music by Kurt Weill.

86 Jephte (excerpt) (ca. 1645–1649)
Giacomo Carissimi (1605–1674)

Revised and edited by
Janet Beat

CD5 Track 35
p. 258

1) Bar 23, Soprano III. ♩. ♪ in A
2) Bar 27, Bass. ♩. ♪ in A

3) Bar 35, Continuo in A reads [notation] but Charpentier has written beneath it the version here given with the legend 'Caris.' (? Carissimi).

4) Bar 37, Continuo in A reads [notation] but again Charpentier has written beneath it the version here given with the same legend.

8) Bar 62, Soprano III. ♪♪ in A

* Bars 70-71. There is much to be said for taking this organ bass an octave higher.

HISTORICUS
Cum vocasset in proelium filios Israel rex filiorum Ammon, et verbis Jephte acquiescere noluisset, factus est super Jephte Spiritus Domini, et progressus ad filios Ammon votum vovit Domini dicens:

When the king of the children of Ammon made war against the children of Israel, and hearkened not unto the words of Jephthah, then there came upon Jephthah the Spirit of the Lord, and he went up against the children of Ammon and vowed unto the Lord, saying:

JEPHTE
Si tradiderit Dominus filios Ammon in manus meas, quicumque primus de domo mea occurrerit mihi, offeram illum Domino in holocaustum.

If thou shalt indeed deliver the children of Ammon into my hands, whatsoever first cometh forth of the doors of my house to meet me, I will offer to the Lord for a burnt offering.

CHORUS
Transivit ergo Jephte ad filios Ammon, ut in spiritu forti et virtute Domini pugnaret contra eos.

Then Jephthah passed over to the children of Ammon, and he fought in the spirit and the strength of God against them.

DUET
Et clangebant tubae, et personabant tympana, et proelium commissum est adversus Ammon.

And the trumpets sounded, and the drums were beaten, when battle was joined against the children of Ammon.

BASS SOLO
Fugite, cedite, impii, perite gentes, occumbite in gladio; Dominus exercituum in proelium surrexit, et pugnat contra vos.

Flee from us, yield to us, impious ones, give away, ye heathen, and fall before our mighty sword; for the God of Israel is risen up to battle and fights against our foes.

CHORUS
Fugite, cedite, impii, corruite, et in furore gladii dissipamini.

Flee from us, yield to us, impious ones, we scatter you, and with our keen and glittering swords we hew you down.

HISTORICUS
Et percussit Jephte viginti civitates Ammon plaga magna nimis.

Jephthah therefore smote them, and took from them twenty cities, and there was a grievous slaughter.

TRIO
Et ululantes filii Ammon, facti sunt coram filiis Israel humiliati.

And he subdued the children of Ammon, for the Lord delivered them to the children of Israel.

* Bars 78-88. There is much to be said for taking this organ bass an octave higher.

Giacomo Carissimi's *Jephte* was one of the most popular of all early oratorios. The Latin-language libretto, based on the book of Judges 11, tells the story of Jephte (also spelled Jephthah), an Israelite general who promises to sacrifice to God the first thing to emerge from his house on his homecoming if God grants him victory in an impending battle. Returning home victorious, Jephte is dismayed to see his only daughter emerge first from his house to greet him. She, virtuously, urges him to fulfill his vow. The work ends with an extended lament by the daughter (who has no name, either in the Bible or in this oratorio) and her companions. This lament, in the view of one mid-17th-century Jesuit observer, "is composed with such skill that you would swear that you hear the sobs and moans of the weeping girls." In Carissimi's setting, a narrator designated as the Historicus—at times a bass, at times an alto—introduces the characters and keeps the plot moving forward in brisk fashion. Except for this narrative device and the fact that it is sung in Latin, *Jephthe* is musically indistinguishable from operas of the mid-17th century. Like them it places a premium on vocal virtuosity and features a quick succession of short movements, some for solo, some for a small group of soloists, others still for chorus.

Performance notes: The ensemble in this recording performs the duet *Et clangebant* (track 38) as a duet of soprano recorders before presenting it vocally. Although marked "organ" in this edition, the continuo part can in fact be interpreted by any chordal instrument. This recording uses at various times theorbo and harpsichord as well as organ.

87 Zadok the Priest (1727)
Handel

CD5 Track 43

p. 261

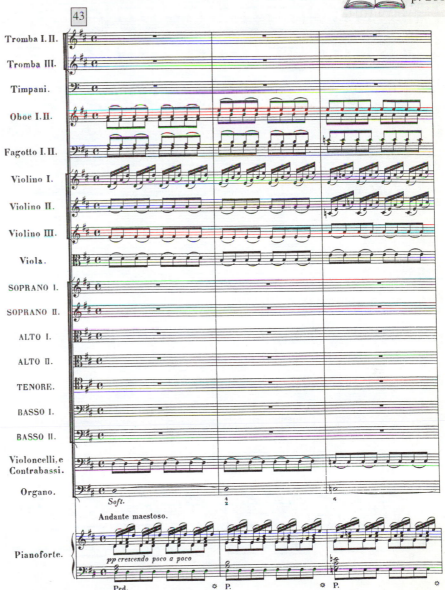

Note: The pianoforte part in this score is for rehearsal purposes only and is not part of Handel's original score.

■   No. 87 Handel: *Zadok the Priest*

No. 87 Handel: *Zadok the Priest* ■ **233**

■   No. 87 Handel: *Zadok the Priest*

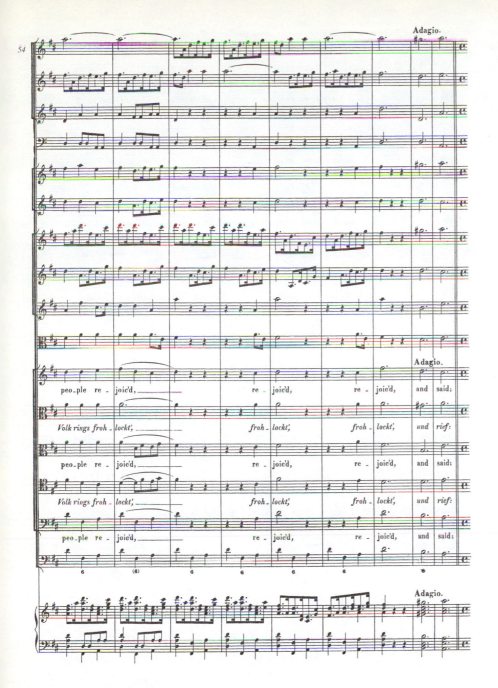

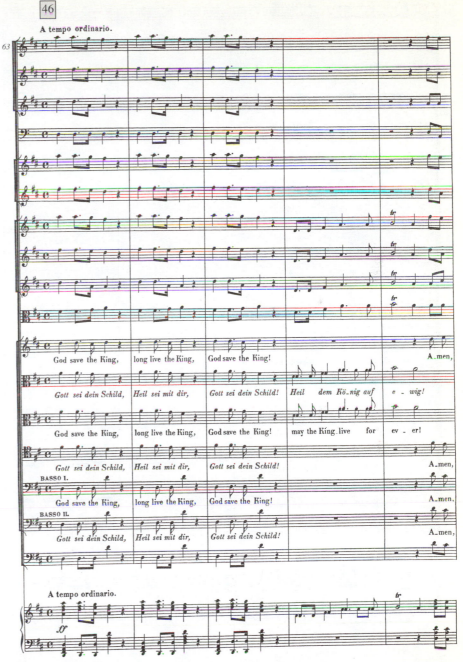

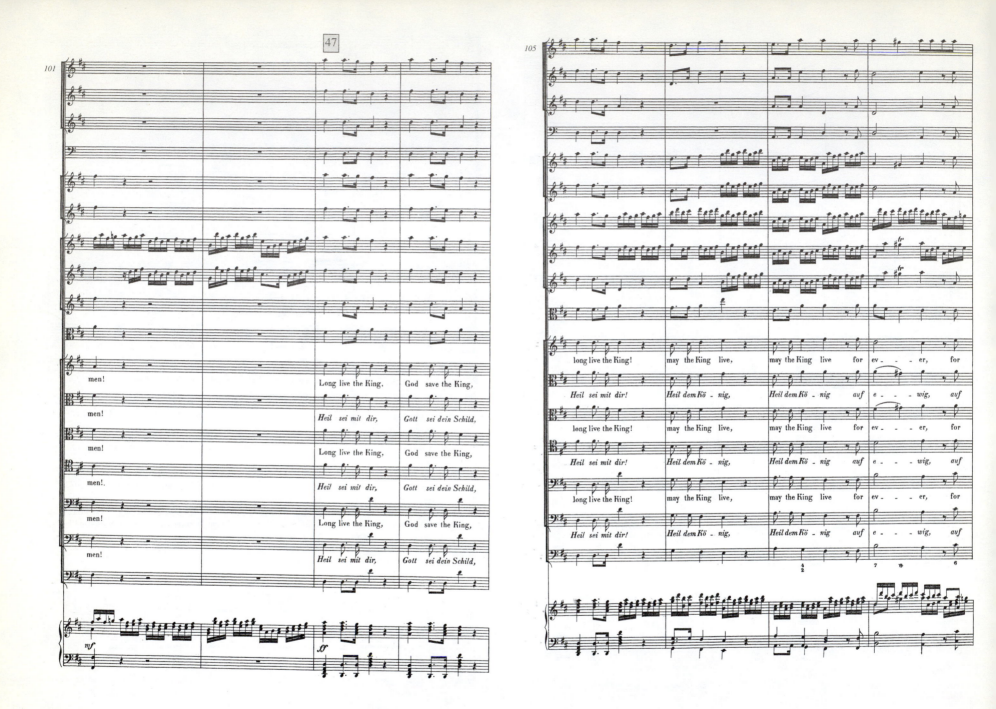

p. 262

88 Jesu, der du meine Seele, BWV 78
(excerpts)
Johann Sebastian Bach (1685–1750)

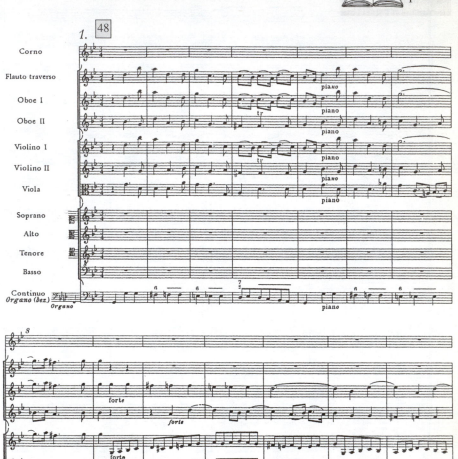

A good deal of sacred music was tailored to fit quite practical needs. The long orchestral introduction to Handel's *Zadok the Priest,* for example, allowed the royal procession sufficient time to make its way down the long center aisle of Westminster Abbey for the coronation of King George II in 1727. The effect of the swelling orchestra, the dramatic entrance of the voices, and the arrival of the new king were of such overwhelming effect that the anthem has been used in every British coronation since that time. The emphasis on chordal declamation reinforces the sense of unity within the chorus and, by extension, with the nation as a whole.

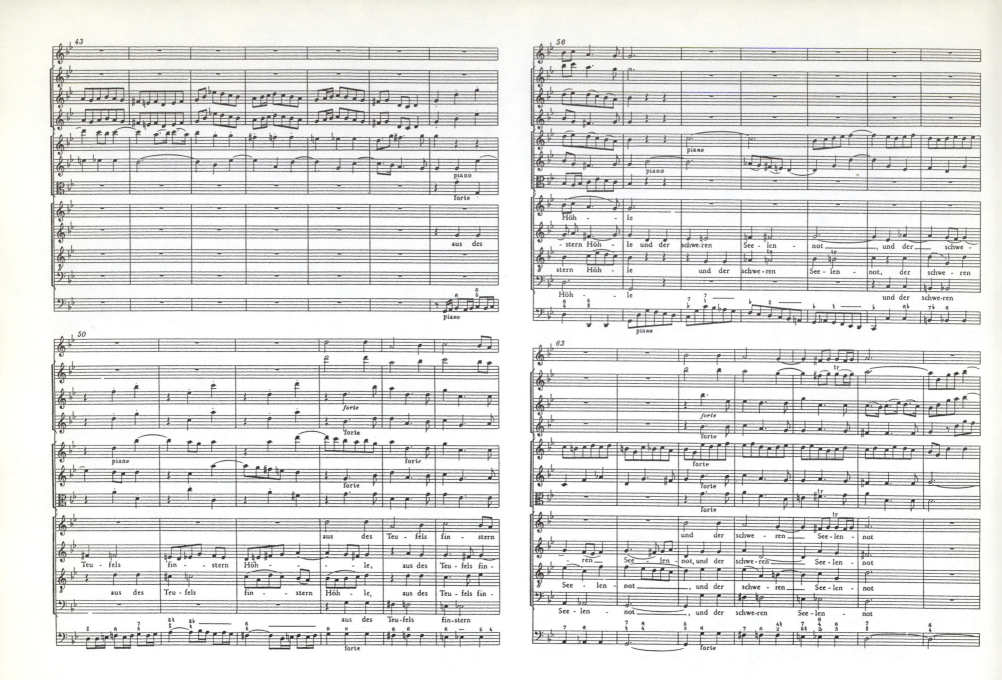

■   No. 88 Bach: *Jesu, der du meine Seele*

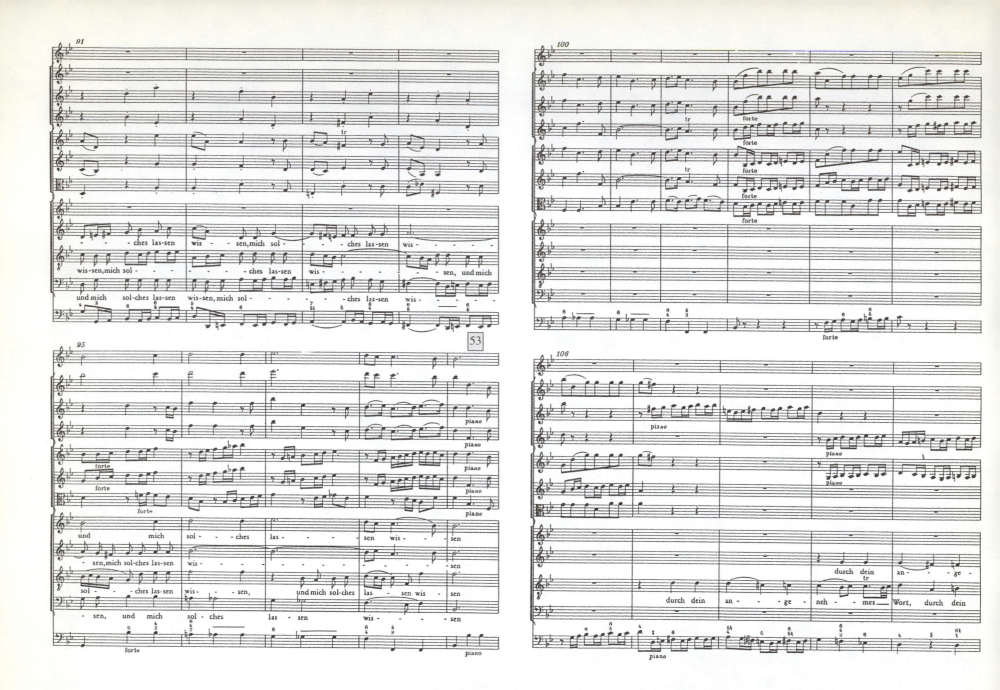

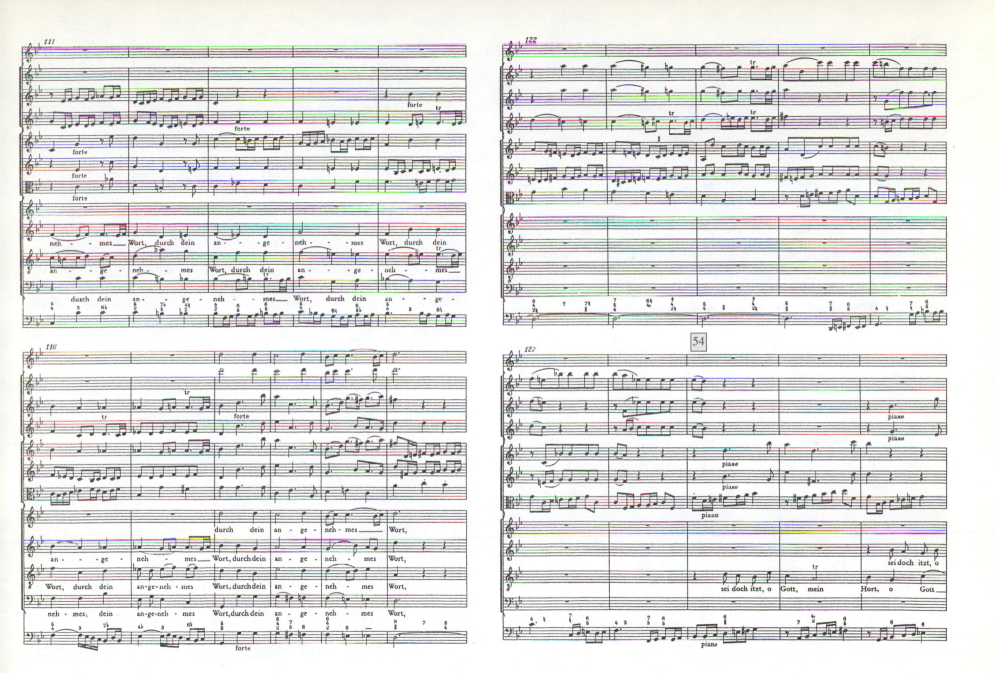

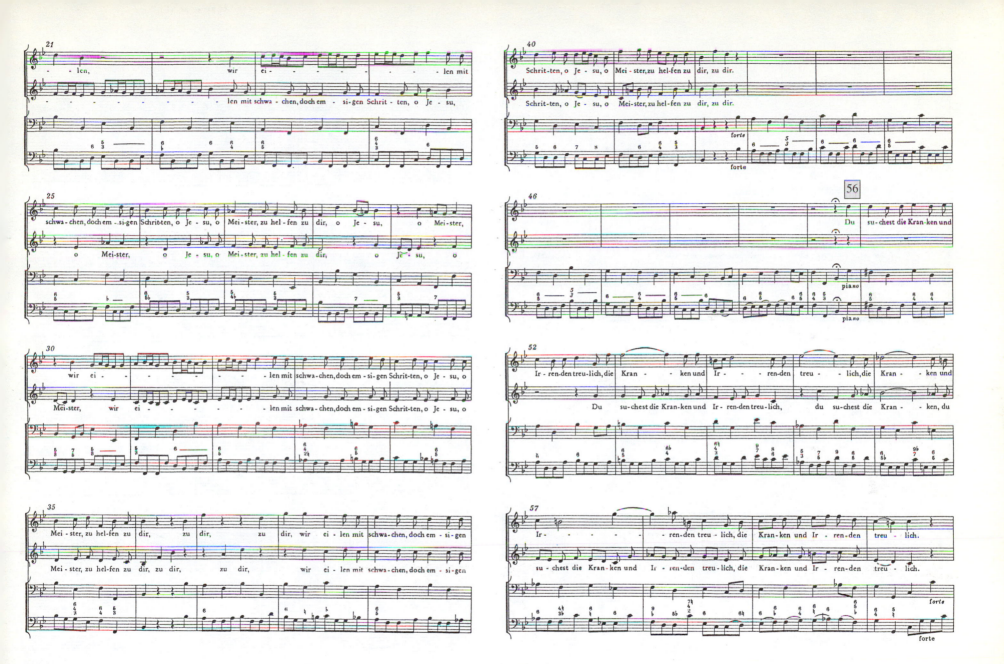

No. 88 Bach: *Jesu, der du meine Seele*   ■   **251**

No. 88 Bach: *Jesu, der du meine Seele*   ■ **253**

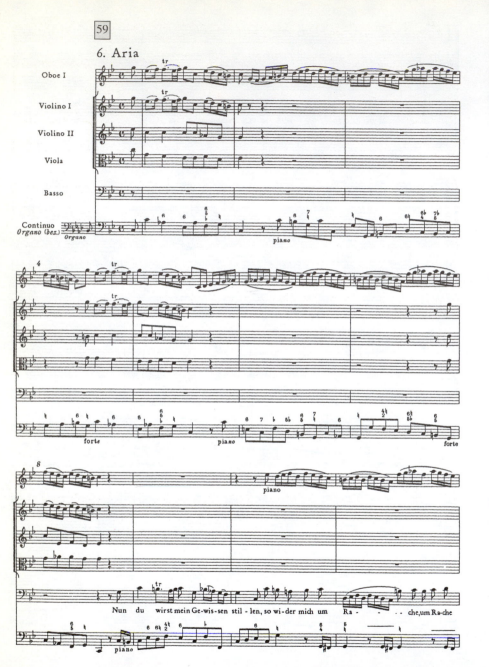

No. 88 Bach: *Jesu, der du meine Seele* ■ **255**

7. Choral

Herr, ich glau-be, hilf mir Schwa-chen, laß mich ja ver-za-gen nicht;
du, du kannst mich stär-ker ma-chen, wenn mich Sünd und Tod an-ficht. Dei-ner Gü-te will ich trau-en,
bis ich fröh-lich wer-de schau-en dich, Herr Je-su, nach dem Streit in der sü-ßen E-wig-keit.

1. Chorus: Jesu, der du meine Seele

Jesu, der du meine Seele hast durch deinen
  bittern Tod

aus des Teufels finstrer Höhle und der schweren
  Seelennoth

kräftiglich herausgerissen,

und mich Solches lassen wissen

durch dein angenehmes Wort:

sei doch jetzt, o Gott, mein Hort!

Jesus, thou who my soul has, through your bitter
  death,

from the devil's dark hell and the severe need of
  the soul

powerfully lifted out,

and gave this known to me

through your comforting word:

Be thou now, o God, my protection!

2. Aria (Duet): Wir eilen

Wir eilen mit schwachen, doch emsigen
  Schritten,
o Jesu, o Meister, zu helfen zu dir.
Du suchest die Kranken und Irrenden treulich.
Ach! höre, wie wir die Stimme erheben,
um Hülfe zu bitten!
Es sei uns dein gnädiges Antlitz erfreulich!

We hasten with weak, yet eager steps,

oh Jesus, oh Master, for help toward thee.
You visit the sick and wayward faithfully.
Ah! hear, how we our voices lift
for help to ask
May us your graceful countenance brighten!

5. Recitative: Die Wunden

Die Wunden, Nägel, Kron' und Grab,
die Schläge, so man dort dem Heiland gab,
sind ihm nunmehro Siegeszeichen,
und können mir erneute Kräfte reichen.
Wenn ein erschreckliches Gericht
den Fluch für die Verdammten spricht:
so kehrst du ihm in Segen.
Mich kann kein Schmerz und keine Pein
  bewegen,
weil sie mein Heiland kennt,
und da dein Herz für mich in Liebe brennt,
so lege ich hinwieder das meine vor dir nieder.
Dies, mein Herz, mit Leid vermenget,
so dein theures Blut besprenget,
so am Kreuz vergossen ist,
geb' ich dir, Herr Jesu Christ.

The wounds, nails, crown, and grave,
the blows, that were given the Saviour there
are to him now signs of victory
and can to me renewed powers give.
If a terrible court
the curse of the damned pronounces:
so shall you reverse it [the curse] into a blessing.
No suffering and no pain can move me.

Because my Saviour knows them [too],
and because your heart for me in love burns,
thus I present back to you my heart.
This, my heart, with suffering heaped,
as your dear blood flows,
as it on the cross poured out,
so give I myself to you, Lord Jesus Christ.

6. Aria: Nun du wirst mein Gewissen stillen

Nun du wirst mein Gewissen stillen,
So wider mich um Rache schreit,

Ja, deine Treue wird's erfüllen,
Weil mir dein Wort die Hoffnung beut.
Wenn Christen an dich glauben,
Wird sie kein Feind in Ewigkeit
Aus deinen Händen rauben.

Now you shall my conscience calm,
Which, against my will, for vengeance screams
  out,

Yes, your faithfulness will fill it,
Because to me your word offers hope.
When Christians believe in you,
No enemy in all eternity
will steal them from your hands.

7. Chorale: Herr, ich glaube

Herr, ich glaube, hilf mir Schwachen,	Lord, I believe, help me, a weakling,
laß mich ja verzagen nicht;	let me falter not;
du, du kannst mich stärker machen,	thou, thou canst me stronger make,
wenn mich Sünd und Tod anficht.	when sin and death assault me.
Deiner Güte will ich trauen,	Your goodness will I trust,
bis ich fröhlich werde schauen	until I gladly see
dich, Herr Jesu, nach dem Streit	you, Lord Jesus, after the battle
in der süßen Ewigkeit.	in sweet eternity

The opening movement is a *tour-de-force* of Baroque compositional techniques, incorporating an ostinato bass into a large-scale ritornello structure, with a chorale superimposed onto choral writing that is typical of a motet. The ostinato passage in the first movement is the four-measure figure in the bass line at the opening of the work that descends by half-steps from G to D. This descending chromatic fourth, known as the *passus duriusculus* ("painful passage"), had long been associated with moments of anguish. Purcell used it in Dido's lament at the end of *Dido and Aeneas,* and Bach himself would later use it in the Credo of his B-Minor Mass for the passage that speaks of Christ's crucifixion. Here it alerts listeners even before a word is sung that the opening movement of this cantata deals with pain and suffering.

The ostinato is stated twice in the bass (m. 1–5 and 5–9) and then migrates to other voices: the first oboe (m. 9–12), second oboe (13–16), and then finally to the singers themselves, who enter in imitation (m. 17ff.). The descending line is then inverted (m. 25ff.) at the first suggestion of hope in the text ("has through your bitter death. . ."), but then reverts to its original descending pattern (m. 28ff.). The figure continues with similar permutations in almost every measure of the movement.

This first movement is also permeated with the melody of the chorale from which the cantata takes its name. The words and melody of *Jesu, der du meine Seele* would have been familiar to any of the parishioners hearing the first performance of this cantata. The melody falls into distinct phrases and is always presented by the soprano (beginning in m. 21). Thus, the chorale melody presents a kind of superstructure above the ostinato figure. The movement opens with an extended passage for the orchestra alone, with a dotted-rhythm melody running above the ostinato in the bass. The rhythm of this triple-meter melody is reminiscent of the sarabande, a dance common to many instrumental suites. This material functions as a ritornello throughout the entire movement, returning between the successive entrances of the chorus, as shown in the following table:

The ritornello structure of Bach, Jesu, der du meine Seele, BWV 78, first movement.

Section	Rit.1	Chorus 1	Rit.2	Ch.2	Rit.3	Ch.3	Rit.4	Ch.4
Measure	1	17	37	49	69	73	85	89
Tonality	g				d		F	

Section	Rit. 5	Ch.5	Rit. 6	Ch. 6	Rit. 7
Measure	99	107	122	129	140
Tonality	B♭	→g		g (G)	

Finally, by dividing the text into six distinct sections, each with its own thematic material, and each with its own set of points of imitation, Bach in effect employs the structure of the motet for the choral portions of the opening movement.

Subsequent movements alternate between aria and recitative. The second-movement duet is a masterpiece of word-painting. The principal thematic idea takes its cue from the text itself ("We hasten with weak, yet eager steps, / oh Jesus, oh Master, for help toward thee"). Bach sets this text to an energetic, upward-moving line that keeps falling back on itself, only to strive ever higher to a constant rhythm of steady eighth notes. The image of "weak, yet eager steps" could scarcely be captured more vividly. The two voices in turn strive with each other to reach their highest pitch.

Formally, Bach constructs this duet as a *da capo* aria:

	Section	Measure nos.	Harmony
A	Ritornello 1	1–8	B♭ major
	Solo 2	9–42	B♭ major
	Ritornello 2	43–50	B♭ major
B	Solo 2	51–60	G minor → C minor
	Ritornello 3	61–64	C minor
	Solo 3	65–80	C minor → D minor
	Ritornello 4	81–82	D minor → F major
	Solo 4	83–98	F major (=V/B♭), ("A" section *da capo*)

The subsequent recitative and aria pair for tenor (omitted from the Anthology for reasons of space) and bass are also full of word-painting. In the bass recitative in the fifth movement, for example, the words *Wunden* ("wounds"), *Nägel* ("nails") and *Kron* ("crown") are set to pointed dissonances; on *Grab* ("grave"), the singer descends to a deep voice register; and the strings present an agitated sixteenth note figure to emphasize the word *erschreckliches* ("terrifying") in m. 8–9. The bass aria is a duet between the vocalist and the oboist. This kind of writing for voice and solo instrument occurs frequently in Bach's music. The cantata concludes with a harmonized setting of the chorale melody *Jesu, der du meine Seele*, which had provided the cantus firmus for the opening movement, rounding out the whole to provide a sense of cyclical symmetry.

89 Concerto grosso in F Major, Op. 6, No. 2 (ca. 1685?)
Arcangelo Corelli (1653–1713)

CD6 Track 1 p. 279

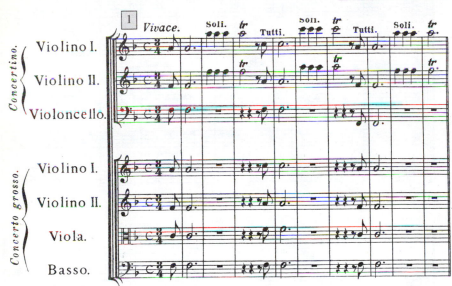

No. 89 Corelli: Concerto grosso in F Major, Op. 6, No. 2 ■ **263**

■   No. 89 Corelli: Concerto grosso in F Major, Op. 6, No. 2

■ No. 89 Corelli: Concerto grosso in F Major, Op. 6, No. 2

No. 89 Corelli: Concerto grosso in F Major, Op. 6, No. 2   ■ **267**

Arcangelo Corelli's concerti grossi are among the earliest works of their kind. Although not published until 1714, a year after the composer's death, at least some of these works were circulating in manuscript in Rome as early as the 1680s. Corelli's concerti grossi feature a ripieno of strings and basso continuo with a concertino (solo ensemble) typical of a trio sonata: two violins and basso continuo. The concertino part is continuous and—as the original title page indicates—can be performed with or without the ripieno forces. The ripieno part, in other words, is not essential to the structural integrity of these works. But without the ripieno, these works lack the timbral variety—the rapid back-and-forth between soloists and ensemble—that gives them their distinctive profile.

The formal structure of these concertos is fluid. The individual movements are not built around recurring themes—ritornelli—like the later concertos of Vivaldi and Bach, but instead move through a series of relatively brief sections that present contrasting thematic ideas in different keys and tempos. The second work of the set (Op. 6, No. 2) falls into four movements, three of which—the first, third, and fourth—have distinct subsections. The first movement moves back and forth between a Vivace fanfare and an imitative Allegro. It also includes two slow sections—one in the middle (m. 40–51), the other at the end (m. 99–107)—each with its own distinct thematic material. The second movement is a continuous and relatively brief (57 measures) Allegro. The third movement opens with a Grave and moves to a thematically distinct Andante Largo. Harmonically, this movement begins in D minor and ends on V/F. It leads without a break into the fourth movement, an Allegro in binary form (consisting, that is, of two repeated sections).

90   Concerto in A minor, Op. 3, No. 8, first movement (1711)
Antonio Vivaldi (1678–1741)

CD6   Track 12

p. 280

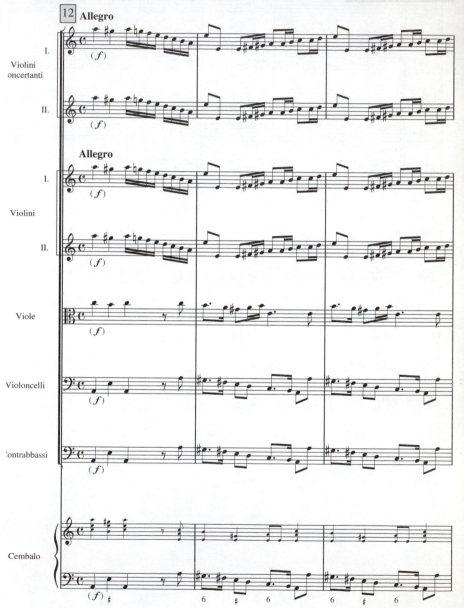

◼ No. 90 Vivaldi: Concerto in A minor, Op. 3, No. 8

■ No. 90 Vivaldi: Concerto in A minor, Op. 3, No. 8

The solo and tutti parts of Vivaldi's Concerto for Two Violins, Op. 3, No. 8, are structurally interdependent: even though the two soloists often double the ripieno violins, these parts diverge at times, as at the beginning of the Solo I section in the first movement (m. 16). In a concerto by Corelli, the ripieno would have simply dropped out entirely at this point.

Thematically, the opening ritornello of Vivaldi's concerto introduces three of the work's four principal thematic ideas (see Example below). The opening unison head motif (1) is typical of many concertos of this era: it presents a memorable, sharply profiled idea that is immediately recognizable whenever it returns over the course of the movement. The middle section of the opening ritornello (2) presents an idea that is more fluid and sequential, while the closing section of the ritornello (3), with its dominant pedal point, clearly signals the arrival of a cadence. These three ideas, taken together, form a self-contained unit consisting of a beginning (1), middle (2), and end (3). Over the course of the movement, however, Vivaldi breaks up the consitutent subunits of the ritornello, combining them with a new idea (4), first presented by the solo violins in m. 16.

In the broadest terms, then, the overall form of this movement consists of an alternation of ritornello and solo sections (see diagram, below). At a more detailed level, however, the form is more complicated than this simple description might suggest. Almost all of the solo and ritornello sections are interrupted at some point by interpolations of an opposing texture. Solo I, for example, is interrupted by a brief return of tutti texture at m. 22, with a brief restatement of the ritornello's closing idea (3). Ritornello II, in turn, is interrupted by a brief solo passage in m. 39–41. The alternation of ritornello and solo is thus more a general organizational principle than a rigid scheme.

Section	Harmonic area	Measures (number of measures)	Thematic ideas
Ritornello I	i	1–16 (16)	(1) (2) (3)
Solo I	i → III	16–36 (20)	(4) punctuated by (3)
Ritornello II	III → iv	37–47 (11)	(2)
Solo II	iv → i	48–67 (20)	(2) punctuated by (1), (3), (4)
Ritornello III	i	68–71 (4)	(1)
Solo III	i	71–78 (6)	(2) punctuated by (3)
Ritornello IV	i	79–93 (14)	(3)

91 Pièces de clavecin (1707): Courante and Gigue (1707)
Elisabeth Jacquet de la Guerre (1665–1729)

CD6   Track 17

p. 286

The suite—a series of dance or dance-like movements—was a favorite genre of instrumental composers in the Baroque era. As in the Renaissance, dances of all kinds were very often in binary form. And binary form, with its built-in repetition, invites variation. Composers usually left the realization of these varied repetitions to the imagination of performers, but occasionally they wrote out altered reprises that constitute, in effect, a variation on the original reprise. The *double* of the courante in Elisabeth Jacquet de la Guerre's *Pièces de clavecin,* for example, offers a considerably more elaborate version of the original courante. In performance, the harpsichord would play the first reprise of the courante, then the first reprise of the *double,* followed by the second reprise of the courante and concluding with the second reprise of the *double.* The gigue in this same collection follows the same pattern, with a *double* far more intricate than its original.

Performance notes: Even with the written-out *doubles,* the score remains a script from which the musician creates a performance. The harpsichordist here adds many details of phrasing, ornamentation, and rhythmic inflection beyond what is notated in the score. Notice in particular the use of *notes inégales* at the opening of the courante. Although notated in straightforward quarter, dotted quarter, and eighth notes, this passage is far more supple and lively in performance than it would appear from the published score. This kind of performance is well documented in musical treatises of the 18th century.

(1737)

Jean-Féry Rebel (1661–1747)

CD6   Track 25

p. 286

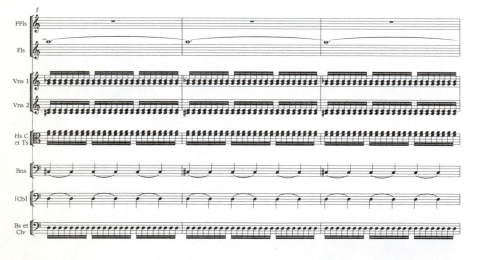

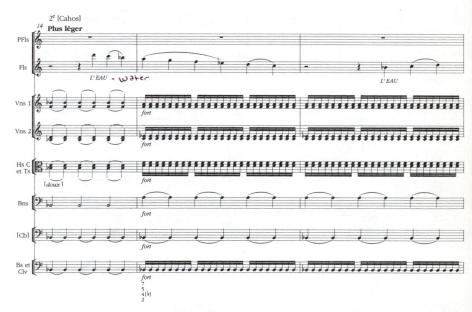

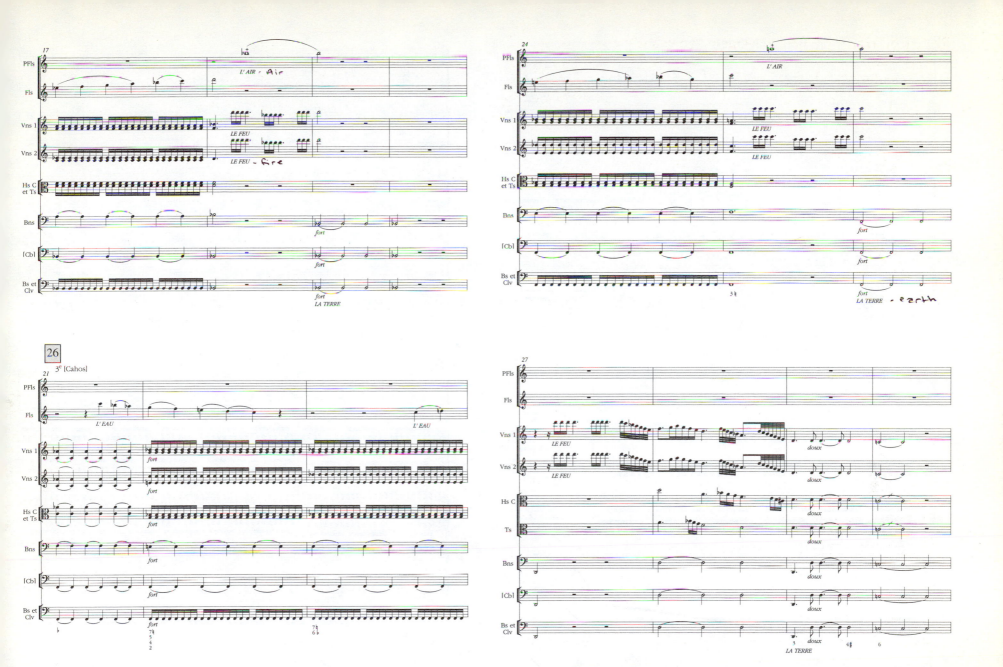

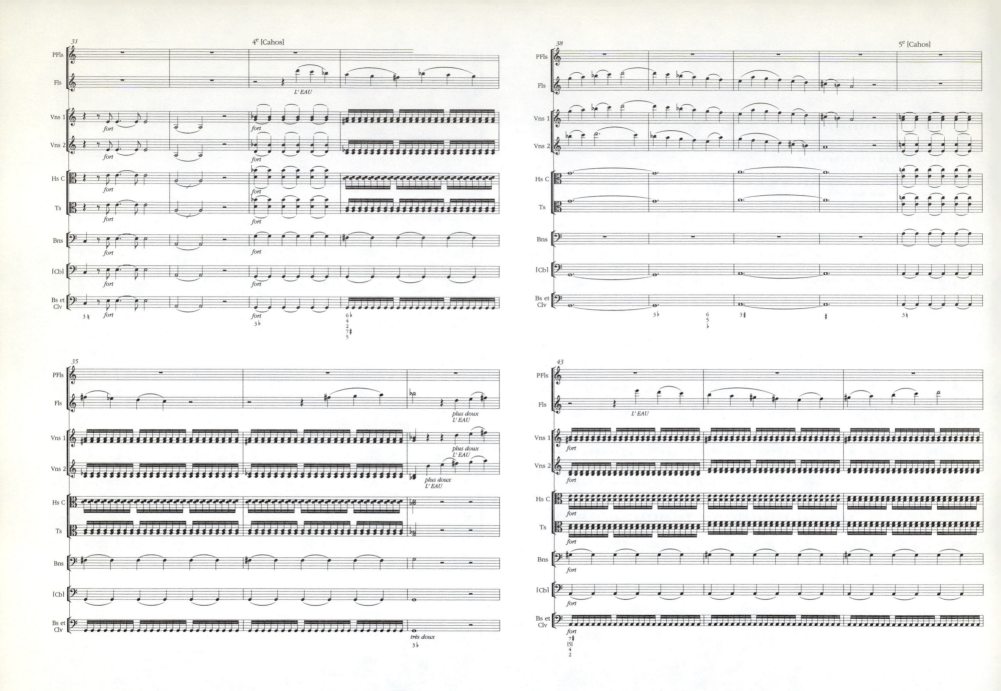

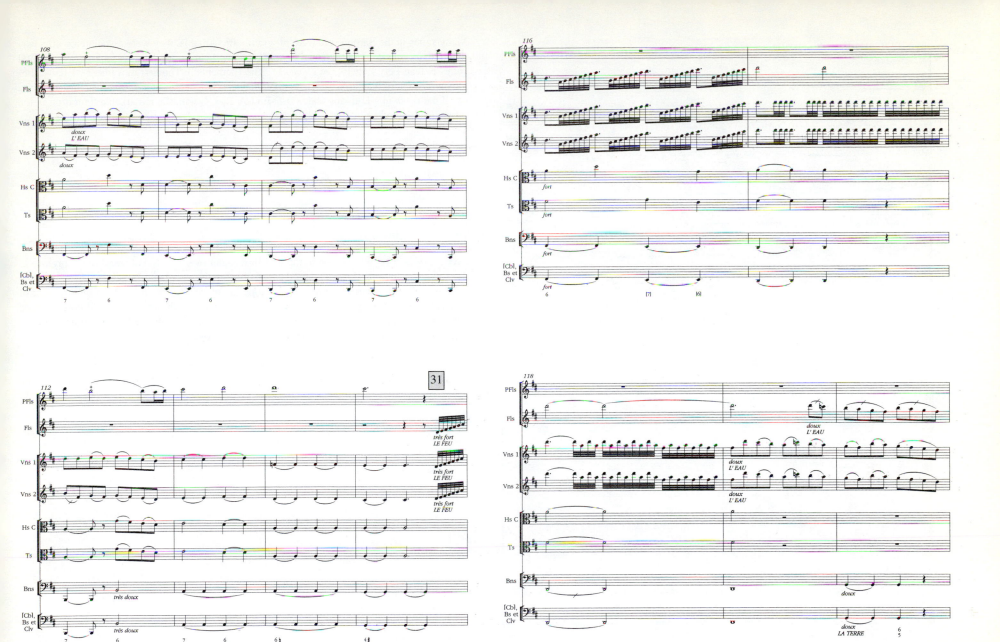

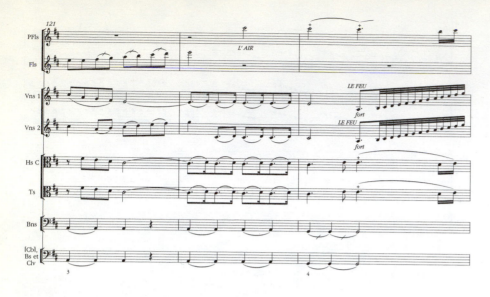

Many suites in the Baroque era were programmatic—that is, they were associated with a particular extra-musical idea, person, or event. Among the most extraordinary of all instrumental suites is Jean-Féry Rebel's *Les élémens* ("The Elements"). The first movement, "Chaos," begins with a chord that strikes even 21st-century ears as chaotic. It is a simultaneous sounding of all the notes in a D-minor scale (D-E-F-G-A-B♭-C♯) with the remarkable figuration in the basso continuo of

$$
\begin{array}{c}
\sharp 7 \\
\flat 6 \\
5 \\
4 \\
3 \\
2
\end{array}
$$

over a low D. The introduction to the first-movement overture, Rebel noted in his preface to the score, "represents the confusion that prevails among the elements before that moment in which, subject to invariable laws, they assume the place prescribed for them by the order of Nature." The bass, he goes on to explain, "expresses the Earth through the tied notes, played percussively. The flutes, with their rising and falling lines, imitate the flow and murmuring of water. The air is depicted by long-held notes followed by cadences in the piccolos. And finally, the violins represent the active nature of fire through their vigorous and brilliant strokes. . . I have dared to connect the idea of the confusion of the elements with a confusion of harmony . . . These notes proceed to a unison in a progression that is natural, and after a dissonance, we hear a perfect chord [i.e., a unison]."

93

Toccata IX from **Il Secondo Libro
di Toccate** (1627)

Girolamo Frescobaldi (1583–1643)

CD6   Track 32

p. 289

■   No. 93 Frescobaldi: *Toccata IX*

*) sic: cf. app. crit.

Non senza fatiga si giunge al fine

The Ninth Toccata from Frescobaldi's *Second Book of Toccatas,* although unusually intricate, is nonetheless representative of the genre as a whole. Rapid passagework combined with freedom of form had long been characteristic of the toccata. Highly episodic, Frescobaldi's toccata moves rapidly through a variety of textures, registers, rhythms, and meters. Some sections last only a few measures. The rhythms are constantly shifting and at times quite intricate (for example, m. 11, 22, 25); the right and left hands occasionally work in cross rhythms (m. 56–60, 65); and the passagework, which is distinctly idiomatic to the harpsichord (as opposed to the organ), is dazzling at times (m. 25–26, 50–54). Small wonder, then, that Frescobaldi should add the remark at the very end of this work: *Non senza fatiga si giunge al fine* ("Not without effort does one arrive at the end").

94

Praeludium in G minor, BuxWV 149
(ca. 1675–1689)

Dietrich Buxtehude (1637–1707)

CD6   Track 37

p. 289

No. 94 Buxtehude: Praeludium in G minor   ■   **297**

Dietrich Buxtehude's Praeludium in G minor for organ (BuxWV 149), written sometime between 1675 and 1689, consists of a series of discrete sections, each with its own distinctive theme and texture. The long imitative sections are typical of the prelude and many other free keyboard genres in the 17th century. Buxtehude's Praeludium ends with an extended rhapsody that sounds almost improvisational.

THE STRUCTURE OF BUXTEHUDE'S PRAELUDIUM IN G MINOR, BUX WV 149.		
Measures	Indicated tempo	Texture
1–20	None	Passagework in hands; ostinato figure in pedals
21–54	Alla breve	Imitative
55–78	Allegro	Free, running bass against chords
78–141	Largo	Imitative, triple meter
142–59	Largo	Free, quasi-improvisatory

Buxtehude's Praeludium exhibits three different kinds of virtuosity:

- compositional, reflected in the wide range of techniques the composer deploys, from rapid passagework to strict polyphonic imitation;
- performative, as reflected in the extreme technical demands of the writing;
- instrumentational, as reflected in the way it calls on almost all the resources of the organ, from shifts in register to demanding pedalwork.

(excerpts) (1722)

J. S. Bach

CD6   Track 42

p. 293

Prelude and Fugue No. 1 in C Major, BMV 846

3 part starts

Oder:

10

44 Stretto (chain of strettos)

15

20

25

Prelude and Fugue No. 4 in C# minor, BWV 848

Companion CD   Track 11

p. 293

5

10

15

The two books of Bach's *Well-Tempered Clavier* present a rich variety of imitative and non-imitative keyboard pieces. Each book consists of a series of 24 paired preludes and fugues, with one pair in each of the 24 major and minor keys. No one is exactly certain what the "Well-Tempered" of the title means. Some believe it reflects Bach's advocacy of equal temperament, a system of tuning that allowed keyboard players to play in any key (see Focus: "Systems of Temperament"). Others maintain that "Well-Tempered" is a vague term that leaves much to the discretion of the performer to use whatever tuning system is appropriate to the work at hand. Bach's purpose in writing the *Well-Tempered Clavier,* according to this line of thought, was to demonstrate the feasability of writing and performing works in all 24 keys, leaving the question of tuning to the performer. There were many systems of temperament at the time that could accommodate a wide variety of keys reasonably well, even if Bach's contemporaries disagreed on the precise limitations of reasonableness. Much depended on a performer's willingness to tolerate certain imperfections of certain intervals in certain keys.

In any event, Bach organized each book of the *Well-Tempered Clavier* according to the ascending chromatic scale, with major-mode works in each key followed by a corresponding work in the minor mode:

Prelude and Fugue in C Major

Prelude and Fugue in C minor

Prelude and Fugue in C♯ Major

Prelude and Fugue in C♯ Minor

Prelude and Fugue in D Major

Prelude and Fugue in D Minor

Prelude and Fugue in E♭ Major

Prelude and Fugue in E♭ Minor

Prelude and Fugue in E Major

Prelude and Fugue in E Minor

and so on.

Reflecting Bach's passion for exploring the many possibilities of a self-imposed limitation, all the preludes and fugues are different from one another. The C-Major Prelude follows a pattern of broken chords in a manner known as style brisée ("broken style"), adopted from the arpeggiated ("broken") chords and figures typically found in lute music. Not coincidentally, this piece remains a favorite among guitar players. The Prelude in C♯ minor is in the style of a sarabande, a slow dance in triple meter. Some analysts have discerned subtle thematic or motivic links between certain preludes and their associated fugues, but in general these, too, are musically independent of each other.

By the same token, there is no standard pattern for the fugues. Some of them—especially the longer ones—have more than one subject, and these do not necessarily all appear at the outset. A new subject enters the Fugue in C♯ minor of Bach's *Well-Tempered Clavier,* Book I, for example, in m. 36, still another in m. 49.

Chorale prelude on the **Magnificat peregrini toni** (late 17th century)
Johann Pachelbel (1652–1706)

CD6   Track 45

p. 294

Chorale preludes were written to serve as instrumental introductions to the congregational singing of a chorale in church. Given this fucntion, these works tend to be brief and relatively straightforward. Johann Pachelbel's chorale prelude *Magnificat peregrini toni* is typical of the genre. The chorale melody had been adopted from the Ninth Psalm Tone of the Roman Catholic liturgy (the *tonus peregrinus* or "pilgrim tone," so called because it moves from one recitation tone in its first half to a different one in its second). In Protestant services, this melody was commonly associated with the Magnificat, the words uttered by the Virgin Mary when she learns from the annunciating angel that she is to bear the Christ child ("My soul doth magnify the Lord," Luke 1: 47–55). In Pachelbel's setting the tune is stated in its entirety in long notes in the upper voice, with the other voices weaving around it. The two measures of introduction present a brief point of imitation on the opening of the theme; once the melody enters in m. 3, the two lower voices engage in antiphonal passagework that is flowing but unspectacular: the focus of attention here, after all, is on the melody in the upper voice. The middle voice again introduces a brief point of imitation in m. 9, anticipating the first notes of the second phrase of the chorale melody while the upper voice pauses between the phrases. But once again, the imitation soon breaks off. The rhythmic acceleration in m. 12–13 provides variety, and the whole concludes with a *tièrce de picardie* (picardy third)—a major third at the end of a work otherwise in minor mode—in m. 19. Such endings had become commonplace for works in the minor mode by 1700. Evidence suggests that even if a sharpened third was not explicitly notated on the final cadence in a score, performers were expected to provide it— a late vestige of musica ficta.

Chorale prelude on **Meine Seele erhebt den Herren,** BWV 648 (1748)

J. S. Bach

Johann Sebastian Bach's chorale prelude on the same melody as Pachelbel's *Magnificat peregrini toni* exhibits a very different approach to the genre. Originally written as part of Cantata 10 in 1724 and published for organ in 1748, this brief work also places the melody in the upper voice in long note values. The three lower voices, however, are considerably more chromatic and intricate than the lower voices in Pachelbel's setting. The two measures of introduction in Pachelbel's version are replaced here by an eight-measure fugal exposition on a chromatic theme unrelated to the chorale. Once the chorale melody enters (m. 9), the imitation in the lower voices continues. The brief pause within the chorale melody—a single measure's rest in Pachelbel's version—expands here to eight full measures, once again on the independent chromatic motive. Even after the chorale melody concludes, we hear an additional seven measures of imitation, with the piece ending as it had begun, a statement of the chromatic countersubject in the pedals.

The effect of all this is strangely haunting. We can at once appreciate Bach's incomparable contrapuntal skills even while sympathizing with the reaction of many of his contemporaries, who found such preludes disconcerting. Early in his career Bach was called to task for the way in which he harmonized chorales being sung by parishioners. According to the letter of reprimand, Bach had "made many curious *variationes* in the chorale, and mingled many strange tones in it, and … the Congregation has been confused by it."

98 Aria mit dreißig Veränderungen,
BWV 988 ("Goldberg" Variations)
(excerpts) (1742)

J. S. Bach

CD6   Track 47

p. 298

Johann Sebastian Bach's *"Goldberg" Variations* offer perhaps the most spectacular example in the entire history of music of the elaborations possible within the framework of a simple bass line. For many years, it was believed that Bach wrote this set of harpsichord variations on behalf of one of his pupils, Johann Gottlieb Goldberg, who in turn was employed by a certain Baron von Keyserlingk. Legend has it that the Baron had trouble getting to sleep at night and that these variations were designed to help him while away the evening hours. But the story is demonstrably false, because Goldberg was only about 14 years old when Bach wrote this work.

The *"Goldberg" Variations,* like the *Well-Tempered Clavier* and the late, unfinished *Art of the Fugue,* exemplifies Bach's passion for writing encyclopedic works. In the *Well-Tempered Clavier* he explored the permutations of free preludes and imitative fugues in every possible key. In the *Art of the Fugue* he would explore various ways in which different fugal devices can be brought to bear on a single subject. In the *"Goldberg" Variations* he systematically explored the technique of both variation and canon.

The variations take us through an astonishing set of permutations on a single idea. The source of that idea is elusive. Bach's use of the term "aria" to designate the opening variation draws our attention to the soprano line, but the theme, spelled out here, is actually in the bass:

Measure	1–8		9–16	
Theme	‖: G-F♯-E-D-B-C-D-G		G-F♯-E-A-F♯-G-A-D :‖	
Tonality	I		I I	V

Measure	17–24		25–32	
Theme	‖: D-B-C-B-G-A-G-E		C-B-A-D-G-C-D-G :‖	
Tonality	V	iii	ii6	I

Bach further concealed the theme with added notes, even on its first presentation in the aria. In the first reprise, the theme's pitches mostly coincide with the longer notes on the downbeats in the bass line (predominantly half notes and dotted half notes); in the second reprise, the notes of the theme do not coincide with the downbeat nearly as often.

Bach uses this bass progression as the foundation for all subsequent variations. In Variation 1, for example, the theme is readily apparent on the downbeat of every measure in the first reprise, but harder to follow in the second reprise.

Another structural device Bach uses throughout this set is a series of canons. Every third variation (Numbers 3, 6, 9, 12, etc.) presents a canon in the two upper voices, creating a trio-sonata texture with two high voices and a bass. The bass line operates independently of the canon, though always providing the necessary notes of the theme in the proper order. Each canon, moreover, is written at an interval one step greater than the one before. Thus, the first canon (Variation 3) is at the unison: the second voice enters one measure after the first, but at the same pitch. The second canon is composed at the interval of a second (no easy task), with the second voice entering one whole step above the first and a measure behind. The third canon is a canon at the third, and so on.

In a third level of complexity, Bach incorporates a variety of musical styles within the "Goldberg" Variations. Variation 16, for example, which opens the unlabeled second part of the work, is in the style of a French overture. Number 10 is a fugue. Number 7 is a gigue. In addition, the work contains many dazzling passages, as in Variation 14, that require a virtuoso to perform.

Performance notes: Like the organ, the more sophisticated harpsichords of Bach's era included multiple stops, settings that could alter the sound of the instrument's tone. The dual manual harpsichords of the day even featured a second keyboard; by setting the stops in advance, a player could thereby alter the tone of the instrument quite rapidly simply by moving from one keyboard to the other. In this recording, the harpsichordist Blandine Verlet plays the first reprise of the opening theme on the lower manual, its repeat on the upper manual, thereby creating a higher, contrasting sound; she follows the same pattern in the two presentations of the second reprise. The dual manual harpsichord also helps the performer avoid some serious problems of hand-crossing that can occur in this particular work for any musician who performs it on a single-manual instrument like the piano.

CREDITS

1. Epitaph of Seikilos. Text and translation reprinted with permission of the publisher from Thomas J. Mathieson, *Apollo's Lyre: Greek Music and Music Theory in Antiquity and the Middle Ages.* (Lincoln: The University of Nebraska Press, p. 149). Copyright © 1999 by the University of Nebraska Press.

2. Plainchant, Mass for Easter Sunday. *Sequence Victimae paschali laudes,* text and translation from *Liber usualis missae officii.* Paris and Tournai: Descee, 1964, p. 780.

3. Plainchant, Vespers on Easter Sunday. *Antiphon Laus deo Patri* and *Psalm 112 Laudate pueri,* text and translation from *Liber usualis missae officii.* Paris and Tournai: Descee, 1964, p. 150 and pp. 914–915.

4. Plainchant, Hymn *Pange lingua gloriosi corporis mysterium.*

5. Hildegard von Bingen, *Ordo virtutum* (excerpt). Text and translation © Hildegard Publishing Company. Used by permission of the publisher.

6. Beatriz de Dia, *A chantar.* Text and translation reprinted with permission of the author from Hendrik van der Werf, *The Extant Troubadour Melodies* (Rochester, NY: Author, 1984).

7. Cantigas de Santa Maria, no. 140: *A Santa Maria dadas.* Reprinted with permission of the publisher from Martin Cunningham, ed., *Alfonso X El Sabio, Cantigas de Loor* (Dublin: University College Dublin Press, 2000).

8. Walther von der Vogelweide, *Palästinalied.*

9. Kyrie *Cunctipotens genitor deus.* Codex Calixtinus, Cathedral of Santiago de Compostela, f. 190. Reprinted with permission from Heinrich Husmann, ed. *Medieval Polyphony: Das Musikwerk,* vol. 9. (Cologne: Arno Volk Verlag, 1962). © 2003 by Laaber-Verlag, Laaber, Germany. English translation: © Jeremy Yudkin.

10. Léonin (?), Organum *Haec dies.* Reprinted with permission from Heinrich Hussman, ed., *Die mittelalterliche Mehrstimmigkeit: Das Musikwerk,* vol. 9. (Cologne: Arno Volk-Verlag, n.d [1960?]). © 2003 by Laaber-Verlag, Laaber, Germany.

11. Clausula *In saeculum.* Reprinted with permission from Heinrich Hussman, ed., *Die mittelalterliche Mehrstimmigkeit: Das Musikwerk,* vol. 9. (Cologne: Arno Volk-Verlag, n.d [1960?]). © 2003 by Laaber-Verlag, Laaber, Germany.

12. Motet *Lonc tens ai mon cuer/In seculum.* Text and translation: p. 34 in *The Montpellier Codex,* Part 3: *Fascicles 6, 7 and 8,* edited by Hans Tischler, Recent Researches in the Music of the Middle Ages and Early Renaissance, vol. 6 & 7. Madison, WI: A-R Editions, Inc., 1978. Reprinted with permission from Hans Tischer.

13. Motet *Huic main/Hec dies.* Text and translation: p. 6 in *The Montpellier Codex,* Part 3: *Fascicles 6, 7 and 8,* edited by Hans Tischler. Recent Researches in the Music of the Middle Ages and Early Renaissance, vol. 6 & 7. Madison, WI: A-R Editions, Inc., 1978. Reprinted with permission from Hans Tischer.

14. Motet *A Paris/On parole/Frese nouvelle,* pp. 189–90 in *The Montpellier Codex,* Part 3: *Fascicles 6, 7 and 8,* edited by Hans Tischler. Recent Researches in the Music of the Middle Ages and Early Renaissance, vol. 6 & 7. Madison, WI: A-R Editions, Inc., 1978. English translation of text by Alfonso d'Avalos from *The European Musical Heritage, 800–1750* [compiled by Sarah Fuller]; consulting editor in music, Alan W. Schindler, 1/e. NY: Knopf, © 1987. By permission of The McGraw-Hill Companies.

15. Conductus, *Flos ut rosa floruit.* London: British Library, add. 27630. Text and translation reprinted from Jeremy Yudkin, *Music in Medieval Europe,* 1st edition, © 1989. Reprinted by permission of Pearson Education, Inc., Upper Saddle River, NJ.

16. Philippe de Vitry (?), *Garrit Gallus / In nova fert / Neuma* from *Roman de Fauvel.* Text and translation from *Anthology of Medieval Music* edited by Richard Hoppin. Copyright © 1978 by W.W. Norton & Company. Used by permission of W.W. Norton & Company, Inc.

17. Guillaume de Machaut, *La Messe de Nostre Dame* (Kyrie). Reprinted with permission from Leo Schrade, ed. Guillaume de Machaut, *Oeuvres completes,* vol. 3: *La Messe de Nostre-Dame* (Monaco: Editions de l'Oiseau-Lyre, 1977).

18. Guillaume de Machaut, *Je puis trop bien ma dame comparer.* Reprinted with permission from Leo Schrade, ed. Guillaume de Machaut, Oeuvres completes, vol. 4: *Les Ballades, Les Virelais* (Monaco: Editions de l'Oiseau-Lyre, 1977). English translation reprinted by permission of the publisher from *The Historical Anthology of Music—Vol. 1: Oriental, Medieval and Renaissance Music,* edited by Archibald T. Davidson and Willi Apel. (Cambridge, MA: Harvard University Press). Copyright © 1946, 1949 by the President and Fellows of Harvard College.

19. Guillaume de Machaut, *Douce dame jolie.* Reprinted with permission from Leo Schrade, ed. Guillaume de Machaut, *Oeuvres completes,* vol. 4: *Les Ballades, Les Virelais* (Monaco: Editions de l'Oiseau-Lyre, 1977). English translation by permission of Hyperion Records Ltd. from *The Mirror of Narcissus.*

20. Guillaume de Machaut, *Ma fin est mon commencement.*

21. Baude Cordier, *Tout par compas.* Reprinted with permission from Gordon J. Greene, ed. *French Secular Music: Manscript Chantilly, Musee Conde 564: Polyphonic Music of the Fourteenth Century,* vol. 18 (Monaco: Editions de l'Oiseau Lyre, © 1981; © 1982). English translation by Howard B. Garey, courtesy of New Albion Records from *Ars Magis Subtilter: Secular Music of the Chantilly Codex, NA 021.*

22. Francesco Landini, *Ecco la primavera* Reprinted with permission from Leo Schrade, ed., *Francesco Landini, Complete Works,* vol. 1: *Two-Part Ballate* (Monaco: Editions l'Oiseau-Lyre, 1982). English translation by Giovanni Carsaniga from *I am Music: Works by Franceso Landini,* Move Records, Carlton, South Australia, 1997.

23. Jacopo da Bologna, *Non al suo amante.* English translation from *The European Musical Heritage: 800–1750* [compiled by] Sarah Fuller; consulting editor in music, Allan W. Schinder. 1/e. NY: Knopf © 1987. By permission of the McGraw-Hill Companies. English translation of text by Alfonso d'Avalos from *The European Musical Heritage, 800–1750* [compiled by Sarah Fuller]; consulting editor in music,

Alan W. Schindler, 1/e. NY: Knopf, © 1987. By permission of The McGraw-Hill Companies.

24. Lorenzo da Firenze, *A poste messe*. In Nino Pirrotta, ed., *The Music of Fourteenth-Century Italy,* vol. 3: Corpus mensurabilis musicae, 8-3 (American Institute of Musicology, 1962). Reprinted with permission. English translation courtesy of Vanguard Classics, © 1971, 1974.

25. Johannes Ciconia, *Doctorum principem / Melodia suavissima / Vir mitis.* Text and translation reprinted with permission from Margaret Bent and Anne Hallmark, ed. *The Works of Johannes Ciconia* (Monaco: Editions de l'Oiseau-Lyre, 1982).

26. Anonymous, *Sumer is icumen in.* From *A Cappella: An Anthology of unaccompanied choral music from seven centuries.* Compiled and edited by John Gardner and Simon Harris. © Oxford University Press 1992. Used by permission. All rights reserved.

27. Anonymous, *Edi be thu, heven-queene.* Reprinted with the permission of the publisher from Frank LI. Harrsion and E. J. Dobson, eds., *Medieval English Songs.* Copyright © 1979. Reprinted with the permisson of Cambridge University Press and Faber & Faber Ltd. English translation: From E. J. Dobson and F. LI. Harrison, Medieval English Lyrics. London, 1979.

28. *La quinte estampie real.* Paris, BN fond francais 844 ("Chansonnier du Roi"). Published in Timothy McGee, ed., *Medieval Instrumental Dances* (Bloomington: Indiana University Press, 1989).

29. John Dunstable, *Quam pulchra es.*

30. Guillaume Du Fay, *Flos florum.* In Heinrich Besseler, ed., *Guillaume Du Fay, Opera Omnia,* vol. 1: *Motetti,* Corpus mensurabilis musicae 1-1 (American Institute of Musicology, 1966). Reprinted with permission. English translation by Hans Heimler, © 1975 Deutsche Grammophon GmbH, from LP Archiv Producktion 2533 291, by kind permission of Deutsche Grammophon, Hamburg, Germany.

31. Du Fay, *Conditor alme siderum.*

32. Du Fay, *Nuper rosarum flores.* English translations from *Norton Anthology of Western Music,* Vol. 1, edited by Claude V. Palisca. NY: W.W. Norton & Company, Inc.

33. Josquin des Prez, *Ave Maria . . . virgo serena,* English translation MEB.

34. Du Fay, *Se la face ay pale.* English translation MEB.

35. Du Fay, Kyrie and Gloria from *Missa se la face ay pale.* In Heinrich Besseler, ed., *Guillaume du Fay, Opera Omnia,* Corpus mensurabilis musicae, 1-3 (American Institute of Musicology, Middleton, Wisc., 1962). Reprinted with permission.

36. Johannes Ockeghem, Kyrie from *Missa prolationum.*

37. Antoine Busnois (?), *Fortuna desperata.* Text and translation from pp. 3–4 in *Fortuna Desperata: Thirty-Six Settings of an Italian Song,* edited by Honey Meconi, Recent Researches in the Music of the Middle Ages and Early Renaissance, vol. 37. Madison, WI: A-R Editions, Inc., 2001.

38. Josquin *Missa Fortuna desperata,* (Kyrie and Agnus Die). Reprinted from *Werken van Josquin des Prez,* Missen, Ser. 3, Deel 1 (Amsterdam: G. Alsbach, 1929).

39. Josquin, *Kyrie* from *Missa pange lingua.*

40. Josquin or Pierre de la Rue, *Absalon, fili mi. The Collected Works,* vol. 14: *Motets on Texts from the Old Testament.* Ed. Richard Sherr. Utrecht: Netherlands: Koninklijke Vereniging voor Nederlands Muzeikgeschidedenis, 2002, pp. 1–4.

41. Du Fay, *Adieu ces bons vins de Lannoys.* English translation by Keith Anderson from Dufay Chansons. Courtesy of Naxos of America.

42. Hayne van Ghizeghem, *De tous biens pleine.* Text and translation from Barton Hudson, ed. *Hayne van Ghizeghem: Opera Omnia,* Corpus mensurabilis musicae, 74. (American Institute of Musicology, 1977). Reprinted by permission. English translation from pp. 3–5 in *De tous biens plaine: Twenty-Eight Settings of Hayne van Ghizeghem's Chanson,* edited by Cynthia Cyrus, Recent Researches in the Music of the Middle Ages and Early Renaissance, vol. 36. Madison, WI: A-R Editions, Inc., 2000.

43. Heinrich Isaac, *Hélas, que pourra devenir.* Reprinted with permission of the publisher from Howard Mayer Brown, ed., *A Florentine chansonnier from the rime of Lorenzo the Magnificent:* Florence, Biblioteca nazionale centrale, MS Banco rari 229 (Chicago: University of Chicago Press © 1983). English translation by permission of Bernard Thomas (Bradford, UK: London Pro Musica).

44. Marchetto Cara, *Hor venduto ho la speranza.* Reprinted from Bevenuto Disertori, ed., *Le frottole per canto e liuto intabulate da Frqanciscus Bossinensis* (Milan: Ricordi, 1964). English translation from *Renaissance Music from the Courts of Mantua & Ferrara circa 1500* (Musical Heritage Society, 513401 K), translation by Peggy Forsyth, © 1984, London.

45. Josquin (?), *El grillo.* Reprinted with permission from A. Smijers et. al., Josquin Wereldlijke Werken II/5 (Amsterdam: Vereniging voor Nederlandse Muziekgeschiedenis, 1968). English translation by Tinelot Wittermans. Used by permission.

46. Claudin de Sermisy, *Tant que vivray.* In Gaston Allaire and Isabelle Cazeaux, eds., *Claudin de Sermisy, Collected Works,* vol. 4: *Chansons II,* Corpus mensurabilis musicae, 52–4 (American Institute of Musicology, 1974). Reprinted with permission. English translation by Lawrence Rosenwald, Anne Pierce Rogers Professor of English, Wellesley College. Used by permission.

47. Jacob Arcadelt, *Il bianco e dolce cigno.* In Albert Seay, ed., *Jacobi Arcadelt: Opera Omnia,* vol. 2, *Madrigals I,* Corpus mensurabilis musicae, 31–2 (American Institute of Musicology, 1970). Reprinted with permission. English translation of text by Alfonso d'Avalos from *The European Musical Heritage, 800–1750* [compiled by Sarah Fuller]; consulting editor in music, Alan W. Schindler, 1/e. NY: Knopf, © 1987. By permission of The McGraw-Hill Companies.

48. Cipriano de Rore, *Da le belle contrade d'oriente.* English translation from The European Musical Heritage: 800–1750 [compiled by] Sarah Fuller; consulting editor in music, Allan W. Schinder. 1/e. NY: Knopf © 1987. By permission of the McGraw-Hill Companies.

49. Madalena Casulana, *Morir non può il mio cuore*. Reprinted with permission from Beatrice Pescerelli, *Madrigali di Maddalena Casulana* (Florence: Leo S. Olschki, 1979). English translation MEB.

50. Luca Marenzio, *Solo e pensoso*. English translation MEB.

51. Luzzasco Luzzasch, *T'amo mia vita*. Reprinted with permission from Adriano Cavicchi, ed., *Monumenti di Musica Italiana,* Ser. II, Vol. 2 ed. (Brescia: L'Organo; Kassel: Barenreiter, 1965). English translation from *Women Composers: Music Through the Ages* edited by Martha F. Schleifer and Sylvia Glickman, G. K. Hall ©1996 G. K. Hall. Reprinted by permission of the Gale Group.

52. Orlande de Lassus, *Matona mia cara*. Text and translation reprinted by permission of Bernard Thomas, ed. (Bradford, U.K.: London Pro Musica Edition).

53. Ludwig Senfl, *Zwischen Berg und tiefem Tal* English translation MEB.

54. Hans Sachs, *Silberweise*. Reprinted from *Jahrbuch fur Liturgik und Hymnologie,* vol. 21 (Kassel: Johannes Stauda Verlga, 1977), by permission of Lutherisches Verlagshaus Hannover. English translation prepared for A-R Editions, Inc., by Salvatore Calomino. Copyright © 2003.

55. Luis Milán, *Al amor quiero vencer*. Reprinted with permission from Charles Jacobs, ed., Luis de Milan, El Maestro (University Par: Pennsylvania State University Press, 1971). Copyright 1971 by The Pennsylvania State University Press. English translation by Nicki Kennedy from *Music for Philip of Spain and his four wives,* Signum Records Ltd. 1998.

56. Thomas Morley, *Now Is the Month of Maying*. Reprinted from Bernard Thomas, ed., *Thomas Morley, Balletts* (1595): *Selection II* (Bradford, UK: London Pro Musica Edition, 1986), by permission of Bernard Thomas.

57. John Dowland, *Come, Heavy Sleep*. Reprinted with permission of the publisher from David Greer, ed., John Dowland, *Ayres for Four Voices* (London: Stainer and Bell, 2000). © 2000 by the Musica Brittanica Trust and Stainer and Bell, Ltd. London, England.

58. Johann Walter, *Ein feste Burg ist unser Gott* Reprinted with permission from Otto Schroder, ed. *Johann Walter, Samtliche Werke,* vol. 1, ed. (Kassel: Barenreiter, 1953). English translation: *Evangelical Lutheran Hymn-Book with Tunes,* ed. 1919 (St. Louis: Concordia Publishing House). Translation composite.

59. Thomas Tallis, *Verily, Verily I Say Unto You*. Music by Thomas Tallis. Taken from *Renaissance Masters: English Anthems*. Edited by Peter Phillips. Copyright © 1995 Novello & Company Limited. International copyright secured. All rights reserved. Reprinted by permission of G. Schirmer, Inc. (ASCAP).

60. William Byrd, *Sing Joyfully Unto God*. Reprinted with permission of the publisher from Craig Monson, ed., *The Byrd Edition,* vol. 11: *The English Anthems* (London: Stainer and Bell, 1983). © 1983 Stainer & Bell Ltd., London, England.

61. Giovanni Pierluigi da Palestrina, *Missa Papae Marcelli:* Credo.

62. Antonio Cabezón, *Diferencias sobre el canto de la Dama le demanda*. Reprinted from Felipe Pedrell, ed. Rev. Higino Angles, *Antonio de Cabezon, Obras de musica para tecla...* vol. 3, *Monumentos de la Musica Espanola,* 29 (Barcelona: Consejo superior de investigaciones cientificas, 1966).

63. Francesco Spinacino, *Ricercar*. Reprinted by permission of the publisher from Stanley Beutens, ed., *Lute Recercars by Dalza, Spiancino, Bossinensis & Capirola* (Menlo Park, CA: Instrumenta Antiqua Publications, 1968).

64. Andrea Gabrieli, *Ricercar del duodecimo tuono.*

65. Tielman Sosato, *La Morisque*. Nikolas Delius, ed. © 1989 Schott Musik International. All rights reserved. Used by permission of European American Music Distributors, LLC, sole U.S. and Canadian agent for Schott Musik International.

66. Michael Praetorius, Dances from *Terpsichore*. Reprinted from Gunther Oberst, ed., *Michael Praetorius, Gesamtausgabe der musiklischen Werke,* vol. 15: *Terpischore* (Wolfenbuttel-Berlin: Georg Kallmayer, 1929).

67. Orlande de Lassus, *Prophetiae Sibyllarum*. Reprinted from Joachim Terstappen, ed., *Orlando Lasso, Prophetiae Sibyllarum* (Wolfenbuttel: Moseler Verlag, 1937). English translation by Thomas Binkley from *The Sibylline Prophecies: Prophetiae Sibyllarum: The Penitential Psalms*. Bloomington, IN: Focus, © 1985, 842 Focus. Reprinted by permission of Ragland Binkley.

68. Orlande de Lassus, *Cum essem parvulus*. From *Anthology of Renaissance Music,* edited by Allan W. Atlas. Copyright © 1998 by W.W. Norton, Inc. Used by permission of W.W. Norton & Company, Inc.

69. Giacopo Peri, *Dunque fra torbid' onde* from *Il Canto d'Arione*. Reprinted from D. P. Walker, ed., *Musique des intermedes de "La Pellegrina."* (Paris: Editions du Centre National de la Recherche Scientifique, 1963). English translation by Cecile Stratta. © 1998 Sony Classical, a division of Sony Music Entertainment, Inc.

70. Giulio Caccini, *Sfogava con le stelle*. Text and translation reprinted with permission of the publisher from H. Wiley Hitchcock, ed., *Giulio Caccini, Le nuovo musiche,* Recent Researches in the Music of the Baroque Era, vol. 9. (Madison, WI: A-R Editions, Inc., 1970).

71. Giacopo Peri, *Al fonte, al prato*. From pp. 4–5 in *Jacopo Peri, Le Varie Musiche and Other Songs,* edited by Tim Carter. Recent Researches in the Music of the Baroque Era, vol. 50. Madison, WI: A-R Editions, Inc., 1985.

72. Monteverdi *Cruda Amarilli* from *Madrigals,* Book Five. English translation MEB.

73. Monteverdi, *T'amo mia vita* from *Madrigals,* Book Five. Edited and translated by Lynn George. Copyright © 1968 (renewed) by G. Schirmer, Inc. (ASCAP). International copyrights secured. All rights reserved. Reprinted with permission. English translation from *Women Composers: Music Through the Ages* edited by Martha F. Schleifer and Sylvia Glickman, G. K. Hall, © 1996 G. K. Hall. Reprinted by permission of The Gale Group.

74. Monteverdi, *Zefiro torna e di soavi accenti*. Text and translation reprinted by permission of European American Music Distributors, LLC, sole US and Canadian agent for Universal Edition, from G. F. Malipiero, ed. *Claudio Monteverdi, Tutte le opere,* vol. 9. © 1929 by Universal Edition. © renewed. All rights reserved.

75. Francesca Caccini, *Lasciatemi qui solo*. Modern edition and English translation © Suzanne G. Cusick. Used by permission.

76. Barbara Strozzi, *Tradimento!* English translation by Carol Plantamura © 1985, Leonarda Productions, Inc. http://leonarda.com

77. Etienne Moulinié, *Enfin la beauté que j'adore*. Reprinted by courtesy of the publisher from Andre Vechaly, ed., *Airs de cuor pour voix et luth (1604–1643)* (Paris: Publications de la Societe de Musicologie, 1989). English translation © Ellen Hargis.

78. Monteverdi, *Orfeo: Favola in Musica*, excerpt from Act II from *Tutte le opera di Claudio Monteverdi*, edited by G. F. Malipiero. © 1929 by Universal Edition © renewed. All rights reserved. Used by permission of European American Music Distributors, LLC, U.S. and Canadian agent for Universal Edition. English translation by Robert Stuart, Chester © 1923. 1934 (renewed), J. & W. Chester Ltd. By permission of G. Schirmer, Inc. & Associated Music Publishers, Inc., a division of Music Sales Corporation. International copyright secured. All rights reserved. Reprinted by permission.

79. Monteverdi, *L'incoronazione di Poppea*, Act I, Scenes 2 and 3. Libretto by Giovanni Busenello. Edited by Alan Curtis. Copyright © 1989 Novello & Company Limited. International copyright secured. All rights reserved. Reprinted with permission of G. Schirmer, Inc. (ASCAP).

80. Heinrich Schütz, *Singet dem Herren ein neues Lied*. Reprinted with permission of the publisher from Werner Bittinger, ed., *Heinrich Schutz, Neue Ausgabe samtlicher Werke, Bd. 15* (Kasse: Barenreiter, 1964). English translation from *Dedication Service for St. Gertrude's Chapel, Hamburg, 1607,* edited by Frederick K. Gable, Recent Researches in the Music of the Baroque Era, vol., 91 (Madison, WI: A-R Editions, Inc., 1998).

81. Schütz, *Saul, was verfolgst du mich*. Reprinted with permission of Carus-Verlag Stuttgart GmbH, Sielminger Str. 51, D-70771 Leinfelden-Echterdingen, Germany; from Stuttgarter Schutzausgabe, ed. G. Graulich, English text by Derek McCulloch. © 1969 by Hanssler Verlag, Neuhausen-Stuttgart.

82. Jean-Baptiste Lully, *Armide,* Act II, Overture and Scene 5 Lully, *Oeurvres completes,* serie III, vol. 14; Hildesheim: G. Olms, 2003.

83. George Frideric Handel, *Giulio Cesare,* Act I, Scenes 5–7. English translation © Harmonia Mundi S.A.

84. Henry Purcell, *Dido and Aeneas,* Act I, Scene I (excerpt).

85. John Gay and Johann Christoph Pepusch, *The Beggar's Opera* (excerpts). From *The Music of John Gay's The Beggar's Opera*. Edited and arranged by Jeremy Barlow. © Oxford University Press 1990. Used by permission. All rights reserved.

86. Giacomo Carissimi, *Jephte* (excerpt). Edited by Janet Beat. Copyright © 1974 by Novello & Company Limited. International copyright secured. All rights reserved. Reprinted with permission of G. Schirmer, Inc. (ASCAP).

87. Handel, *Zadok the Priest.*

88. Johann Sebastian Bach, *Jesu, der du meine Seele,* BWV 78 (excerpts). Reprinted with permission of the publisher from Neue Bach Ausgabe © 1953 Barenreiter-Verlag. English translation MEB.

89. Arcangelo Corelli, Concerto grosso, Op. 6, No. 2

90. Antonio Vivaldi, Concerto in A minor, Op. 3, No. 8, first movement. Copyright © 1965 by G. Ricordi & E. Editori, Milano. All rights reserved. Reprinted by permission.

91. Elisabeth Jacquet de la Guerre, *Pièces de clavecin,* Courante and Gigue.

92. Jean-Féry Rebel, *Les élémens:* first movement, ("Le cahos"). Reprinted with permission from edition by Catherine Cessac (Paris: Editions Salabert, 1993).

93. Girolamo Frescobaldi, *Toccata IX* from *Il Secondo Libro di Toccate*. Reprinted with permission of the publisher from Etienne Darbellay, ed. *Girolamo Frescobalid, Opere complete,* vol, 3: *Il secondo libro di Toccate* (Milan: Edizioni Suvini Zerboni, 1979).

94. Dietrich Buxtehude, Praeludium in G minor, BuxWV 149.

95. J. S. Bach, *The Well-Tempered Clavier,* Book I, excerpts.

96. Johann Pachelbel, Chorale prelude on the *Magnificat peregrini toni.*

97. J. S. Bach, Chorale prelude on *Meine Seele erhebt den Herren,* BWV 648, from *Sechs Choräle von verschiedener Art* (the "Schübler" chorales).

98. J. S. Bach, *"Goldberg" Variations* (excerpt).